ANYONE CAN TEACH ART

HOW TO CONFIDENTLY TEACH ART IN YOUR CLASSICAL HOMESCHOOL

JULIE B. ABELS

~

Anyone Can Teach Art; How to Confidently Teach Art in your Classical Homeschool

Ridge Light Ranch Press

7850 N. Silverbell Rd #114-159

Tucson, AZ 85743

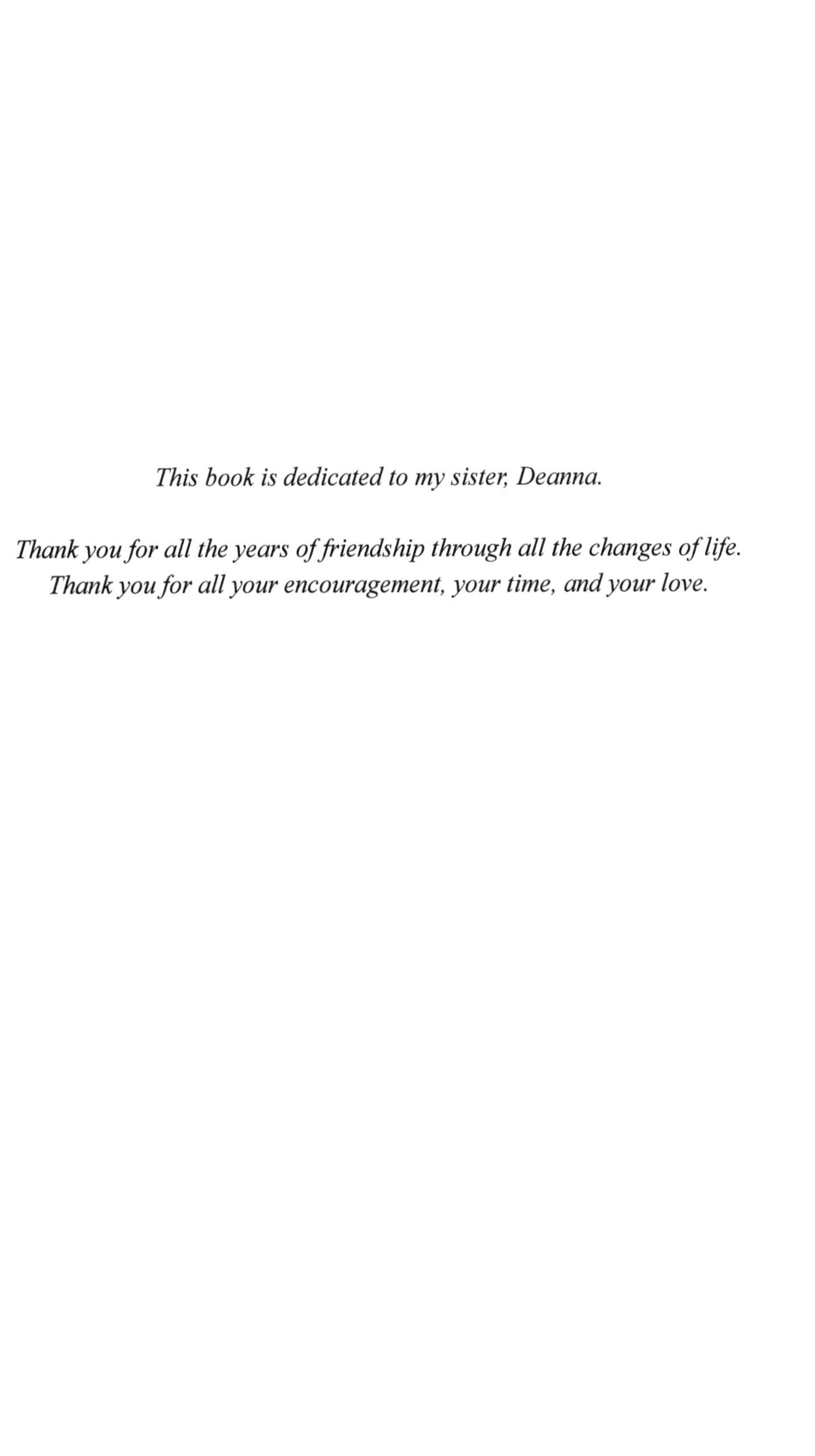

This book is dedicated to my sister, Deanna.

Thank you for all the years of friendship through all the changes of life.
Thank you for all your encouragement, your time, and your love.

CONTENTS

FREE ART TEACHER KIT DOWNLOAD

Thank you for reading this book. I'm so glad you're interested in teaching your children art and I want to help you in any way I can. You can find helpful free art content at the RidgeLight-Ranch.com website and on our free podcast, *Anyone Can Teach Art*. (You can listen on iTunes, Stitcher, GooglePlay, or on our website.)

At the webpage, **RidgeLightRanch.com/Art-Teacher-Kit**, you'll find a printable PDF of the famous works of art pictured in this book. (No email sign up needed.) This allows you to easily print beautiful full-color public domain images of most of the world's best-known works of art. You'll find this especially helpful if you're reading on a small e-reader or reading the black and white version of this book.

Since I'm so passionate about helping you teach art, I've also put together an Art Teacher Kit. I sell the items in this kit separately for $24, but you can download it for free when you sign up for my email list.

The Art Teacher Kit includes a set of six printable art posters to hang up in your homeschool room or classroom. The posters include:

- Elements of Art
- Principles of Design
- Color Wheel
- Common Compositional Structures
- Art History Overview
- Methods of Perspective

Download your free Art Teacher Kit at: **RidgeLightRanch.com/Art-Teacher-Kit/**

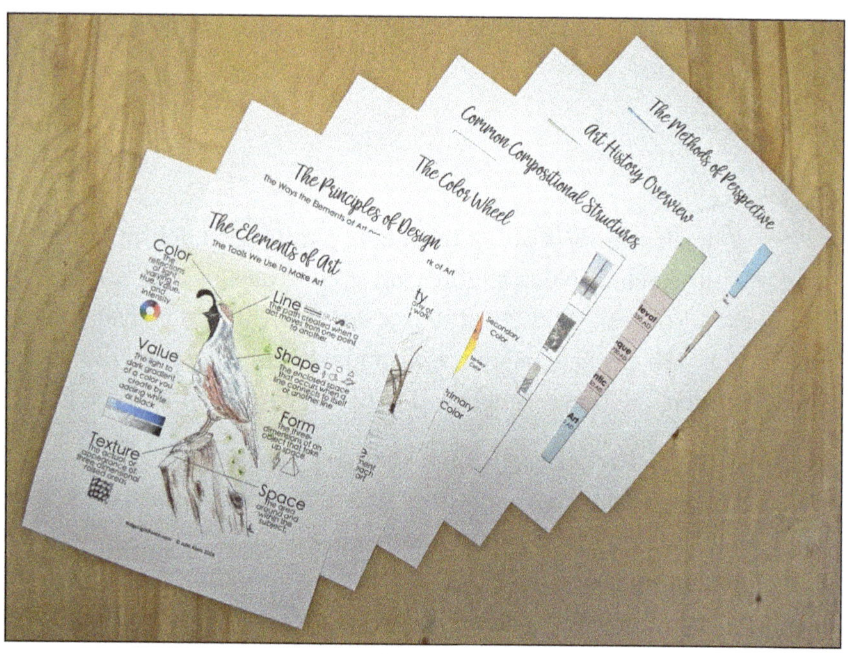

Download these beautiful printable posters, free with your purchase of this book!

When you sign up for our email list you:

- Get access to all our exclusive subscriber-only discounts and deals.
- Are the first to know about our newest art projects and lesson plans.

- Learn about our favorite art products.
- Keep up to date on all the free content we give away.
- Receive our tips, tricks, and strategies to make teaching art easy and fun!

Your privacy is important to us. We'll never sell your info. You can opt-out any time.

INTRODUCTION

Something great happened last year. My older son—the one who used to refuse to draw, the one who scribbled over all his attempts to draw—he finally started enjoying art. He draws to help himself organize ideas, to entertain himself, to make others laugh, and to express himself. As an artist myself, this is more than just a thing that brings me joy—it's a relief!

I didn't think of myself as an artist when I was young and I didn't know much about teaching art to children when we started homeschooling. When I realized art was one of those subjects I would need to teach my children, I started reading more about art and working through some of my own misconceptions about art.

Early on, I realized that what I was doing for art education was mostly just colorful hands-on projects without any fundamental art principles. Don't get me wrong—I enjoy coloring, cutting, and pasting (as long as it's not too messy). However, I could see that this approach was selling our students short of what they could be learning in art.

As my own knowledge of the classical model of education grew, I started seeking out and teaching the basics (the grammar) of art education. I loved seeing the true growth that instruction in art principles provided our students.

I've been teaching art in our homeschool community and to my own (sometimes reluctant) children at home for several years now. I started creating art lesson plans that combined three main components: art basics, an art project, and an integrated non-art subject matter (like history or science). I've been selling these art lesson plans on my website for several years (they're available to you too), and now I'm excited to share with you what I've learned and still am learning about teaching art.

I'm writing this book to all my fellow homeschooling parents who are trying to teach all the subjects even though they don't know it all themselves. Every homeschooling parent I've talked to seems to share similar struggles in knowing what and how to teach. None of us are professionals or experts in all the subjects, especially art. However, with good curriculum, we can teach anything! (I'll explain why I know this to be true later in the book.) I hope this book will become a key resource for you and the backbone of your art curriculum as you incorporate art into your students' education.

I love hearing from parents who have used my art lesson plans with their own children and in their homeschool co-ops and communities. I hope you'll use them as you teach your children art! Check out all the resources on our website, RidgeLightRanch.com, including our free podcast called *Anyone Can Teach Art*. You can also join us in our 'Anyone Can Teach Art' Facebook group as we post photos of our projects, ask art-related questions, and encourage each other.

I'm also hopeful that parents whose children attend traditional schools will be able to use this book to teach their children art at home. The sad truth is that art is often cut from school budgets. If traditionally-educated children are to receive any art education, it will probably need to be at home. Fortunately, creating art together as a family can have a beautiful bonding effect as you learn side by side. As the parent, YOU are your children's first and most influential teacher. That doesn't stop when they head off to the local school.

So, I hope you're able to find time to learn art together, whether it's after school, on the weekends, or over the summer. When I refer to your 'students' or your 'classroom,' that includes you, the non-homeschooling parent too. Your home is naturally a school, whether you homeschool your children or not.

There may also be those of you who take what you learn in this book and want to teach more than just your own children. Fabulous! You can volunteer at a local school, host your own art camp, or simply invite some friends over for an art day. Whenever and however you bring art into others' lives, you bless them. So please, make time for art!

WHAT YOU'LL FIND IN THIS BOOK

First and foremost, you'll find a lot of encouragement in this book. You CAN teach art. It is as easy and simple as any other subject.

Part One of this book explains why it's so important to include art in your children's education. I hope this section will inspire and encourage you!

Part Two explains the classical model of education and how to use it to teach all the basics of art education. The classical model is why you don't have to be an art expert or a famous artist to teach art. *This section should be a reference for you going forward.* It includes all the art grammar, the dialectic ways to think about art, and examples of using art in the rhetoric layer of learning. Highlight and bookmark away. Be sure to download the free Art Teacher Kit that goes along with the book to make implementation easier! (RidgeLightRanch.com/Art-Teacher-Kit/)

Once you know the basics, it's all about practice.

Part Three gives you practical art exercises to help develop your students' skills in art creation and art appreciation. You can do these exercises by themselves or use them within a more formal art lesson that includes integration with another subject.

FAMOUS WORKS OF ART

You'll see I've included many examples in the form of famous works of art to illustrate the concepts I explain and make it easier to understand.

Most of the included works of art could serve as examples of almost every concept, but I've tried not to duplicate the works so that this book would contain a collection of some of the best-known works of art. A printable, full-color PDF of these famous works of art is included in your free Art Teacher Kit, as explained on page 3.

You won't see any art from modern or contemporary artists like Pablo Picasso, Salvador Dali, Andy Warhol, or Jackson Pollock because their art is still under copyright and I lack the resources needed to obtain permission to reproduce the art of these more recent artists.

WHAT'S NOT INCLUDED IN THIS BOOK

This book is the '*why, what,* and *how*' of teaching art. It's written directly to you, the art teacher, rather than to an elementary-aged student. Once you read this you'll be ready to use art projects from library books, Pinterest, or your own imagination while incorporating the basic principles (the grammar) of art education. If you purchase our lesson plans from RidgeLightRanch.com, you'll quickly see how we've incorporated these art principles into our lessons and how they build a solid art foundation.

I'm leaving out any discussion of art supplies in this book. We have information about supplies on our website (RidgeLightRanch.com/Art-Supplies/) and in our podcast. Every artist has their favorite supplies, each medium has numerous brands, and there are countless types of art supplies to choose from. For most exercises in this book, the simplest paper and pencil work beautifully. Start with whatever you have on hand—you'll have many years to try different types of supplies.

START NOW

This book is designed to get you and your family creating in a way that brings all of you joy and confidence. Use this book to start learning the fundamental elements of art and keep building. Please don't wait! Start small so you don't get overwhelmed. Don't let busyness or fear of messes (art does NOT have to be messy!) or anything else hold you back. Teaching your children art is so very doable and it's sooooo worth it. Art can make your world beautiful, refresh your children's education, and give them a new way to look at learning.

When my previously reluctant son started enjoying and using art in his life, it made his education more well-rounded, rich, beautiful, and valuable to him and those around him. You'll have your own kinds of 'wins' when you incorporate art education into your family's life. They won't be the same as mine, but they will be good.

Let's learn about teaching art!

I

WHY WE ALL NEED ART

1

WHAT'S THE PURPOSE OF EDUCATION?

There are many compelling reasons we need art, but before I dive into all the juicy benefits, I want to ask you one question —and I hope you'll take a few minutes to think through your answer:

What is the purpose of education?

Have you ever sat back and formulated an answer to this question? Here's a collection of further questions that are interrelated: *Why does it matter if our children are educated? Why does it matter if the citizens of our country are educated? What does it mean to be educated? How will we know if and when we have effectively educated our children? Do standardized tests show us? Is success in a career evidence of education?*

These questions have shaped my whole approach to homeschooling, and to parenting in general. In fact, they've changed how I spend my personal time as well.

By some standards, I'm a well-educated person. I have a Bachelor's and a Master's degree. However, the diplomas are in a drawer somewhere and no one has asked to see them in many years. In my life as a home-schooling mom, art teacher, and online business owner, no one really cares about my degrees. Should they? I don't think they should. I learn what I need to teach my children from the curriculum I purchase. I learn what I need to teach art from art books, other artists, and non-credit classes. I learn what I need to run an online business from friends, YouTube, and online training programs.

So then, what does it mean to be well-educated? When I started my website years ago, I didn't know how to create a website or write a compelling ad to run on Facebook. When I started teaching my son how to parse and diagram sentences, I didn't even know what those words meant. When I started painting with acrylics, I had no idea how to make the best use of them or even where to start. Was I uneducated then?

I believe the key is to separate 'training' and 'education' in our minds. Training teaches us how to do a specific thing well, while education teaches us how to think so we can become wise and virtuous. Virtue may sound like a religious answer, and while I find it inherent to my faith, even secular Humanists agree our society is built on some agreed tenants of morality.

I really love the definition that the CIRCE Institute[1] (a wonderful source of additional information about education) gives: "Education is the cultivation of wisdom and virtue by nourishing the soul on truth, goodness, and beauty." The Bible tells us we are all created in God's image (Gen. 1:27), capable of wisdom and virtue. The Bible also tells us we are to do "all for the glory of God" (I Cor. 10:31) and to "Rejoice in the Lord always" (Phil. 4:4). So, when we learn how to think, we must also learn in a way that moves us toward the act of glorifying God and enjoying Him.

My favorite definition of 'education' comes from a source I stumbled upon one day: The Mother of Divine Grace School. On their website, they take the definition a step further:

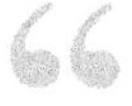

> "Classical education is the cultivation of wisdom and virtue by nourishing the soul on truth, goodness and

> beauty, so that, in Christ, the student is better able to know, glorify, and enjoy God."

What do you think of these definitions? I believe these definitions and the Christian perspective bring to light six important facts about education:

1. Education should nourish the soul, not just inform the person.
2. Education should focus on wisdom and virtue, apart from whatever might be on the latest and greatest standardized test.
3. Since education results in wisdom and virtue and because it almost always takes place within relationship, the worldview of the teacher is important. No human can teach you how to think —or lead you to wisdom and virtue—without including at least some of their own worldview.
4. Education should look to the true, the good, and the beautiful as sources of knowledge.
5. Every student is capable of wisdom and virtue.
6. Our life purpose is to glorify God and enjoy Him.

How does this connect to your understanding of the purpose of education?

The facts we learn about any subject are important, of course. However, what we learn must serve the ultimate goals of education. Art is important in the same way; its value lies in how it helps us grow into wise and virtuous people. Throughout this part of the book, as I cover the skills art teaches us, the ways we can use art to teach other subjects, and the benefits of an art-filled life, I'll refer back to some of these components regarding what education should be. I hope you'll see how perfectly art helps fill in the gaps in an education that leads to a good and beautiful life.

~

Chapter Summary

- Our view of the nature of education drives what we do in our homeschools, our families, and our lives.
- Education does more than convey information; it forms us into people who can learn and live well.
- Art education is an important part of how we accomplish this very high goal.
- A great summary of the purpose of education is: "Classical education is the cultivation of wisdom and virtue by nourishing the soul on truth, goodness, and beauty, so that, in Christ, the student is better able to know, glorify, and enjoy God."

2

WHAT DOES ART TEACH US?

We know intuitively that art is important to life, that it somehow feeds our soul, and that it's part of the human experience. The benefits of learning to create and appreciate art are numerous and intertwined, but it can be difficult to articulate exactly how art benefits our school-aged students. Our society as a whole has not solidified the importance of art education, so we often see it cut from public schools and homeschools alike.

I want us to change that. Together, we can be ambassadors for art. In order to get started on that, I want to not only inform you of art's many advantages, but also inspire you to create a little time for art in your students' lives and your own life. The benefits transcend childhood and will impact you and your students' whole lives. Art can be beneficial no matter what age you are.

I like to break down the benefits of art into three categories, which I'll explain in this chapter and the next two chapters:

- The skills art teaches us
- The ways art can integrate with other school subjects and facilitate learning

- The inherent positive effects of an art-filled life

This chapter is not a comprehensive list of all the benefits of art. Art is so connected to who we are as humans that it touches every part of life in countless ways. Each person's experience with art is inherently unique, so I can't predict how art will touch your life or your students' lives. However, I hope I can show you enough value to energize you to make art a part of your everyday life. Many of these benefits can be experienced in all forms of art (music, dance, visual art, etc.), but for the purpose of this book, I've focused only on the visual arts.

THE SKILLS ART TEACHES US

1. Noticing Details

Art has many elements, but learning to draw is a fundamental building block that forms the basis of many other skills. Learning to draw is all about learning to see and notice details. Noticing details is a key lifelong skill used in many other subjects, activities, and careers.

Noticing details is not only inherently valuable; it also promotes curiosity. The more you know about a subject, the more interesting it becomes.

The fact that drawing helps you notice details, which fosters creativity, is explained well in Samuel H. Scudder's "Look at Your Fish" story[1]. It's about a budding scientist whose professor told him to look at a Haemulon fish (figure 2.1). After ten minutes the student was bored and thought he'd seen everything there was to see about this fish. After a few hours of noticing nothing new, it finally occurred to him to draw the fish. Only then did he start noticing more and more of the fish's features. When his professor returned, he approved saying, "That is right, a pencil is one of the best of eyes." Our brains are designed to be efficient. We can easily skim over details until we need those details for the task at hand. Drawing is one way to create a situation where we will focus on the details.

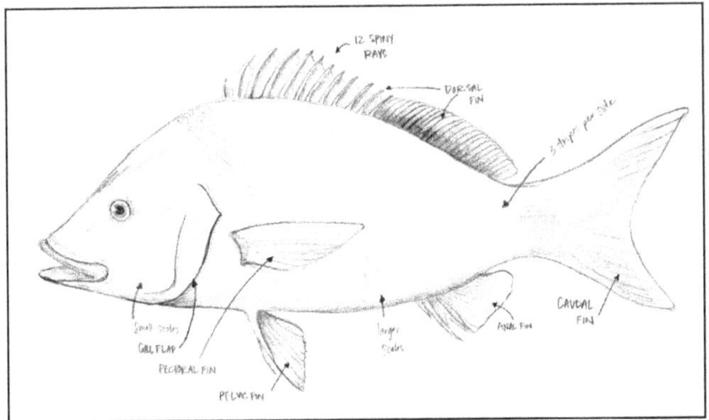

Fig. 2.1 - This sketch I made of a Haemulon fish may be similar to Scudder's own sketch of the fish as he tried to notice more and more details.

Malcolm Gladwell also talks about the way the brain works in his book, *Blink*. He discusses how, after years of paying close attention to details of a certain subject, the subconscious will make use of vast amounts of information in that subject area and will help the brain make informed decisions, even if the conscious brain doesn't really know what's going on. This helps us understand how developing the habit of noticing details gives us a wealth of knowledge, which our brains then use to make decisions.

2. Motor Skills

Each time we do something a little different with our fingers, our brains learn a new skill. Activities like cutting, painting, drawing, building, sculpting, sewing, and braiding build both fine and gross motor skills. The more you do one activity, the better you become at it. At the same time, your neural and muscular systems are also learning more general skills. These motor skills make other, not-so-artsy activities, like hand-writing, measuring, and dissecting easier.

. . .

3. Visual Literacy

In her book, *The Doodle Revolution,* Sunni Brown defines traditional literacy as "using printed and written materials in various contexts." She then draws a parallel between traditional literacy and visual literacy, defining visual literacy as "using visual material in various contexts."

In teaching and promoting visual literacy, Brown has found that people have such strong insecurities when she uses words like 'draw' or 'sketch' that she must use the word 'doodle' instead. She defines 'doodle' as "making spontaneous marks to help yourself think."

In her work increasing visual literacy by teaching people basic drawing skills (which she calls doodling), she has found a wealth of benefits for her students.

The benefits for the individual include increased:

- Information recall
- Information comprehension
- Insight
- Creativity
- Focus
- Relaxation
- Imagination of new possibilities

Brown has also seen doodling help groups of people perform better by:

- Giving them better access to the big picture of the problem they're trying to solve
- Promoting deeper group engagement
- Improving creative, strategic, and tactical thinking
- Pulling all parties into innovative problem solving
- Increasing the group's mental efficiency
- Giving the group a shared visual record

One reason for all these benefits is that drawing connects four modes of learning: visual, auditory, reading/writing, and kinesthetic. Learning to draw can give our students all the same advantages Brown talks about in her work on visual literacy.

4. Creativity

No one denies that art helps us with creativity, but what is creativity? Creativity can be a loaded word because it seems to mean different things to different people. Since words are important and some words have much broader interpretations than others, take a moment and have a discussion with someone nearby as to what they think when they hear the words 'creativity' or 'artistic.'

In the interest of communicating effectively, let me tell you what I mean when I use these two words:

- **Creativity:** the divine ability to imagine new combinations of things
- **Artistic:** a way to describe a work created or imagined for the purpose of communicating a deep, complicated, or multifaceted concept

These two words are key to many art concepts, so allow me to elaborate on a few things about my definitions. This will not only help us understand the benefits of including art in education, but also help us actually teach art!

- Creativity is a divine trait. All humans have it because it is part of what it means to be created in the image of God. (Obviously, those with a secular worldview would define the word differently.) Since creativity is part of what it means to be human, nothing can completely remove all creativity from a person. However, many things can stifle creativity: stress, pressure, busyness, distractions, fatigue, etc. (you know, all the things that are part of everyday life in the 21st century). I believe that's why we see so many people struggle with creativity. It's not a muscle that flexes well when rushed. Like almost any other skill, creativity takes focus and time until the muscle grows and creative habits are developed.

- Creativity is something that takes place in the mind. We often experience the results of someone else's creativity in a painting, song, or movie. However, we assign creative credit to the person or group who imagined it, who birthed the idea—even if they hired someone else to help them execute their creative vision.
- Creativity is not imagining new things, it's imagining new combinations of things. As Solomon said in Ecclesiastes 1:9, "there is nothing new under the sun." Austin Kleon restated this idea in his insightful book, *Steal Like an Artist,* when he confessed, "I know something that a lot of artists know but few will admit to, and that is: nothing is completely original. All creative work builds on what came before. Every new idea is just a remix or mash-up of one or two previous ideas."
- Creativity is broader than the arts. Creativity is not limited to art. For example, we can creatively build a structure, creatively invent a product, or creatively solve a math problem. (I'll cover this idea more in the next benefit, 'Problem Solving.')
- Not everything that is artistic is creative. If I recreated a famous work of art it might still be artistic in its ability to communicate a transcendent concept, but it wouldn't take much creativity on my part. That's okay and it's still a valuable exercise, since we learn a lot by copying great works of art! It's a way of inputting information into our mind. Once that information is in our minds, our divine spark of creativity works it over and rearranges it into new, creative combinations. So, when copying great works of art, be sure they are the types of things you'll want your mind to dwell on and incorporate into your thoughts.
- 'Creative' and 'artistic' do not necessarily determine the price of a work of art. Something is not valuable simply because it is a novel combination of things. (Some modern art critics certainly

> disagree with me there.) Neither is it valuable because of its ability to communicate an idea. Price is simply how much someone is willing to pay for something. In my opinion, if a work of art convincingly communicates a lie, it's worse than worthless—it's damaging! However, there may be other people willing to pay a high price for that same work of art.

You might then realize our beginning art lessons often don't use a lot of creativity or have a lot of artistic elements in them. Even so, there are creative benefits of doing those lessons. At the beginning, we're teaching our students the building blocks of art so that they can later be artistic and creative. We can see an example of this in teaching a musical instrument—we learn to play the notes and scales before doing more creative work.

In Part Two of this book, I'll explain the classical model of education and you'll be able to see how producing an artistic, creative work of art is a very advanced step. Not to worry. The seeds of creativity are in all of us. When we include art in education, it exercises the students' creativity muscles and helps them grow stronger, even if we can't see the growth at first. As we teach our students, we give them all the tools and techniques they need to later exercise their own creativity. Then we give them time to try out, experiment with, and perfect what they've learned. This is why we include 'creativity' in the list of benefits of including art in education.

5. Problem Solving

As I mentioned before, exercising your creativity muscles can lead to creative problem solving as well. In her book *Drawing on the Right Side of the Brain*, Betty Edwards noted that once individuals learn to think and see creatively, that skill carries over to all areas of their life. For example, in her experience, teaching average office workers how to draw a portrait resulted in them being able to think up more creative solutions for unrelated problems at work.

The more often you find ways to creatively solve problems, the more likely you are to see problems as opportunities, energizing you to engage in solving the problems instead of hiding from them. Each time you willingly engage in problem solving you grow your perseverance.

6. Patience / Focus / Perseverance

Anytime we do something challenging and stick with it, we grow the muscles we use. This isn't only true for physical muscles; it's also true for mental muscles. In the book *Willpower Instinct,* Kelly McGonigal talks about how willpower works like a muscle in the brain. We need to exercise our willpower for it to grow. Patience, focus, and perseverance work the same way.

Patience is the ability to be content when something is progressing slowly. We would all love to have a supernatural endowment of patience, but it doesn't work that way. I often try to remind myself that it's only in a situation that demands patience that I can develop patience. Art is one of those situations (and the most pleasant one, in my opinion). While art can be great fun, it also tends to be a fairly slow process. So, we flex and build our patience muscles each time we create art.

Focus is the ability to keep working on one task without getting distracted and pulled away. Because of its slower pace, most art creation also demands a level of focus, forcing us to confront our own lack of concentration. Sometimes we learn that we need to change the circumstances (for example, turn off the TV to focus) and other times we learn more self-discipline within the circumstances.

Perseverance is the ability to continue working on something over the long haul and not give up. Art gives us an opportunity to practice perseverance. Ira Glass spoke about persisting in his art form (writing) in a 2009 interview[2] and it applies to the visual arts as well. He said many people who begin a creative work start off excited but quickly notice their taste exceeds their skill. They become disappointed and want to quit. However, that gap between taste and skill is normal and every creator has to pass through it. The solution is daily practice. It's only by creating a large volume of work that you'll close that gap and your work will become as good as your ambitions. It's normal for this season of practice to take years, so you have to fight your way through the initial disappointment and frustration.

Art gives us a perfect place to grow our patience, focus, and perseverance muscles every time we start learning a new art subject, skill, technique, or medium. This process, in turn, increases our confidence.

7. Confidence

Confidence is the peace you get when you know something is going to work out in the end, even if it looks like a disaster at the moment. For Christians, our primary confidence comes from trusting that the good, all-powerful God of the universe loves us. However, we can also learn to gain confidence in our own ability to use the gifts God has given us.

Art gives us a great way to learn this confidence. It's one thing to grow in confidence because you got the exact same answer to a math problem as everyone else, but it's another layer of confidence when you create a drawing or painting, notice it's a little different from everyone else's, but know it's what *you* wanted it to be. You can start to see how God can work uniquely through you to create something beautiful.

In almost every area of life you'll make mistakes, but in art mistakes don't have a high cost. Art is a great place to learn how to fix a mistake and how to learn from failure. This is another unique type of confidence.

Finally, when you gain confidence in one area, it is easier to gain confidence in other areas too. Confidence in your ability to use your gifts and in God's faithfulness to make good use of any situation can also increase your comfort with ambiguity. Confidence and comfort with ambiguity help us to find peace in the uncertainty of life.

Our students will benefit from the skills that art teaches for years to come. In the next chapter, we'll learn how art can be used to help us learn other subjects as well.

CHAPTER SUMMARY

One of the benefits of including art in education is the specific set of skills art teaches us. Creating and appreciating art teaches us:

- To notice details, which fosters curiosity, allows the brain to form more connections, and helps us remember more
- Is fundamental in many careers and a lifelong love of learning
- Fine and gross motor skills, making other hands-on activities easier
- Visual literacy, which has numerous benefits for individuals and groups
- Creativity, which is the divine ability to imagine new combinations of things
- Problem solving, even for problems with no connection to art
- Patience, focus, and perseverance, which can only be developed in a situation requiring those traits
- Confidence to use the skills God gave us and to learn from mistakes

3

USING ART TO LEARN OTHER SUBJECTS

One of the many benefits of art is that it helps us teach and learn other subjects. Although we're focusing on the visual arts, this is true for all the arts, including music, dance, and drama. Incorporating the arts in education makes learning other subjects easier due to the different modes of learning the arts employ. For example, drawing is both a kinesthetic activity and a visual activity. The act of creating also connects the learning in our minds with our emotions and souls. We can see this in general academics as well as in specific subjects.

OVERALL IMPROVED ACADEMIC PERFORMANCE

You've probably seen or heard about at least one of the many studies[1] that show a correlation between the presence of art in education and lower high school dropout rates, fewer disciplinary problems, and better grades in Reading, Writing, and Arithmetic. These studies consistently indicate that the arts add to overall academic success in addition to providing knowledge and skills in specific artistic areas. I believe this is because our whole being needs balance between the left-brained academic subjects and the right-brained creative subjects, just as our physical bodies need both activity and rest.

BENEFITS WITHIN SPECIFIC SUBJECTS

We can also see the benefits of art education in each of the following subjects:

History and Culture

Looking at a particular civilization's art helps you understand that culture's beliefs, values, priorities, and worldviews. While diving deep into the story behind the art, you don't have to know a lot about the artist or the artwork to get a gut feel for the culture. This is true for ancient civilizations as well as modern-day cultures. Their art is a visual representation of life through their eyes.

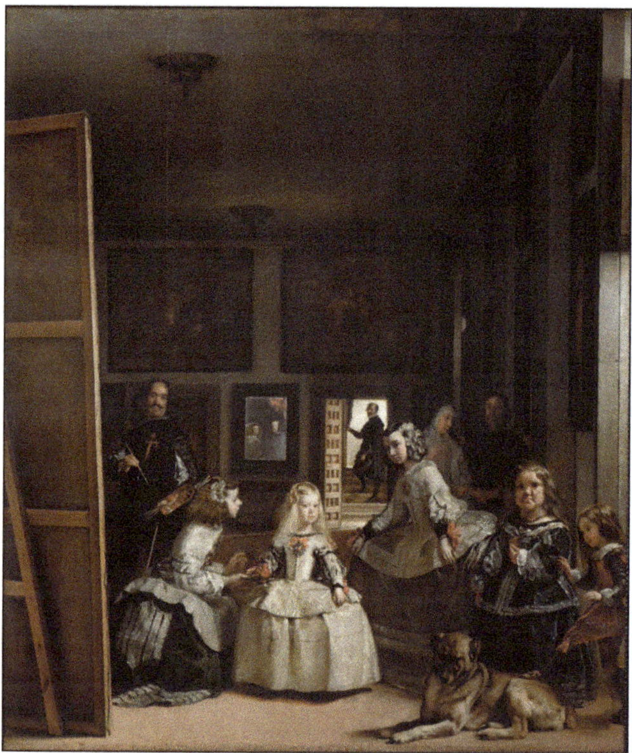

Fig. 3.1 - *The Maids of Honor* (1656) by Diego Velazquez gives us a sense of the Spanish court in the mid 1600s.

For example, Diego Velazquez's 1656 painting, *The Maids of Honor* (figure 3.1), shows King Philip IV's daughter. She is wearing an elaborate dress with a full petticoat and she is surrounded by servants ready to serve her, all while an artist paints her portrait. Looking at this painting, we can get a feel for the formality of the Spanish court and the deference paid to royalty during this time period.

In comparison, Renoir's 1881 painting, *The Luncheon of The Boating Party* (figure 3.2), helps us get a feel for the casual, pleasant culture of his day, as diners sit and stand around a table in the midst of conversation. In the front right corner, a man sits in a chair turned backwards. On the left side, a woman holds a small dog which is partially sitting on the table next to bottles of wine and fresh fruit. These details, along with the light colors and outdoor atmosphere, give us a tangible feel for that place and time.

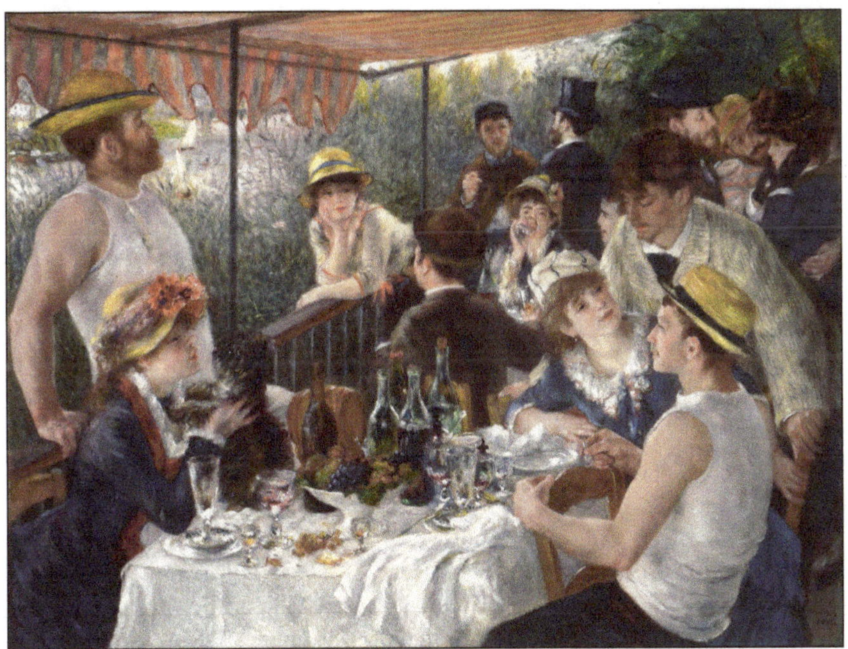

Fig. 3.2 - *The Luncheon of the Boating Party* (1881) by Renoir gives us a feel for the culture of the late 1800s in Europe.

Since art can both reflect and influence culture, we can often see the way ideas spread through and between cultures by examining their art. In fact, when studying any artist, it's always good to investigate which past artists influenced him or her.

Art can also help us understand and appreciate the complexity of historical periods and events as they take us to that time and place.

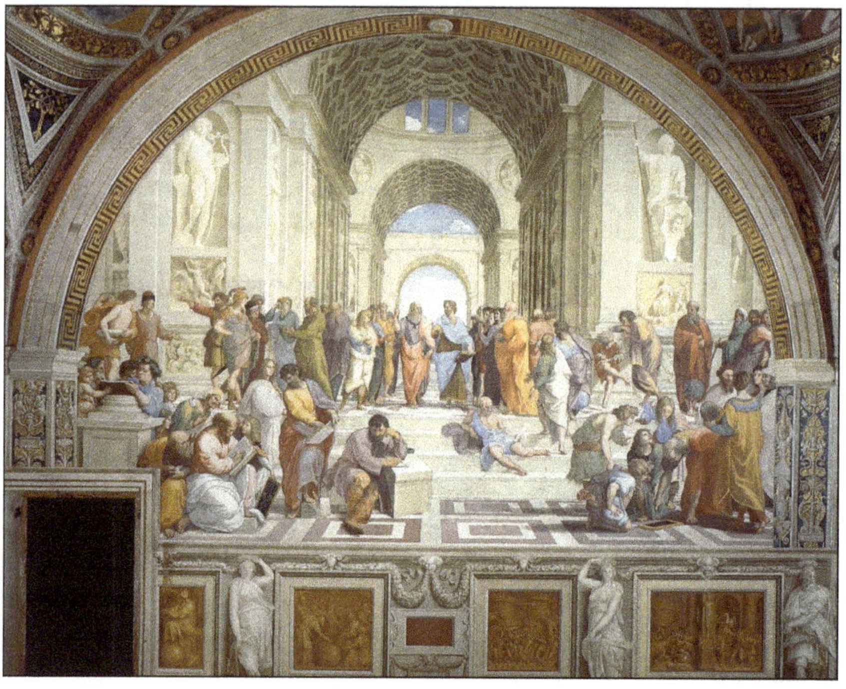

Fig. 3.3 - *The School of Athens* (1511) by Raphael is a Renaissance painting of the most famous ancient Greeks and Romans with the faces of important Renaissance men, showing just how deeply the people of the Renaissance admired the ancient Greeks and Romans.

For example, observing *The School of Athens* (figure 3.3) by Raphael gives us a better sense of the respect Renaissance people had for the ancient Greek and Roman philosophers and teachers. This painting is a who's-who of the ancient Greek world. Interestingly, Raphael painted each of the ancient Greek figures with the faces of one of his contemporaries. For example, the central figure on the left is the ancient Greek philosopher, Plato, holding a copy of his own book. However, he has the face of the Renaissance legend, Leonardo di Vinci. Similarly, the man sitting alone in the front center of the painting is the Greek philosopher Heraclitus of Ephesus, also known as the lonely weeping philosopher. However, he has the face of the notoriously solitary sculptor and painter Michelangelo. Raphael's painting helps us see how much the people of the Renaissance admired and aspired to be like the ancient Greeks and Romans.

Whenever you're studying a historical time period, be sure to look at the art of that era and geographical location.

Geography

Artistic skills can also be used in a practical way to help us learn geography. For example, at home we trace (figure 3.4) and then draw maps (cartography), committing not only the places' names to memory, but also the shapes of their borders and physical features, such as rivers and mountain ranges. You can find additional cartography resources at RidgeLightRanch.com/cartography-for-geography.

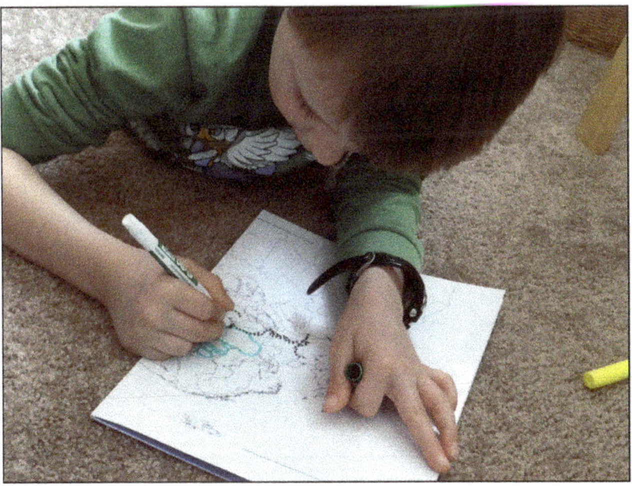

Fig. 3.4 - Tracing maps helps students learn the names and shapes of geographic areas and their features.

Language Arts

Art can be used in teaching each of the components of language arts: handwriting, reading, spelling, and writing. In handwriting, students learn to draw simple shapes as they learn each individual letter. This helps develop fine motor skills and hand strength. Drawing simple pattern shapes can also help teach pattern recognition, a key skill when learning reading and spelling.

When learning spelling, some students find they can remember how to spell a word when they've converted it to a picture. For example, after struggling to spell the word 'restaurant' for years, I created this visual (figure 3.5) and now I can finally remember!

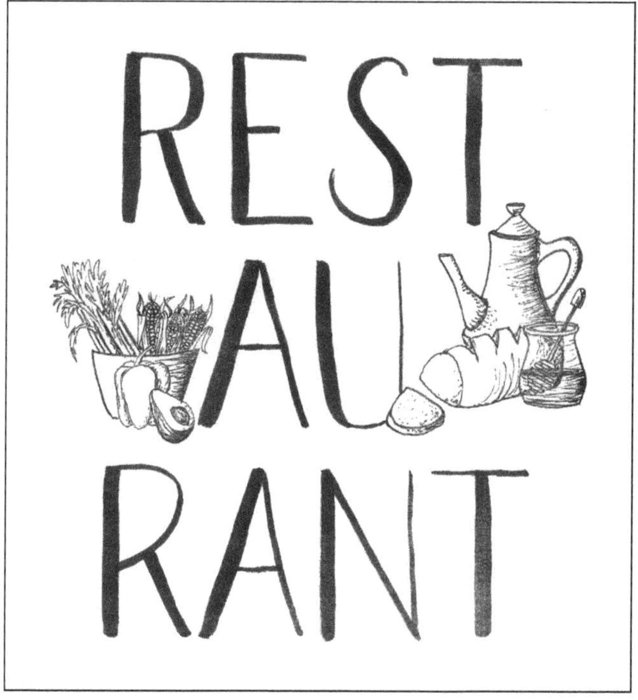

Fig. 3.5 - Drawing a word in a creative way, like this drawing of 'restaurant,' can help you remember how to correctly spell the word.

Art can also bring a great book to life and provide a fun way to dig deeper into a work of literature. This can take many forms and it's great to mix in multiple forms to appeal to different students.

In chapter two of his book *Why Gender Matters*, Leonard Sax explains that from a very young age, "girls draw nouns and boys draw verbs" because of the difference in the neural pathways of boys and girls. Girls can usually describe *what* a subject is while boys are better at telling you *where* it is and how it *moves*. In chapter five, Sax discusses differences in boys' and girls' reading subject preferences. He explains that girls tend to prefer fiction stories where they can discuss a character's motives and behaviors. Boys, however, tend to prefer non-fiction books with exciting events or detailed explanations of how things work.

Keep these ideas in mind as you're incorporating art projects with literature. Sax shares an example where a teacher assigned his classroom of boys the job of drawing maps for the island in *The Lord of the Flies*. This engaged the boys' spatial brain and made them much more interested in the book. (Sax's book is fascinating and I highly recommend it!)

Andrew Pudewa, in his Institute for Excellence in Writing (IEW) curriculum, recommends that students occasionally create a 'polished copy' of their paper with an illustration. I've made creating an illustration for a paper optional for my own children, but offered extra credit (aka, extra screen time) as an incentive. They've both chosen to do it a few times and it's been a fun experience! (You can watch a few videos on the RidgeLightRanch YouTube channel showing how to draw some of the subjects we've chosen for these papers.)

Math

Art can help students learn math as well. Art is easily used in developing pattern recognition skills. Pattern recognition is a key skill in all levels of math. Early math generally includes colors and shapes along with numbers and patterns, so math and art may feel indistinguishable to students at that stage. From first grade on, drawing what's going on in a math problem can help make a complex idea seem concrete and understandable. This can work with simple addition, fractions, geometry, or calculus. In fact, my sister, an engineer, assures me that pattern recognition is the key to understanding calculus!

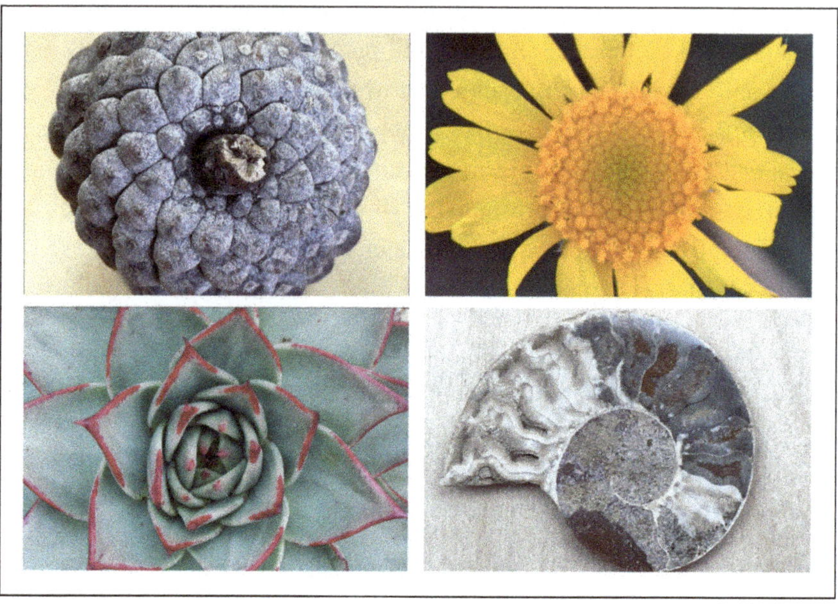

Fig. 3.6 - Fibonacci's number sequence and resulting mathematical patterns show up frequently in nature.

Math can also include studying the amazing and beautiful patterns that occur in nature. Many natural laws can be expressed as mathematical formulas. For example, Fibonacci's number sequence and the resulting mathematical patterns have been found in a mesmerizing number of places in nature, like pinecones, flowers, seashells, and succulents (figure 3.6). The increasing size of the spiral seen in these objects follows the same pattern as the numbers in Fibonacci's sequence. Due to the natural beauty found in Fibonacci's number sequence, we can also see it show up in famous works of art, like *The Great Wave* (figure 3.7) and the architecture of the Greek Parthenon (figure 3.8)!

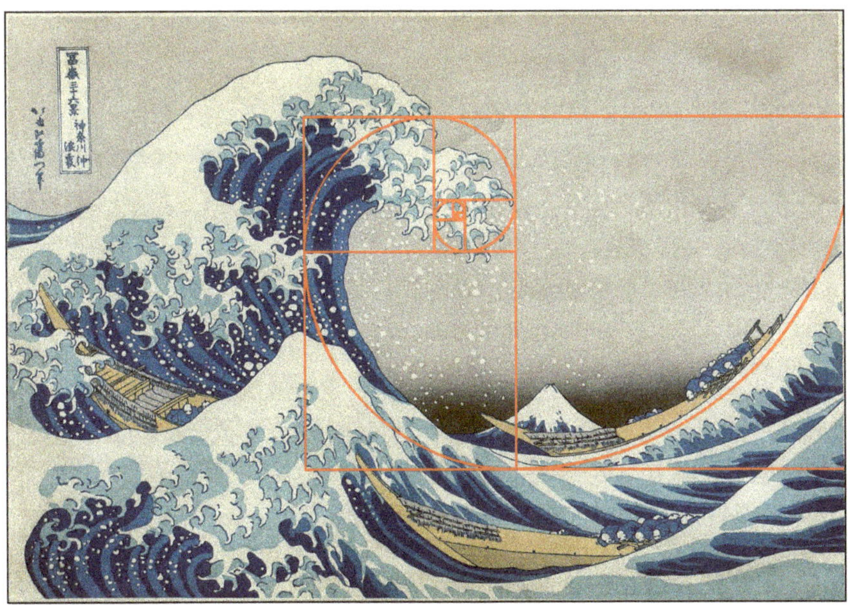

Fig. 3.7 - Fibonacci's number sequence shows up in the spiral of *The Great Wave* (c.1832) by Hokusai.

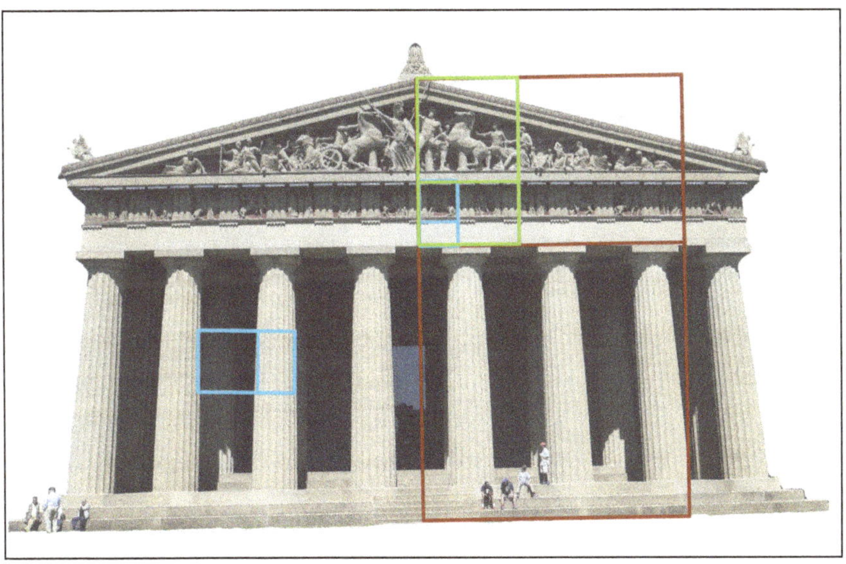

Fig. 3.8 - Fibonacci's number sequence shows up in the ratios of the Greek Parthenon by Iktinos & Callicrates.

Science

A science textbook without any pictures would be so much less interesting and less effective. Illustrations and photographs help explain complex ideas and identify the components of systems and organisms.

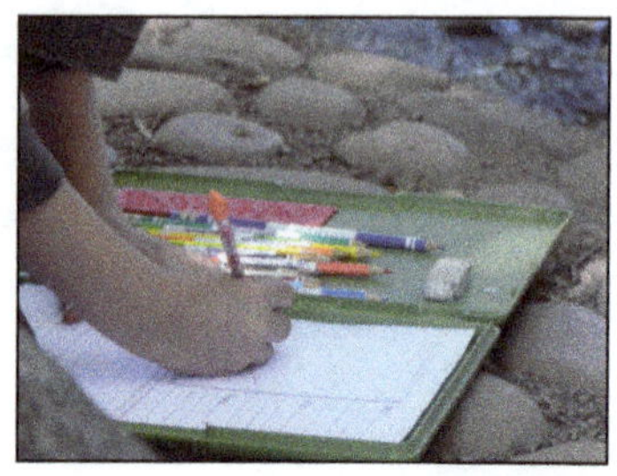

Fig. 3.9 - Nature journaling is a great way to use art to teach science.

Much of science is about observation. Drawing helps us become more observant, document our observations, and communicate them to others.

Art is a great way to encourage students to look for more detail in the subject they're studying. This is seen in the "Look at Your Fish!" story I shared with you in chapter two. If you're on a nature walk, bring paper and pencil with you and take time to draw what you see (figure 3.9).

If you're conducting a science experiment, encourage students to sketch what they see. Students who can't read or write can still sketch. Even if you have no idea what they drew, it will have encouraged them to look longer and notice more.

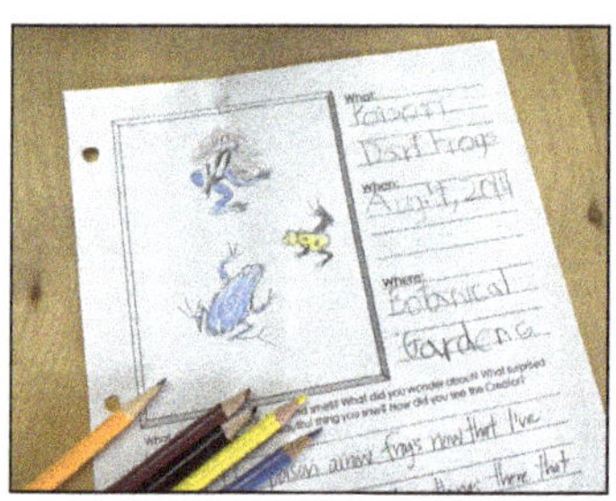

Fig. 3.10 - This nature journal, created by my son when he was six years old, solidified his memory of the frogs and the trip to the Botanical Gardens.

When I asked my own children about a specific trip we took to the Tucson Botanical Gardens over four years ago, the first thing they remembered was what they sketched in their nature journal: poison dart frogs (figure 3.10).

What's more, when I asked them about a trip we took to the Phoenix Zoo that same year, they couldn't remember any solid details. We didn't take our nature journals with us to the zoo, so we didn't do any sketching. Now, they don't remember any details from that trip.

Drawing can also make memorizing details faster and easier. Trace or draw, then label the respiratory system a few times and you'll be amazed at how much you remember. (Later, you can wow your friends with your ability to quickly sketch a pair of lungs.)

CHAPTER SUMMARY

- Art improves overall academic performance as it helps balance the left-brained academic activities with the right-brained creative activities.
- It can also be used as a tool to help us learn specific subjects like social sciences (culture/history/geography), language arts (reading/spelling/handwriting), math, and science.

4

THE BENEFITS OF LIVING AN ART-FILLED LIFE

As we saw in chapter two, art teaches us many skills and develops our creativity and artistic nature. Likewise, as we learned in chapter three, we can use art to teach other subjects and gain depth and understanding in those subjects. However, the greatest benefit of including art in education is learning to embrace an art-filled life. Art in education provides a lifelong gift of a deeper appreciation of art. It impacts our personal lives, our experiences as a community, and our relationships with God.

ART BENEFITS US PERSONALLY

Art can become an accessible method of self-expression for every individual. The process of creating art can enrich your life, help you relax, and restore your soul. If this sounds far-fetched, consider the rise in popularity of adult coloring books in 2015. Many people discovered that coloring is a great introductory way to relax. We experience our lives in scenes and colors, so learning to draw and use color taps into this fundamental way of interacting with and influencing the world around us.

Art can also be a satisfying way to preserve memories. I love drawing and painting while traveling. It helps me notice more and connect with my surroundings in the moment. It also helps me disconnect from the stress of traveling and find beauty in the world around me. I find when I add some art to my travels, I enjoy the whole trip more.

Drawing is a kinesthetic activity, so it aids in memorization, no matter what we're drawing. I'll never forget the view of Grinnell Lake in Glacier National Park, Montana, because I sketched it there on the spot. Even though my sketch (figure 4.1) was very rough and light (Really, it's barely visible!), it still helped me to remember the trip, the hike, and the location. Now when I look back at the pictures and sketches of that location, I can remember the wonder and beauty as well (which is much better than remembering the ups and downs of traveling logistics, right?).

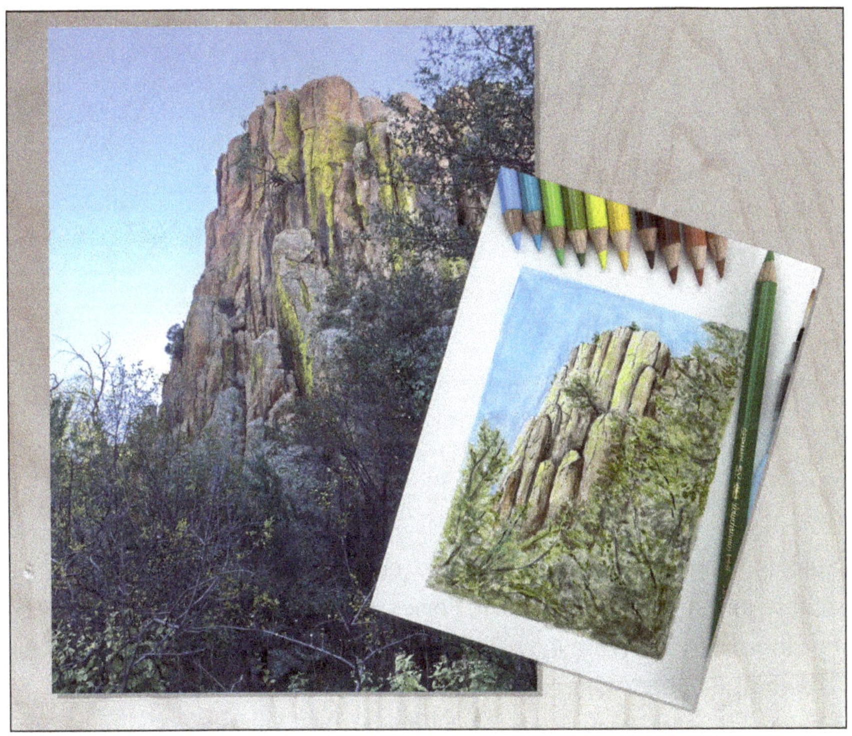

Fig. 4.1 - Sketching while traveling has many benefits! This quick painting I created while in Prescott, AZ using Faber Castell's watercolor pencils reminds me of the location and the trip!

Do you have a favorite hobby? Incorporating or reflecting that hobby in the visual arts can be very rewarding. If your hobby involves plants or animals, sketching your favorites is a great way to get to know your subjects better and share your love of them with friends. If you love hiking or golfing, try sketching those amazing views. If you love music, try capturing the feeling of a favorite song using colors and shapes like Wassily Kandinsky (figure 4.2).

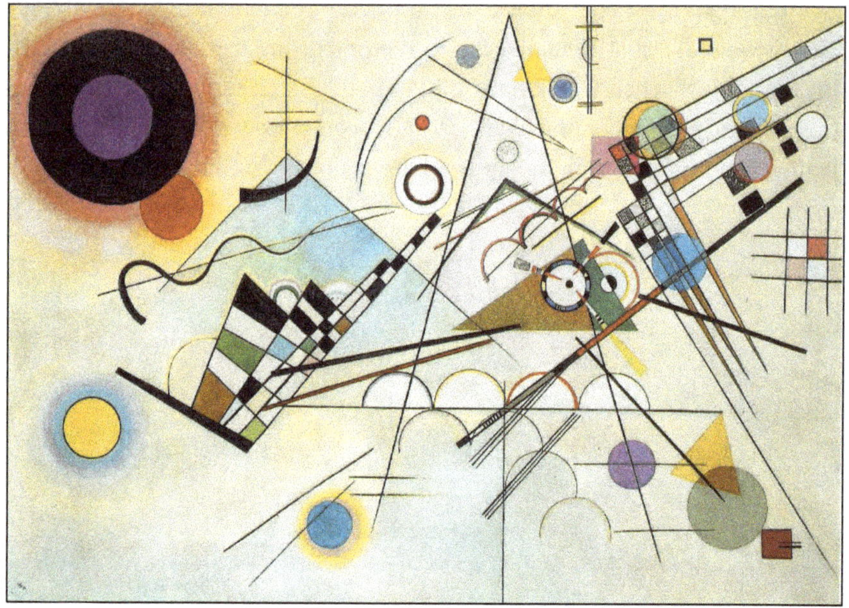

Fig. 4.2 - Wassily Kandinsky is known for hearing color and seeing music. He created art, like this painting, *Composition 8* (1923), as a visual representation of songs he enjoyed listening to.

Studying famous works of art also connects us to our *own* personal culture and our cultural history. For example, *The Battle of Bunker Hill* by Howard Pyle (figure 4.3), *The Death of General Montgomery* by John Trumbull (figure 4.4), and *Washington Crossing the Delaware* by Emanuel Leutze (figure 4.5) each depict the American Revolutionary War differently.

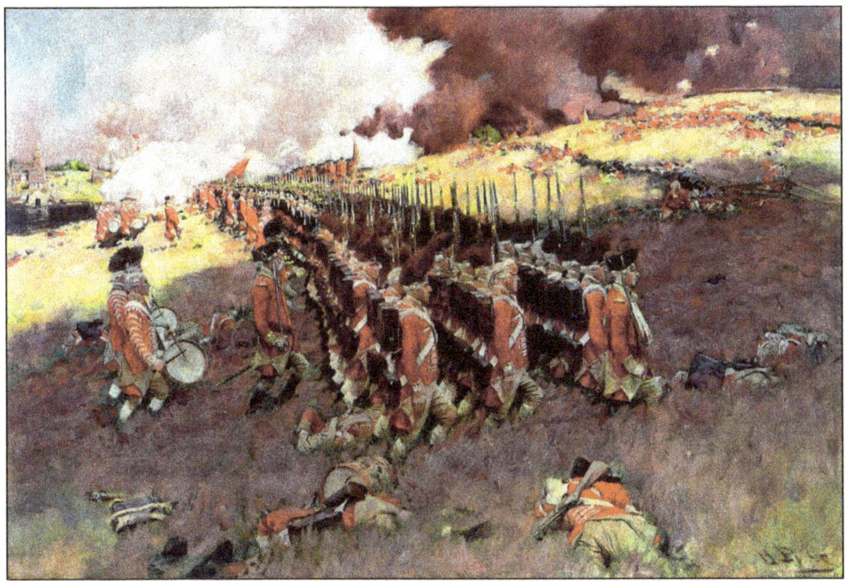

Fig. 4.3 - Painted by Howard Pyle in 1897, *The Battle of Bunker Hill* shows the red coats marching systematically toward their deaths.

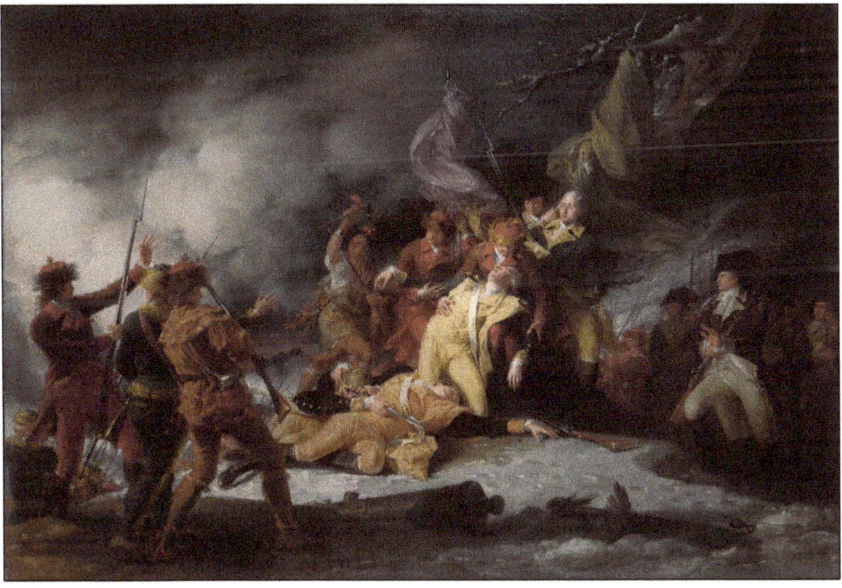

Fig. 4.4 - *The Death of General Montgomery in the Attack on Quebec, December 31, 1775* by John Trumbull in 1786 shows the death of an American hero and the effect it had on his comrades.

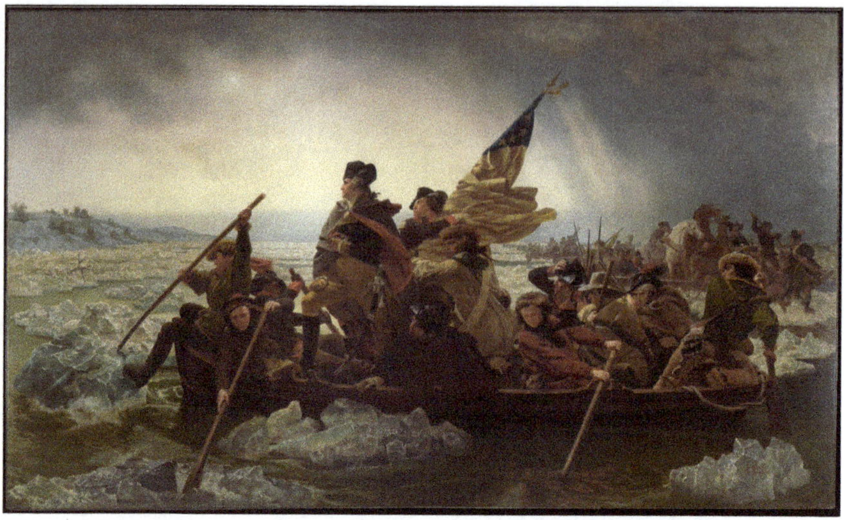

Fig. 4.5 - In 1851, the German, Emanuel Leutze, painted *Washington Crossing the Delaware* in hopes of inspiring European reforms. It depicts a turning point in the American Revolutionary war when Washington bravely crossed the Delaware River to mount a surprise attack on the British.

As an American, looking at all three of these artworks together gives me a more complete understanding of my country's heritage.

As a bonus, when we study famous works we'll finally get all the jokes and cultural references made about art, like this remake of Grant Wood's *American Gothic*, called *American Coffee* (figure 4.6). (The original, *American Gothic*, is pictured in chapter 15.)

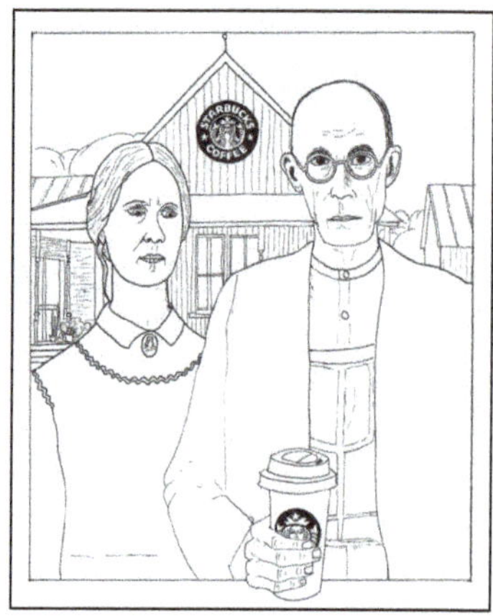

Fig. 4.6 -*American Coffee* (2017) by Julie Abels is an example of a joke using a cultural reference. Studying *American Gothic* (1930) by Grant Wood helps this drawing make sense.

ART BENEFITS FAMILIES AND WHOLE COMMUNITIES

When we create art together or discuss great art as a family, we grow together through the shared experience. This creates emotional bonds that connect us beyond what is merely logical.

As a community, art-filled lives can help preserve the best elements of our culture and our heritage. Art preserves memories for future generations and is a great way to 'hear' the stories of the past. Creating is part of being human in all civilizations, so help it flourish in your own community.

ART HELPS US KNOW AND GLORIFY GOD

A life surrounded by art encourages us to contemplate divine beauty. Who is God that he chose to create such a beautiful world? Who is God that he made his creatures creative? Contemplating divine beauty helps us better know our Creator.

In the story of creation, God creates light and substance from nothing, but after gathering the waters and creating dry land, God begins to call his creation to create. He says, "Let the land produce vegetation" (Gen. 1:11), "Let the water teem with living creatures" (Gen 1:20), and "Let the land produce living creatures" (Gen 1:24). God doesn't hoard all the creativity for himself—even the earth produces, and every living creature creates more of its kind. God pours creativity into us and gives us the ability to pour it into others. We were created by the Spirit of God, by a creative Creator, and given the ability and impulse to create. When we create, it helps us know, glorify, and enjoy our Creator.

AN EDUCATION WITHOUT ART IS SOULLESS AND INCOMPLETE

Did I say that too strongly? I don't think so. At the end of our lives, if we've memorized our math facts but have failed to connect with others, we will have missed the purpose of life. Life is about relationships—first with God, then with others. Art helps us connect with each other and see the beauty around us. Why do we have art on our walls? Why do we care what our homes look like? The items with which we surround ourselves not only display our preferences but also affect our moods and attitudes. Art is fundamentally part of the human experience, so to neglect art in education is to neglect a major part of our own humanity.

Now that you know *why* you should teach art and all the ways art benefits us as human beings, you'll learn *what* to teach in part 2 of this book. Don't panic or feel like I'm giving you more to add to your homeschool calendar! Since art is a natural and fundamental element of the human experience, you don't have to add another subject to your list. Changing your point of view on how to include art in education will make life easier *and* more fulfilling—just wait and see! In chapter 18 I'll explain how art can easily and simply integrate into your current studies. But first, let's begin to understand *what* to include in art education with a look at the classical model of education and how it relates to art.

CHAPTER SUMMARY

- The benefits of living an art-filled life are personal, relational, and spiritual.
- Personally, art can aid in memory retention, increase the joy we experience, and connect us with our culture and history.
- Relationally, art can create shared experiences that connect us and preserve our joint heritage.
- Spiritually, art can help us come to know our Creator as we live out our calling to create!

II

TEACHING ART USING THE CLASSICAL MODEL OF EDUCATION

5

WHAT IS THE CLASSICAL MODEL?

I'm excited to tell you how to use the classical model of education to teach art, but first I want to provide a quick overview of the classical model of education. It's this model that makes teaching art simple and straightforward, no matter how little experience you have.

Starting in chapter 7, we'll quickly get into the specifics of what to include in your classical art curriculum. If you're not already familiar with art education, this is where you'll learn the basics of art. I suggest you read this section and focus on learning the basics of art yourself. Then you can refer back to it as you teach art to your students.

The overview of basic art concepts in this part of the book (Part Two) does not include specific art skills such as shading a sphere, drawing a specific animal, or blending colors. Knowing how to implement those types of specific art skills is something that we learn through guided practical exercises, which I'll cover in Part Three of this book.

THE HISTORY OF CLASSICAL EDUCATION

Classical education began with the Greek culture, although it may have had Egyptian roots.[1] When the Romans adopted it, they altered it and added the names of the Seven Liberal Arts, which we now call the Trivium (grammar, rhetoric, and dialectic) and the Quadrivium (arithmetic, geometry, music, and astronomy).

As Christianity emerged within the Roman Empire, Christians were being persecuted for their faith. Many strongly spoke out against classical education because it was a pagan educational model, not centered on God. However, after Constantine legalized Christianity around 300 AD and Christians gained power, they adopted the model of classical education and altered its goals and assumptions. It became a path to God's Truth instead of something that could only teach pagan Greek and Roman ideas. From there, classical education became the most common educational structure in the European Medieval period (around 400 AD to around 1300 AD) and beyond.

In the early 1800s, the Prussians invented the industrial model of education, and Howard Mann introduced it to the United States in the mid-1800s. Near the end of the 1800s, "The Committee of Ten" standardized education in the US. By the early 1900s, John Dewey and other progressives introduced our current "modern" model of education, which differs a great deal from the classical model.

Today classical education is making a comeback. Many educators are learning about and incorporating this model. Since it has both pagan and Christian roots, you'll see it used in both Christian and secular settings.

CLASSICAL EDUCATION TODAY

The simplest way to describe the classical model is to tell you about the Trivium.

"Trivium" is a Latin word that means the three paths, or the place where three roads meet. In reference to the classical model of education, the

Trivium includes the three layers of learning: grammar, dialectic, and rhetoric (figure 5.1). (I've heard many synonyms used in place of "layers," such as stages, phases, paths, or types.)

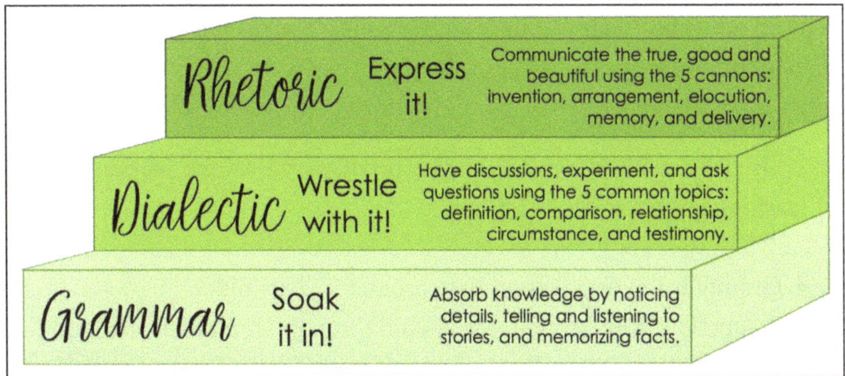

Fig. 5.1 - The Trivium is the three ways or the three layers of learning.

In the **grammar** layer of education, we emphasize training the brain to retain information. This is done by teaching students how to soak in information and remember it. We do this by spending our time noticing details, telling and listening to stories, and memorizing facts.

In the **dialectic** (also called "logic") layer of education, we emphasize training the brain to reason. This is where we teach students to wrestle with each subject by asking questions, having deep discussions, and experimenting. It's only through this wrestling with the material that students can arrive at a rich and nuanced understanding of the topic.

In the **rhetoric** layer of education, we emphasize training the brain to express what it has learned and discovered. While students accumulate knowledge in the grammar stage and grow in understanding in the dialectic stage, they then use that knowledge and understanding to persuasively express what is true, good and beautiful in the rhetoric stage. They do this by creating (inventions, books, songs, paintings, etc.), teaching, and leading others.

THE TRIVIUM AND BRAIN DEVELOPMENT

The Trivium is *extra* genius in how it aligns with the natural progression of brain development. Not only do these layers of learning go along with how an adult best learns a new subject, they also follow the brain development of children. This is the way our brains were designed to learn and grow. As children age, their brains go through different stages.

In each stage, a child's mind will be predisposed to one particular layer of learning:

- Grammar Layer: younger than around 9 years old
- Dialectic Layer: around 9 years old through around 15 years old
- Rhetoric Layer: usually over 15 years old

We focus on grammar with our youngest students because their brains are best suited to it. However, even six-year-olds will often master all the grammar of a subject they love and be ready to add on the dialectic layer. Both of my sons mastered the grammar of Legos at a very young age and were ready to move into the dialectic layer in this subject. I frequently overheard them, as early as four and six years old, having dialectic discussions about the best storage systems for Legos, whether or not sets of Legos should ever be mixed to create new designs, and the possible reasons why traditional Lego sets didn't include their favorite weapons.

As we grow in a subject and as we mature as individuals, we layer on dialectic learning and then rhetoric learning. These layers of learning are cumulative, not sequential! As adults, we're predisposed to want to spend all our time in the rhetoric layer, but we'll find value in moving back and forth among the layers when learning a new subject.

Within the Trivium (the three layers of learning), there are two key principles classical educators also utilize. The first principle is to prioritize the methods of learning above the content of what is taught. The second key principle is to integrate all the subjects together as much as possible.

KEY PRINCIPLE 1: PRIORITIZING METHODS OVER CONTENT

In a world where most education prioritizes workplace readiness, classical education prioritizes teaching the student *how* to think and *how* to learn.

However, in the process of teaching a student how to think and how to learn, we still need to practice our learning techniques on something. This is why we need good content. When teaching the skill of memorization, we intentionally pick out the most important information students will need to know and then resolutely memorize that limited information. For example, we've memorized Newton's three laws of motion, which helps us later when we study physics. However, our emphasis is on teaching students *how* to memorize. Our secondary goal is totally committing this information to memory so we can apply it later.

Prioritizing the skill of learning above the subject matter means we often cover **fewer unique subjects** than those in a traditional school setting who use the modern model of education. It's like a small, deep pool of water instead of a large shallow puddle. As a result, people are often impressed by the information our classically-educated children know because they actually remember what they were taught. This is the beauty of the classical model. In focusing on *how* to learn, students strengthen their brains and retain an incredible amount of information in their long-term memory.

The benefits of knowing *how* to learn don't stop there. Knowing how to learn is what grants students the freedom to learn any subject or vocational (career) skills they may need or want to know in the future and gives them the confidence that they *can* learn. As the world changes, they can be confident in their ability to grow and change with it, learning what they need to know for any job or situation.

The classical model also allows anyone to learn without being dependent on a single expert. By contrast, in an educational model that relies on experts, such as the modern model of education, the expert gives the student the answer. Receiving the answer from an expert is a quick way to arrive at a conclusion, but without knowing all the grammar (the basics) of the subject the student remains dependent on the expert to provide the next answer.

In the classical model, we still consider and discuss the ideas of experts, but only within the context of a thoughtful discussion, after we've learned the grammar of the subject. Experts become one of many resources, not the sole source of information on a subject.

For example, in an educational model that relies on experts, students are taught that evolution is responsible for the diversity of life we see on earth. Without any background knowledge, students can't discuss the merits of that claim or skillfully debate the idea. They can only accept or reject the idea as truth. Without any other method to discover truth, their choice is usually determined by who is relaying the content and whether or not they trust that source.

However, in classical education, students are first taught how to gather information (in the grammar layer) and then how to use the principles of logic and debate to discover truth (in the dialectic layer). When introducing students to the theory of evolution, we first teach students the grammar of biology, origin science, DNA replication, fossil creation, carbon dating, and more. Next, we facilitate a rich discussion about the strengths and weaknesses of the theory of evolution. Then students can decide for themselves if they believe that the theory of evolution is the best explanation for the diversity of life. In this way, we teach our students to research facts before they decide what to believe; we prioritize teaching them the method for discovering truth over any specific content.

How Does Prioritizing Methods over Content Relate to Art?

The classical model of education is why I frequently say (and host a podcast titled) "Anyone Can Teach Art." With the classical model, anyone can teach any subject! You don't need to be an expert to lead others through the learning process. Once we understand how learning takes place, any of us can pick up a new subject and 'teach' it as we learn alongside our students.

Art, like all subjects, starts with learning the basics, experimenting with ideas, and then using your knowledge and experience to create, teach, and lead. Most of us were educated under a modern educational system that told us to begin our art education with the last step: "Just create art!" But that's not how we best learn. Music teachers don't teach a child music by handing him/her a violin and saying, "Just create music!" Instead, we need to follow the stages of learning and progress through them, knowing the fruits of our labor will come at the end, not the beginning. You and your students can walk through these steps together. Using the classical model, you can be the 'lead learner' and you can all learn art creation and art appreciation without an art degree or formal art training.

KEY PRINCIPLE 2: THE MAGIC OF SUBJECT INTEGRATION

After prioritizing methods over content, the second key principle within the layers of classical learning is subject integration. All the pieces of information we know naturally intertwine with each other in our daily lives, so they should connect in the learning process as well. When all subjects are presented as ways to learn about the world God created and about God himself, students' brains will naturally make connections between subjects.

In contrast, modern education tends to artificially segment subjects into individual boxes like history, biology, or algebra. Sadly, this results in a diminished understanding of all the subjects, as the brain is stunted from making connections that aid memory and understanding. Of course, some segmentation will occur in all learning because it is a form of categorizing, which helps our brains simplify. However, it's not the same as separating subjects into their respective boxes and closing the lids, without any carryover between them.

To integrate subjects as you teach, simply ask your students if whatever you're learning at the moment reminds them of anything. You'll be amazed at how quickly the brain makes connections when we encourage it to!

How Does Subject Integration Relate to Art?

We explained some of the ways art can facilitate learning in other subjects in chapter 3 but there are also ways other subjects can inspire students to grow their art skills. For example:

- History: Recreate famous works of art or sketch out a scene from a historical event.
- Biology/Ecology: Sketch your subject and label the parts, go on a nature walk and sketch something interesting, or trace and label a diagram.
- Physics/Math: Create a drawing so you can visualize a word problem.
- Literature: Look at the artwork in an illustrated version of the literature you're reading or create your own illustration of your favorite scene from the book.
- Handwriting: Write out a favorite quote or Bible verse in your very best handwriting and hang it on the wall, framed or pinned to a cork board.

There are an infinite number of ways to incorporate art in your education! I'd love to see all the ways you uncover. (Refer to the last page of this book for how to best connect with me!) Next, we'll dive into each of the layers of learning to discover what they are and how to teach art within each layer.

CHAPTER SUMMARY

- Classical education has both pagan and Christian roots and is used in both Christian and secular education today.
- The overarching framework of the classical model of education is the Trivium, which includes the three layers of learning: 1) grammar, where students are trained to retain information, 2) dialectic, where students are trained to reason and 3) rhetoric, where students are trained to express truth, beauty, and goodness.
- The layers of learning align with brain development. However, we never outgrow any of the layers of learning.
- Within the Trivium, educators utilize two key principles: 1) prioritizing the methods of learning over the content learned, and 2) integrating all subjects.

6

THE GRAMMAR LAYER

In the grammar layer of education, we're primarily training the brain to retain information. This is done by teaching students how to soak in and remember information like definitions, lists, formulas, and dates. We retain information best by **noticing details, telling and listening to stories, and memorizing facts.** Let's look at each of these a little closer within the context of art education.

NOTICING DETAILS

We're bombarded with so much information every day. Our brains do us a great service by filtering out any information it deems unimportant. However, the brain doesn't always make the best choices as to what to remember and what to forget. For example, just yesterday I found myself remembering a jingle from a 1980's pizza commercial when what I really wanted to remember was where I set my keys down.

Oftentimes, just taking a few minutes to intentionally notice something will help us remember it. For example, if I take the time to say out loud, "I'm putting my keys inside my purse," I'm much more likely to remember that's where they are. If I were to take it another step further and draw a quick picture of a key in a purse, I definitely wouldn't forget it!

We experience the same effect when we're learning. It's very easy to quickly gloss over something, but we remember much more by looking carefully, listening closely, and noticing the details of the item. We can encourage these habits by naming and drawing what we see when we're on a nature walk or by physically showing, with math manipulatives, what's happening in a math problem.

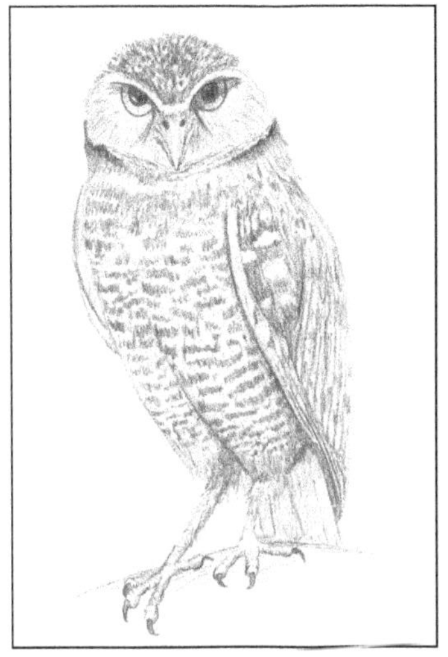

Fig. 6.1 - I learned more about Burrowing Owls sketching this one than I could have by observing it with no intent to sketch.

In art creation, we spend time noticing the details of the subject we're drawing. This is why so many artists say learning to draw is primarily learning to see what is actually there. Our brains want to simplify what we see, often causing us to skim over the details of what we're looking at and reduce the elaborate beauty before us into a simple concept. For example, when we first see an owl, our brains convert the detailed visual image to a single verbal idea: 'owl.' The visual picture of the owl may never even be stored in our memory. However, when we start to draw an owl (figure 6.1), we're forced to look for and notice the details of that visual image. We begin to notice the way its beak curves, the way the feathers overlap, and the way its toes orient themselves.

In art appreciation, we spend time noticing the details within a famous work of art. We do this by talking about a piece of art with a friend, playing "I Spy" games, or recreating famous works of art.

For example, when observing a painting like *The Burial of the Count of Orgaz* by El Greco (figure 6.2) you might first notice that the painting seems to be cut in half horizontally, separating the natural from the supernatural. Next you might look closer at what all the people are doing in the painting.

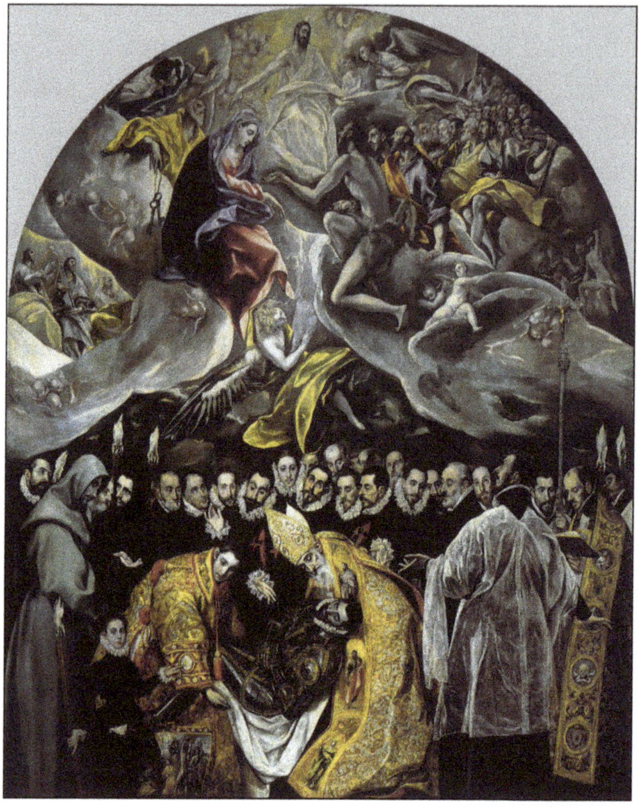

Fig. 6.2 - How many details can you pick out in this painting, *The Burial of the Count of Orgaz* (c.1588) by El Greco? Now ask a friend what details they notice.

Any time you're looking at a painting with your students, ask them what interesting details they see in the painting. You'll probably be surprised by something you missed upon first inspection!

This skill of noticing details can be taught and learned, and it's a foundational skill for visual arts just as it is in other subjects.

STORIES

Stories are another incredible way to help retain information. A story creates a framework within the human brain that makes it much easier to stay focused, understand, and retain the information. Young children love to hear stories, even when they aren't willing to sit still and look at a book. I remember my mom entertaining my children for hours with silly made up stories, even when they were quite young. Now, my sons have taken up the habit and tell each other stories that never end but just continue from day to day!

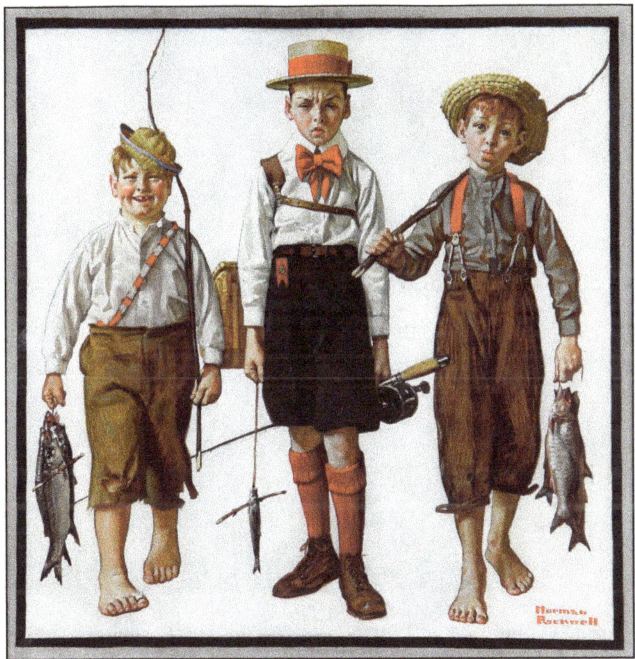

Fig. 6.3 - In *Catch* (1919) by Norman Rockwell, you can 'read' the background story of what happened leading up to this moment in the details of the painting: the boys' clothing and facial expressions, the size of their fish, and the quality of their fishing poles.

Our brains are hardwired to engage with stories. Blogger and podcaster, Mike McHargue (also known as "Science Mike") explains that the human brain tends to spend a large amount of time daydreaming. However, when immersed in a story, he says, the story captivates the brain and we stop daydreaming. This is probably why Jesus spoke in parables and why today's marketers tell a quick story in each commercial. It's also why stories are used extensively in education.

Stories are works of art in and of themselves, but they also focus the brain and engage our full attention. Stories help us remember and facilitate great discussions of ideas and concepts.

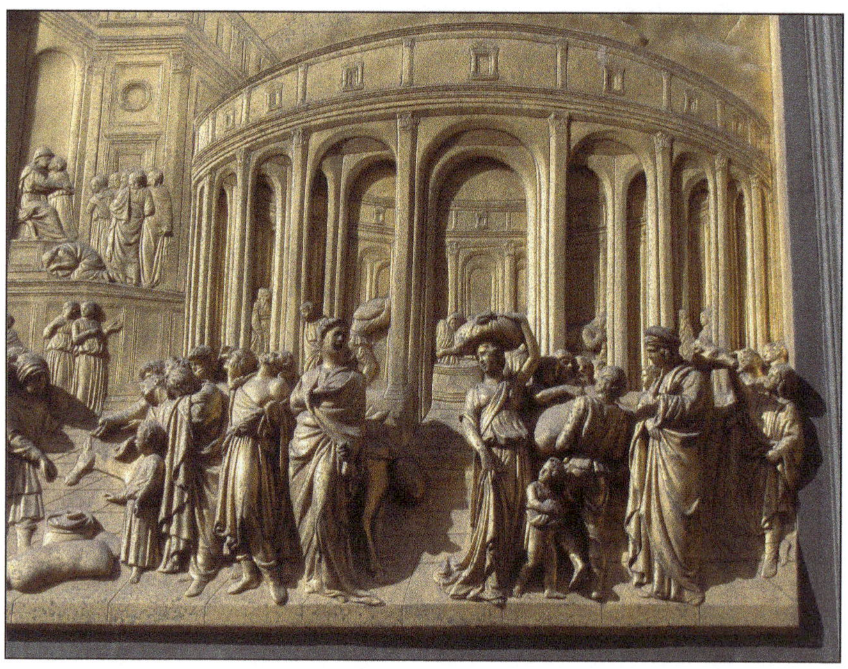

Fig. 6.4 - This gilded (gold-covered) bronze relief by Ghiberti's, made in the 1400s, shows the Biblical story of Joseph, as told in Genesis, by incorporating several scenes from Joseph's life in one panel.

In art appreciation, we can see how artists like Norman Rockwell (figure 6.3) captivate their viewers with a story depicted in their art. In Medieval and Renaissance art, we see Biblical stories depicted on frescos, stained glass, and paintings. These visual stories were used to teach church members about the Bible. For example, Ghiberti's golden doors on the

Florence Baptistry (figure 6.4) depict scenes from the Old and New Testament, which helped the public learn the stories of the Bible.

Similarly, modern-day illustrators bring stories to life with works of art that follow the author's storyline. We're drawn deeper into the story by seeing a visual representation of that moment. The combination of the story and the picture activates our brains to notice and remember.

Use this in your art appreciation time by asking your students what they think might be going on in a painting. What might have happened right before? What might happen right after? Also, reading short story books about a well-known artist helps us remember the artist and his/her artwork.

In art creation, we can use a story to create compelling works of art by imagining what might be happening before and after the moment in time depicted by the picture. Including clues about the story within the art adds interest and fun to the picture.

THE IMPORTANCE OF MEMORIZATION

Memorization is an important element in the grammar layer of a student's education. Our current culture often avoids memorization, probably because so few people are taught *how* to easily memorize. Having never experienced the benefits of memorization, we might believe it's boring, mindless, or useless. However, experience with memorization will teach us that it's valuable and useful because it gives us:

1. An easy place to start learning
2. A framework for our future learning, both within and beyond the time set aside for learning
3. A common language for discussing our ideas with others

1. Memorization give us an easy place to start learning

Memorizing gives us a great place to begin learning any subject, because you don't need to fully grasp a concept or have a deep understanding of an idea in order to memorize a few terms or a summary sentence. Later, as the brain matures and we encounter the ideas again and again, the understanding will layer on top of the memorization.

I see this frequently within my own family. We'll memorize a sentence full of names or terms that mean nothing to us only to start noticing them in unexpected places. I'll never forget the light bulb moment I had in Costco many years ago. It was our first year homeschooling and we'd just memorized a sentence about Simón Bolívar liberating South America when I saw Marie Arana's book *Bolívar* for sale in Costco. I picked up the book and read the back of it. The information was fascinating and I felt curious to know more. Prior to learning one short sentence about Bolívar, I'm sure I would have never noticed the book. If someone had shown me the book it would have seemed overwhelming. However, because we'd started learning about Bolívar with a simple sentence to memorize, the dense 625-page book seemed inviting.

The fact that you don't need to fully understand what you're memorizing is very liberating! It gives you a simple, straightforward place to start learning without the pressure to understand it all. However, many people are hesitant to believe it's true. You may need to experience the beauty of learning via the classical model before you're willing to trust that it works!

2. Memorization give us a framework for our future learning

Memorizing the basics of a subject also helps the brain grasp and notice concepts that would otherwise be missed. How might we miss information on an unfamiliar subject? As I mentioned, our brains process an enormous amount of information every day. In order to function efficiently and not become overloaded with too much input, our brains must automatically filter out some information. The filtering process is a normal part of our lives, so we don't notice we're doing it. However, once we learn the basics of a subject, the information no longer seems irrelevant to our brains. Then, when we encounter the subject again, our brains will notice it and connect it to the basics we previously learned. The most surprising aspect of this process is that it suddenly seems like we're encountering that subject with increased frequency. Experts call this the Baader-Meinhof Phenomenon or the Frequency Illusion.

For example, have you ever been shopping for a car and thought there couldn't be many of a particular make and model of car in your city because you've never seen them? Then once you decide to buy one, you notice them everywhere you go! That's the Frequency Illusion at work.

The way this filtering process affects education is profound. Before we've learned the basic terms and concepts of a subject, our brains will often disregard, or label as irrelevant, any input related to that unknown subject. Then, we memorize a few terms or a summary sentence about that subject and we suddenly begin to notice and remember additional information about that subject. In this way, memorizing basic information, even without a thorough understanding of that information, provides us a foundation on which to build future learning.

We can see these same benefits of memorization in art education. For example, once we memorize the seven methods of perspective in art (covered in chapter 22), we will start to notice them in everyday life as well as in the art around us. We'll notice how the farther clouds are closer to the horizon line and how closer mountains are darker and greener than farther ones. We'll see how a rounded column has a gradual change in tone while the color changes abruptly at the corner of a building. Once we study an art concept, we'll notice references or uses of it everywhere. Our brains can now gather this additional information and file it right next to the memorized grammar. In this way, memorizing introductory information about a subject increases our learning beyond our dedicated study time.

. . .

3. Memorization give us a common language for discussing our ideas with others

Memorizing the grammar (the basics of any given subject) also gives us a common language with others. Having a common language is important for all types and levels of artists because it allows them to collaborate with and learn from each other. Someone might be a child prodigy with an amazing natural gift for creating art or music, but without knowing the common language of the subject, they will be limited in their development because discussing and sharing thoughts and talents with others is an important part of learning.

I've learned so much about art from others that I wouldn't have learned without having memorized the grammar of art. Knowing the grammar facilitates learning, whether it's from an in-person art class, an art book, a YouTube video, or a casual conversation about art with friends. The effect is even more pronounced as art skills advance, because the more advanced instruction assumes the student is familiar with the basics. Educational sources such as textbooks and advanced lectures assume the student is familiar with art terms and therefore no longer define them. Instead, they devote their time and instruction to more advanced concepts. If you have memorized the grammar and can understand the common language, you can continue your learning using advanced instruction.

HOW TO MEMORIZE

Here is the good news: Memorization can be both easy and fun! Our brains are like muscles that grow stronger every time we use them. The more we memorize, the easier memorization becomes.

In the classical model of education, we use repetition, intensity and duration to memorize.

- Repetition: hearing and saying the information again and again
- Intensity: repeating the information in silly, dramatic, or unusual

ways to make an emotional connection in the brain, which makes the information easier to remember (Stories are a great way to create intensity!)
- Duration: repeating the information day after day and week after week in order to move the information from short-term to long-term memory

As we repeat the information with intensity and duration, we use tools that incorporate all the senses as much as possible. These tools include songs, hand motions, visuals, skits, stories, activities, and more.

We can use all the tools with all subjects, but certain subjects lend themselves more readily to certain tools. For example, we use more visuals than songs in art education. However, we tend to use few visuals when memorizing a list of prepositions.

Each student will find they enjoy and have more success with certain tools than others. For example, my older son likes to have a visual and auditory component to his memory work, while I find it's easier to memorize with kinesthetic activities like hand motions and rewriting sentences. The information we memorize in the grammar layer of learning is incredibly valuable, but even more importantly, each student ends up knowing how to painlessly memorize whatever they need to learn in the future.

DON'T FOCUS ON OUTPUT IN THE GRAMMAR LAYER

Starting with the grammar, as the classical method prescribes, may appear to be a slow way to learn since there's no visible output at first. In our results-oriented culture, this can be frustrating (especially for us homeschool parents who feel responsible for producing proof that our children are, in fact, learning something). However, the classical method ends up being the fastest way to arrive at understanding and wisdom–our goals of education.

We can see the logic in the classical approach when we look at other subjects. In music, we start learning scales before we write an original sonata. In writing, we learn the structure and style before we jump in and write a novel.

In art, we need to learn to draw basic shapes and create simple value scales before we create a masterpiece of art. While there are some who say we should "just let the children be creative" and not formally teach art concepts, this leaves students to learn solely through experimentation. Experimentation alone is truly the slowest way to learn, and it results in most students getting frustrated and quitting before they produce a work of art they love. When we start with the grammar, however, we avoid having to learn art solely through experimentation.

In the grammar layer of learning, we teach students to notice details, tell and listen to stories, and memorize facts. We save experimentation for the dialectic layer, where we can productively wrestle with the grammar through questions and discussion. Then in the rhetoric layer, we produce new, creative works of art. Like sowing seeds, the process is simple but the harvest doesn't come until later, after all the work has been put in.

If you have natural talent, then great! You'll find the grammar of art gives words to concepts you knew intuitively but weren't able to explain to others. If you feel like you don't have any natural artistic talent, then get ready–there's a basic set of art knowledge I'm going to teach you that's going to open up your world and turn you into an artist

So, what's the grammar of art? What art-related content can we teach our students (and ourselves), so they don't have to learn art through experimentation alone? In the next chapter, I'll teach you the components of art grammar that you can then turn around and teach your students. In Part Three of this book, I'll give you the tools and exercises I use to teach these basics.

CHAPTER SUMMARY

- In the grammar layer of learning, we train the brain to retain information by focusing on the fundamentals of each subject as we are noticing details, telling and listening to stories, and memorizing facts.
- Memorization gives us an easy place to start learning, a framework for our future learning, and a common language for discussing our ideas with others. In the classical model of education, we use repetition, intensity and duration to memorize.
- All these skills can be taught and learned, and art is a great way to develop them. Trust that the classical process works and be patient. The results will come with time.

7

ART GRAMMAR

Now you have a basic understanding of the grammar layer of the classical model of education and how it relates to the subject of art. Next, you'll need to know what specific information to teach your students in the grammar layer of learning. We refer to this collection of information as the 'grammar' of the subject, also called the 'basics' or 'fundamentals.' In chapters 7-12, I'm going to teach you art grammar so that you can teach it to your students. Then in chapters 13-17, I'll explain what the dialectic and rhetoric layers of learning include in art.

Another way to think of this part of the book is the 'scope' for your introductory art curriculum. Remember, the classical model shows us *how* to teach and learn; it's the method. However, the classical model does *not* tell us *what* content to learn. These next chapters are an overview of *what* to learn in art, or the content of art education.

How do we choose what to learn for each subject, especially a subject like art? We look ahead at what information will be most useful when we're in the dialectic and rhetoric layers of learning. It may be hard to know exactly what information is important later in art (or any subject) if you yourself are new to the subject. However, we can utilize the resources around us (like this book) to pick the content that is most likely to be helpful, knowing we'll keep memorizing new content as we add on the other two layers of learning.

While there's a little variation on what constitutes the grammar of any subject, there's a surprising consensus in most subjects, including art. If you pick up any advanced art book, you'll see the same concepts and vocabulary words sprinkled throughout as you'd find in many state and national visual arts standards. Since this information forms the foundation of art education, it's taught in many elementary art classes. The biggest difference is *how* it's taught. Since most traditional schools don't use the classical model of education, the grammar of art is typically taught as something to be discovered instead of something to be memorized. However, we know helping students memorize the grammar of art will make learning simpler and easier.

Don't be intimidated by the grammar of art. I've taken this opportunity to thoroughly explain each component of art grammar for you so you can teach with confidence. Teaching your students these basic concepts will help them reap all the benefits of art and creativity in their education.

THE MAIN COMPONENTS OF ART GRAMMAR ARE:

1. The seven elements of art
2. The principles of design
3. Techniques/media
4. Skills
5. Purposes of art
6. Art history
7. Art appreciation

As we start to understand the components of this list, we'll see that some of the ideas overlap a little. However, looking at each area individually will allow us to understand the grammar we need for future studies. As they appear in your art creation and art appreciation, you can call attention to them, but there's no need to teach them in this order.

Be sure to cover each one at least once over the course of your entire multi-year art curriculum. If you look back on your art projects and discover you didn't introduce one particular element or component, simply plan an art lesson that incorporates it.

To help students understand how the components of art grammar fit together, I find it helpful to keep posters with these key ideas hung in my classroom. Whenever I mention an item on one of the posters, I point it out and review where it fits. For example, if I'm teaching a lesson that includes 'value,' one of the seven elements of art, I point to the elements of art poster and sing the 15 second song we made up of all seven elements of art.

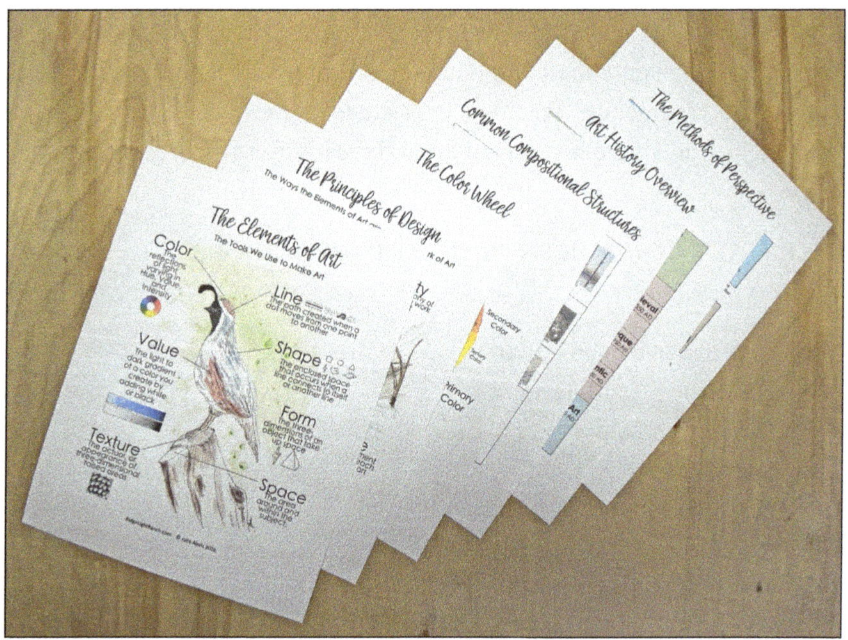

Fig. 7.1 - These posters make great visuals in your school room. You can download them free from my website as explained in the front matter of this book.

You and your students can make your own posters or download printable versions (figure 7.1) included in your free Art Teacher Kit (as explained in the front matter of this book). When you introduce or discuss a component of art grammar, point to the poster and remind the students how it fits into the larger whole.

Over the next five chapters I'm going to explain each of the components of art grammar, starting with the best-known component, the seven elements of art.

CHAPTER SUMMARY

- The main components of art grammar are: the seven elements of art, the principles of design, techniques/media, skills, purposes of art, art history, and art appreciation.
- While they don't need to be taught in order, try to teach each element one or more times throughout your students' art education.

8

ART GRAMMAR: THE SEVEN ELEMENTS OF ART

The most fundamental and widely known component of art grammar is called the elements of art. Think of the elements as the 'tools' we use to draw. Since creating a work of visual art is more about seeing what exists than about what your hands are doing, the seven elements of art could also be thought of as the seven things we look for when observing our subject in order to create art.

THE SEVEN ELEMENTS OF ART ARE:

- Line
- Shape
- Form
- Space
- Value
- Color
- Texture

You'll find the elements most intuitive for your students when you are teaching basic drawing with pencil, so I suggest you introduce them then.

However, we use the elements of art anytime we create art, even in three-dimensional media. Once your students have learned the elements of art in relation to drawing, it will become easier to see how they apply to all forms of visual art.

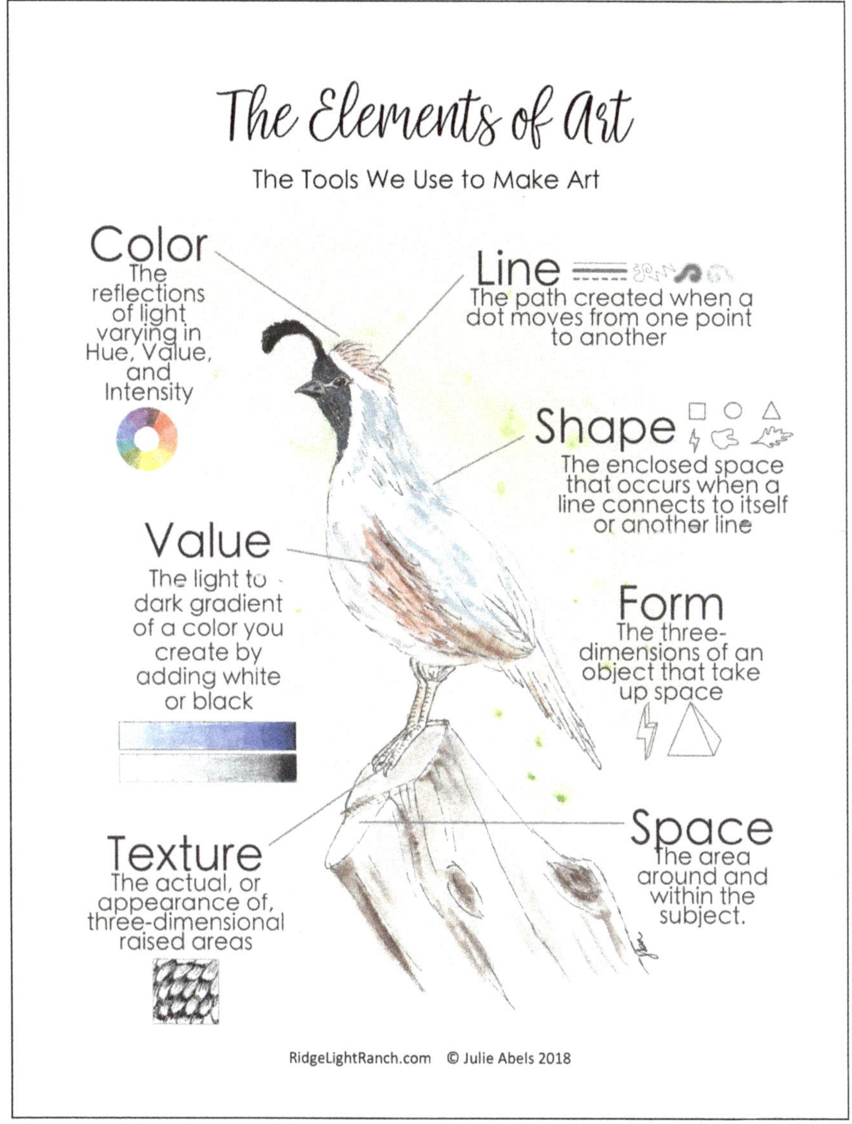

Fig. 8.1 - This poster showing the seven elements of art is a great visual to post in your school room.

The elements work together like different components of a machine, so they feel a little awkward broken apart. However, breaking them down can help budding artists learn in manageable segments.

It's great to discuss each applicable element of art in any art lesson you're teaching. If possible, point them out on a classroom poster (figure 8.1) as you mention them. As students become familiar with these words, they'll have a vocabulary that allows them to learn faster and express themselves with clarity and ease.

Line: the path created when a dot moves from one point to another

A line is defined precisely in math, but much more loosely in art. Lines can be:

- thick or thin
- horizontal, vertical, or diagonal
- solid or broken
- curved, straight, or angled

If there's more than one line, they can be parallel, perpendicular, or oblique. In art, a strict definition of a "line" is not nearly as important as the general concept, so don't spend too much time trying to establish what's a line and what's not a line.

Play around with making different kinds of lines. Think about what kinds of lines make up different letters of the alphabet and what kinds of lines you see in abstract art. Lines can be used to create simple drawings of almost any subject, as seen in numerous cave paintings (figure 8.2 and 8.3). When you're introducing a new medium, like a new kind of pen or marker, have your students practice making different kinds of lines so they get a feel for what the medium is capable of doing.

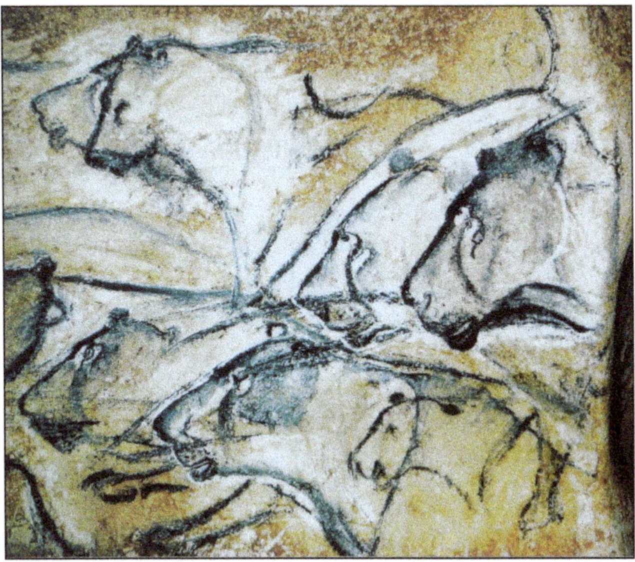

Fig. 8.2 - These prehistoric cave paintings in the Chauvet caves in France by unknown artists are a great example of how much information can be conveyed with simple lines.

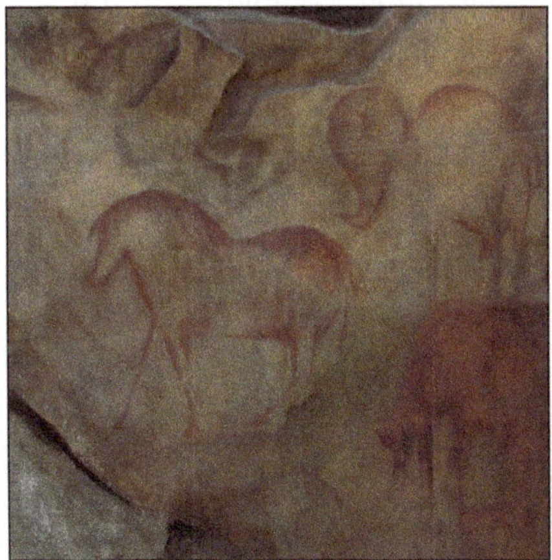

Fig. 8.3 - These prehistoric cave paintings in the Kapova Cave in Southern Ural by unknown artists use a different style of lines as compared to the Chauvet cave paintings.

Shape: the enclosed space that occurs when a line connects to itself or another line

Lines can create shapes. Generally, whenever a line crosses over itself or connects back to itself, we say a shape has been created. Again, don't allow yourself or your students to get too picky regarding what's a shape and what's not. Learning *how* to use this tool is more important than an exact definition.

There are geometric shapes like circles, squares, and triangles, and irregular/organic shapes we might call blobs, splatters, and streaks. We often use organic shapes when drawing nature and geometric shapes when drawing man-made objects.

When drawing with new artists, talk about a specific shape by describing the lines that create the shape. For example, a square is made of four straight, equal lines joining at right angles, while a leaf can be made from two opposite (or mirrored) curved lines.

Start with shapes your students already know how to draw, and then build more complex shapes from the basic ones. For example, start with a circle and a triangle, and then show students how a circle and a triangle come together to form a more complex teardrop shape. Now use these lines and basic shapes to draw a subject.

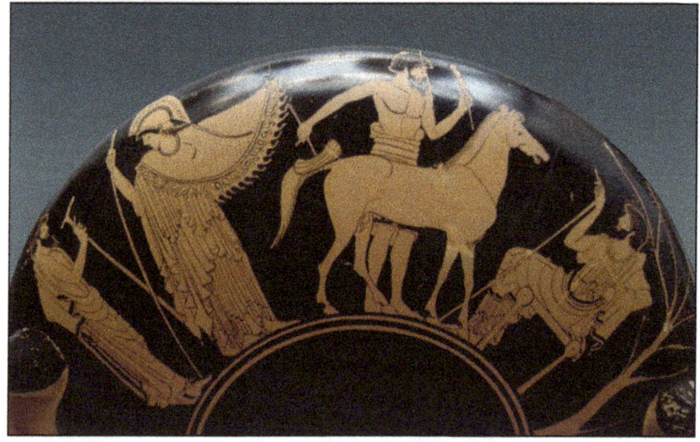

Fig. 8.4 - The simple art on this Archaic Greek pottery uses lines to create shapes.

Keep in mind, many preschoolers are just learning to draw the most basic shapes like circles, squares, and triangles. Have patience and remind your students to have patience with themselves.

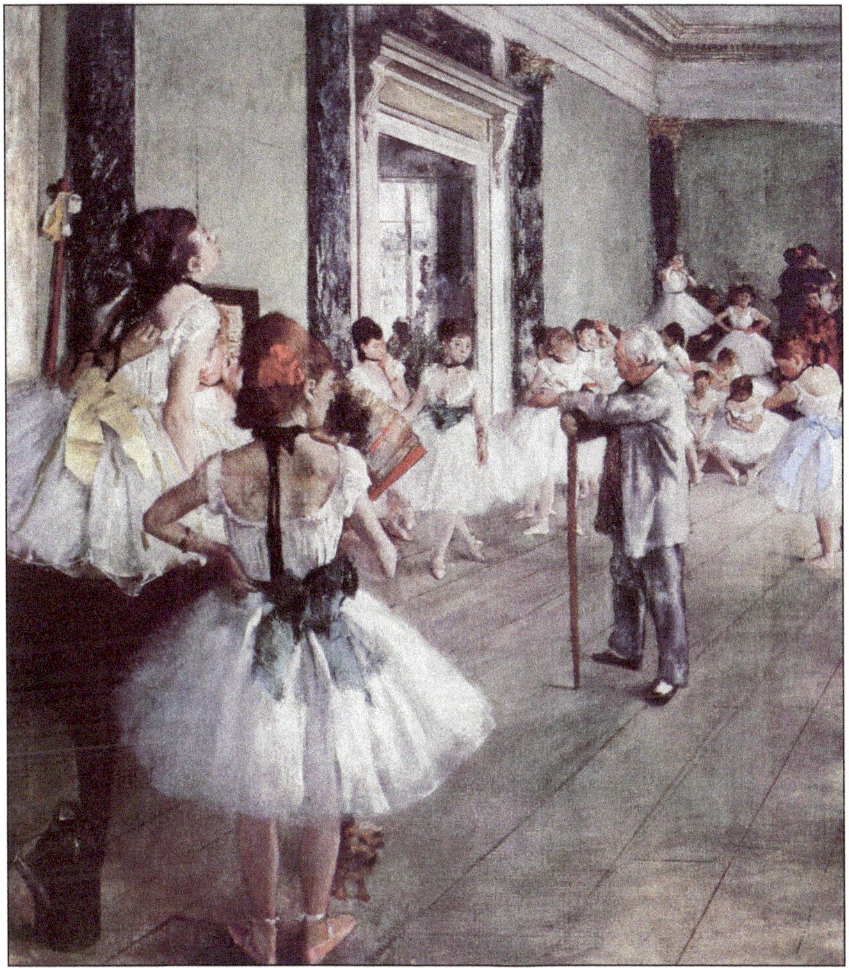

Fig. 8.5 - The elaborate, complex art of Edgar Degas' *The Dance Class* (1874) began with lines creating shapes. Of course, Degas also made use of additional elements of art and principles of design.

Shapes can be seen in almost all art. For example, the simple decorations on Archaic Greek pottery (figure 8.4) are made from lines coming together to form shapes, without additional color, value or texture. A more complex and elaborate work of art, like Degas' *The Dance Class* (figure 8.5), is still drawn using lines that come together to form shapes. The difference is that *The Dance Class* also includes use of all the other elements of art and principles of design.

Form: the three-dimensions of an object that takes up space

Form is three-dimensional. Only three-dimensional works of art like sculptures, paper-mâché, fiber arts, and so on, have actual form. For example, *The Thinker* (figure 8.6) is a marble sculpture with true form.

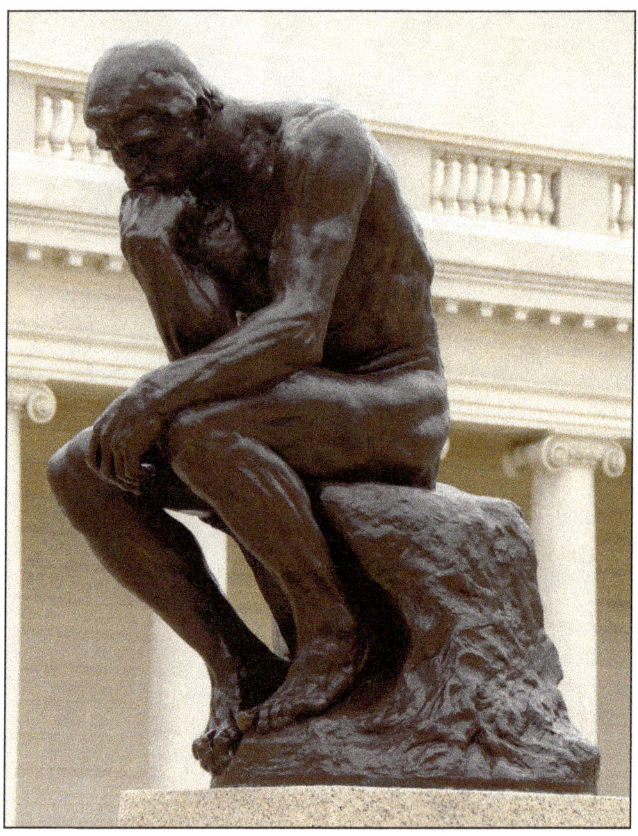

Fig. 8.6 - *The Thinker* (also called *The Poet*), made by Auguste Rodin in 1880, is a three-dimensional cast bronze statue and is a great example of the traditional definition of form.

Two-dimensional art often has the appearance or illusion of form. Be aware that some people are very precise about 'form' being three dimensional while other people will refer to the illusion of form as 'form.' I'm generally not picky about which way students use the word.

We create the illusion of form by using one or more of the 'methods of perspective' in the space of the artwork. (See chapter 23 for more details about creating the illusion of depth using the methods of perspective.)

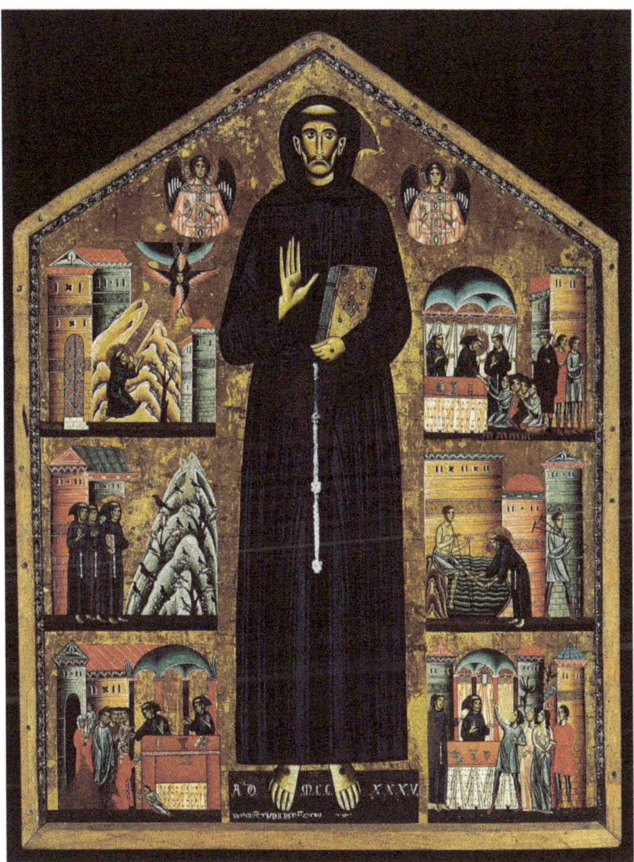

Fig. 8.7 - This medieval painting, *St. Francis of Assisi* (1235) by Bonaventura Berlinghieri, is intentionally flat. The artist purposely avoided using some of the methods of perspective to create a distinctive look with less form.

While most two-dimensional art has the appearance of form, sometimes an artist intentionally limits form and purposely creates 'flat' art. For example, medieval art is often flat like the 1235 painting, *St. Francis of Assisi* (figure 8.7) by Bonaventura Berlinghieri.

You can practice creating true form in three-dimensional art or practice creating the illusion of form in two-dimensional art. I love the variety of creating both types of art. Many students who are easily frustrated with two-dimensional art come alive when the three-dimensional art media comes out.

Space: the area around and within the subject

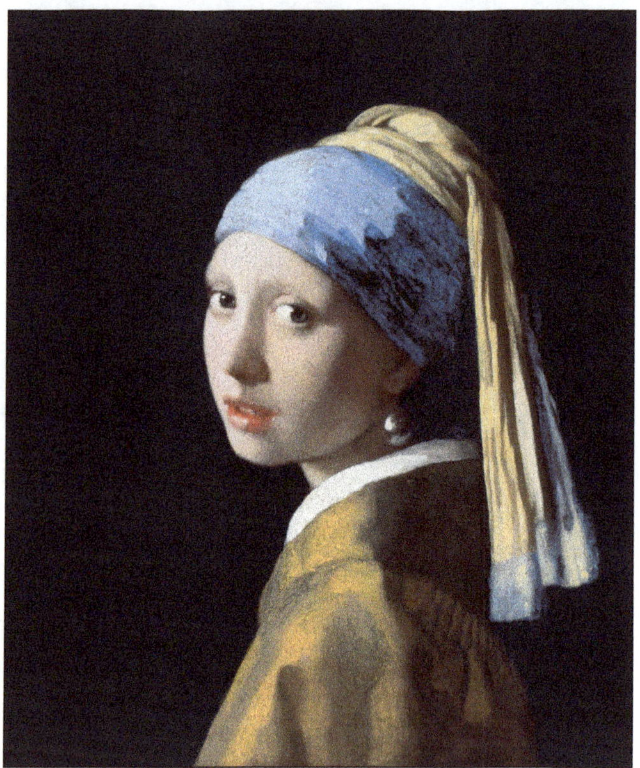

Fig. 8.8 - The blank, black background in *Girl with a Pearl Earring* (1665) by Johannes Vermeer is considered 'white space,' even though it's black. In this painting, Vermeer chose to leave the space around his subject and draw all the attention to the girl.

How we use the space of a work of art will impact the work itself. When teaching art creation, we want students to think about and be intentional with the space in their art. Will they choose to fill the paper or leave a lot of white space (blank space)? Will they draw off the edge of the paper or leave a border? Will they draw big so the subject doesn't fit on the paper or draw small? Do they want to emphasize the foreground (close up), the midground, or background (far away)? Will their art emphasize the positive space (the subject) or the negative space (the space around and behind the subject)?

For example, in *Girl with a Pearl Earring* (figure 8.8), the artist, Johannes Vermeer, left a blank, black background. Even though it's black, we still refer to it as 'white space.' In contrast, Paul Signac used the foreground, midground, and background in his painting, *Notre Dame de la Garde* (figure 8.9).

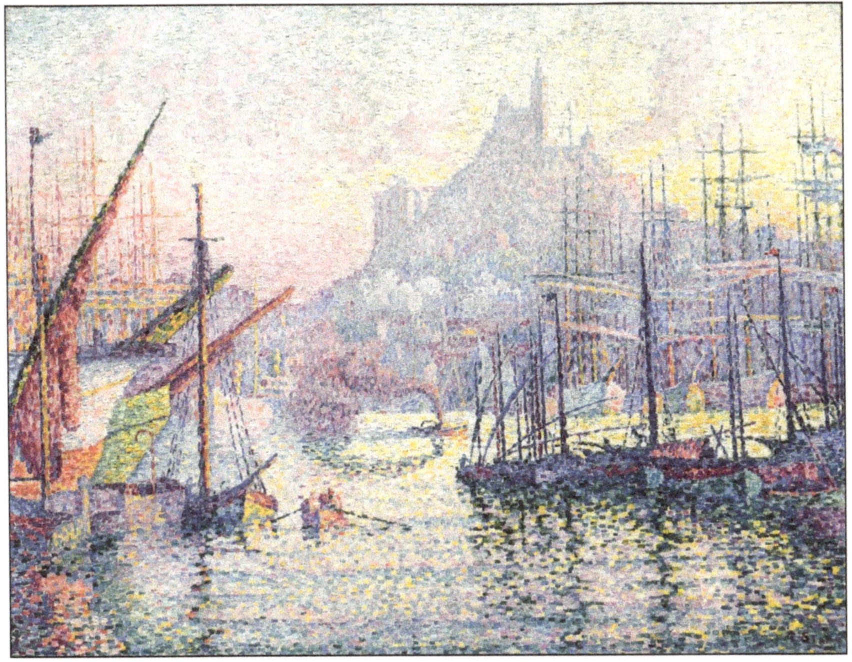

Fig. 8.9 - In Notre Dame de la Garde (1905), Paul Signac made full use of the foreground, midground, and background and painted all the way to the edge, making full use of his canvas.

The concepts of positive and negative space can also be very helpful when learning to draw a subject accurately. Often, we don't fully see the shape of the object we're drawing unless we look at both the shape of the object itself (the positive space) and the shape of the negative space around it. For example, when you look at a pinecone (figure 8.10A), it's hard to see the exact shape of each scale. However, when we look at the negative space around the pinecone (figure 8.10B), our brains can see the actual shape better and our ability to accurately draw it improves drastically!

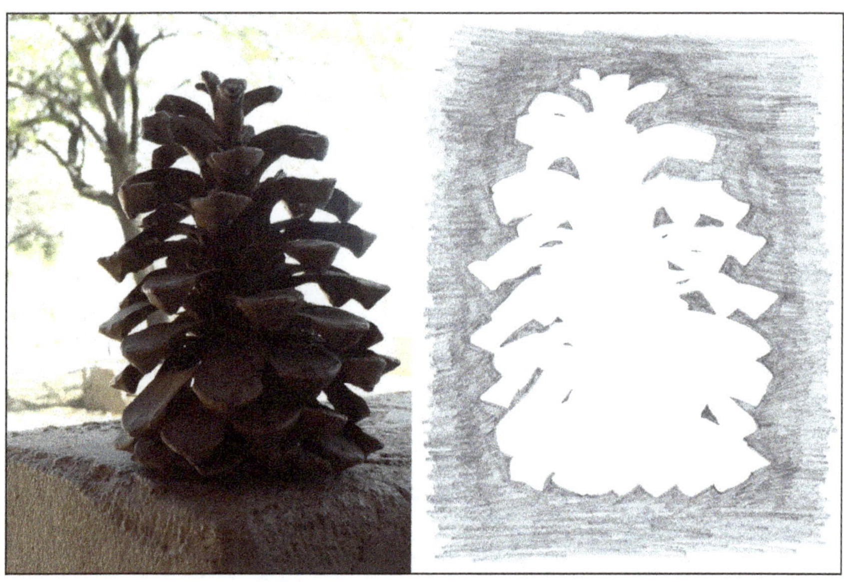

Fig. 8.10 - This photograph I took of a pinecone emphasizes the positive shape of the pinecone while my graphite (pencil) sketch emphasizes the negative space around the pinecone.

Value: the light to dark gradient of a color, typically created by adding white or black

Value, often used synonymously with 'tone,' is the light or dark variation of a color you create by adding white or black. Adding white creates a 'tint' while adding black creates a 'shade.'

With a colored medium, such as colored pencil, we usually create a value scale in one color. With graphite, charcoal, or another colorless medium, we create a simple white to black value scale instead (figure 8.11).

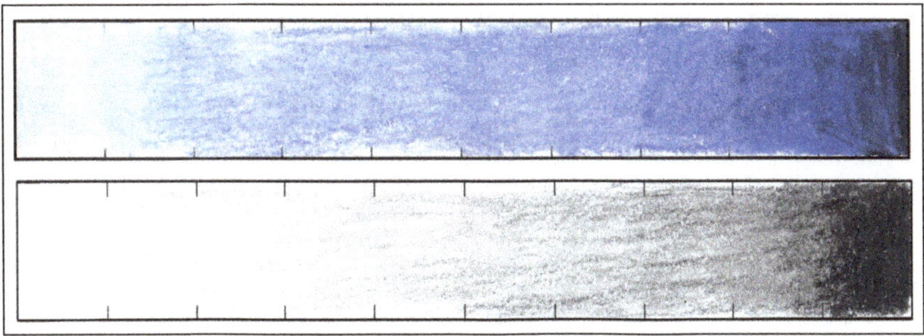

Fig. 8.11 - These two value scales show the full range of values for a graphite pencil and a colored pencil.

Any time you introduce a new medium, try creating a small value scale where you blend from white to black using a color with all the progressive variations in between. (See chapter 21, Drills for Seeing Value, for how to create a value scale.)

Color: the reflections of light varying in hue, value, and intensity

- **Hue:** the purest form of a color
- **Intensity:** the brightness or saturation of a color

Scientifically, color consists of rays of light at different wavelengths. When these rays hit our eyes, they create a sensation which our brains interpret as color. In art, however, color is much more than a sensation. It is such an expansive subject that many books have been written about color alone. The following gives a basic overview of color.

It's best to start with the simple definitions of color, hue, and intensity (above).

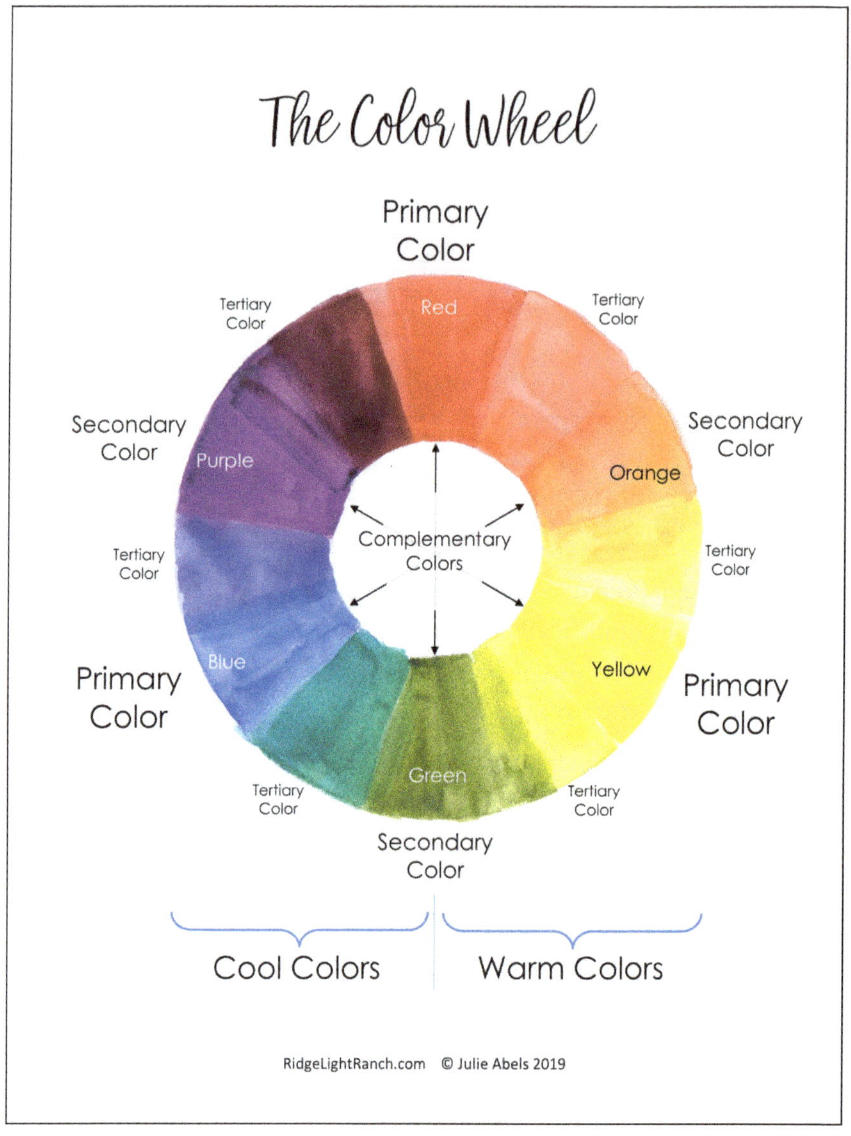

Fig. 8.12 - A color wheel shows the result of mixing colors and often conveys other important information and vocabulary about Color Theory.

Then introduce the color wheel (figure 8.12) and these color groupings:

- **Primary colors:** red, blue, and yellow

- **Secondary colors:** orange, green, and purple
- **Tertiary colors:** colors that fall between each primary and secondary color, like red-orange or turquoise
- **Complementary colors:** colors directly across the color wheel from each other, like orange and blue (Using complementary colors next to each other gives a high contrast look. 'Contrast' is the use of opposite elements of art together to create interest. See chapter 9 for more information about Contrast, one of the principles of design. Mixing complementary colors together results in a brownish, neutral color.)
- **Analogous colors:** colors that are next to each other on the color wheel, like red and purple
- **Warm colors:** red, orange, and yellow (These colors give a high energy feeling.)
- **Cool colors:** green, blue, and purple (These colors tend to be more calming.)
- **Monochromatic colors:** variations in value and/or intensity of the same hue, such as several different blue

In the element of color, we can also learn about color mixing and context of color. The 'context of color' is the perception that a color looks different depending on what other colors are alongside it.

In the classroom, start with the simple exercise of creating your own color wheel. Then practice mixing colors. Next, try a painting project using a color grouping (like warm colors) and then paint the same subject with a different color grouping (like cool colors) to experience the effect colors have on the end result. Look at the results with your students and ask your yourselves how the different combinations make you all feel.

Responses to color are individual in some ways but universal in other ways. For example, in my *America in Color* series (figure 8.13), everyone I asked agreed the *Natural* version was much more calming than the *Impact* version.

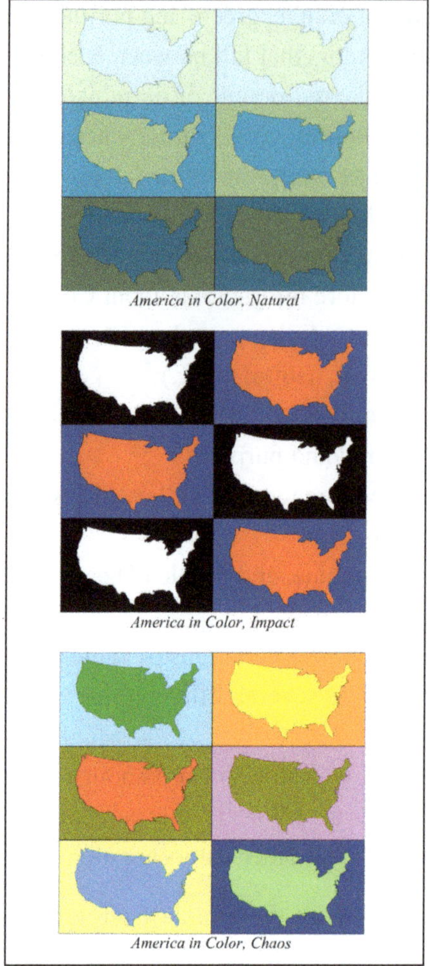

Fig 8.13 - This series of images I created, called *America in Color,* for an art lesson plan about the pop art artist, Andy Warhol, are identical except for their color schemes. What does each color combination make you think or feel?

Artists often work within color themes. Studying a specific artist can provide a great way to learn about color. For example, Pieter Bruegel the Elder's painting *Winter Landscape with Skaters* (figure 8.14) is a great example of an almost monochromatic color scheme. Other artists use bold contrasting colors, as Piet Mondrian did in his painting, *Composition in Red, Yellow, Blue and Black* (figure 8.15).

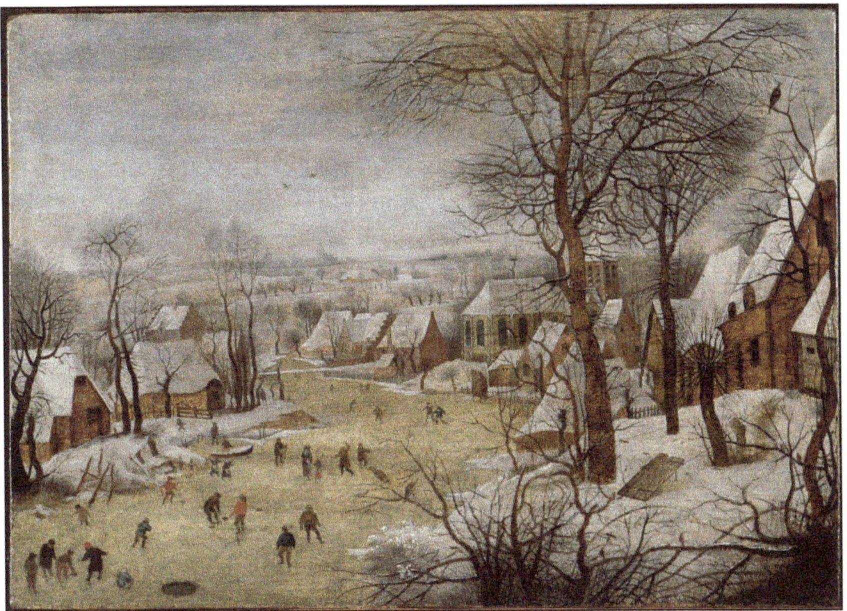

Fig. 8.14 - *Winter Landscape with Skaters* (1565), by Pieter Bruegel the Elder, shows a limited, almost monochromatic color scheme.

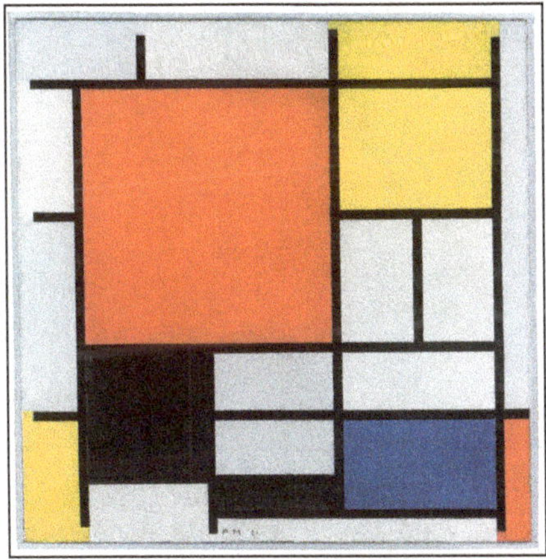

Fig. 8.15 - This 1921 painting by Piet Mondrian called *Composition in Red, Yellow, Blue, and Black* shows a bold use of primary colors.

Some artists go through an extended period of time experimenting and practicing with one color. A famous example of this is Picasso and his blue period.

Claude Monet, like most Impressionists, experimented with color extensively. Monet once said, "Color is my day-long obsession, joy and torment." In his experimentations, he repainted the same subject in different lights by using different colors. For example, he painted 105 different paintings of water lilies (figure 8.16)!

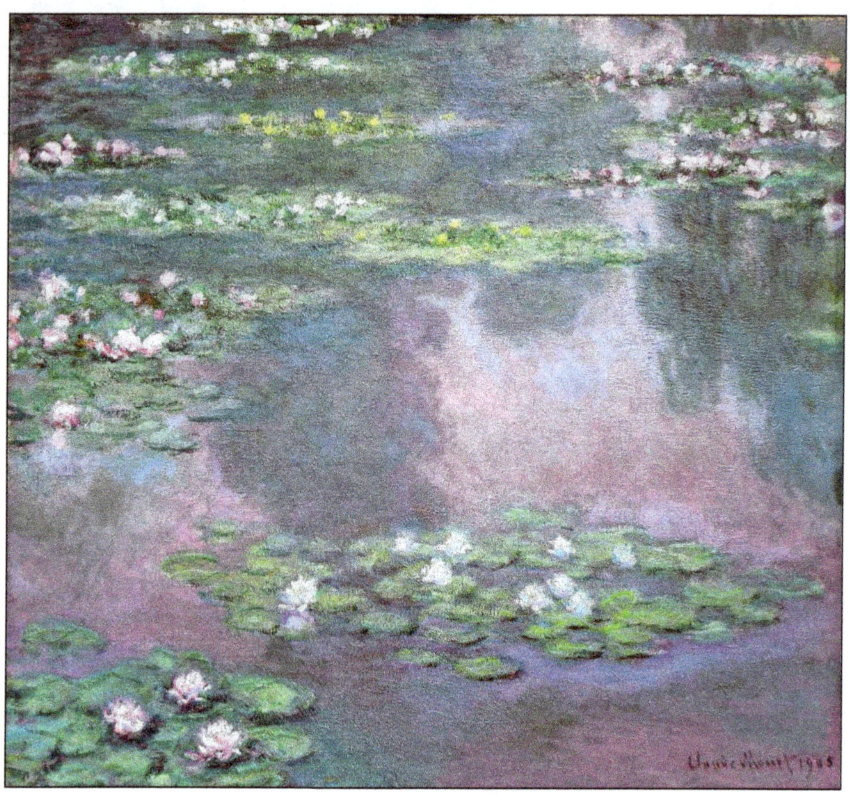

Fig. 8.16 - This 1905 artwork, called *Water Lilies*, is one of a series of 105 paintings of water lilies that Claude Monet created while he experimented with color.

Texture: the actual, or appearance of, three-dimensional raised areas

Three-dimensional art has actual texture while two-dimensional art can have the appearance of texture. We can create the appearance of texture using a combination of lines, shapes, value, and contrast. Notice how the elements of art overlap!

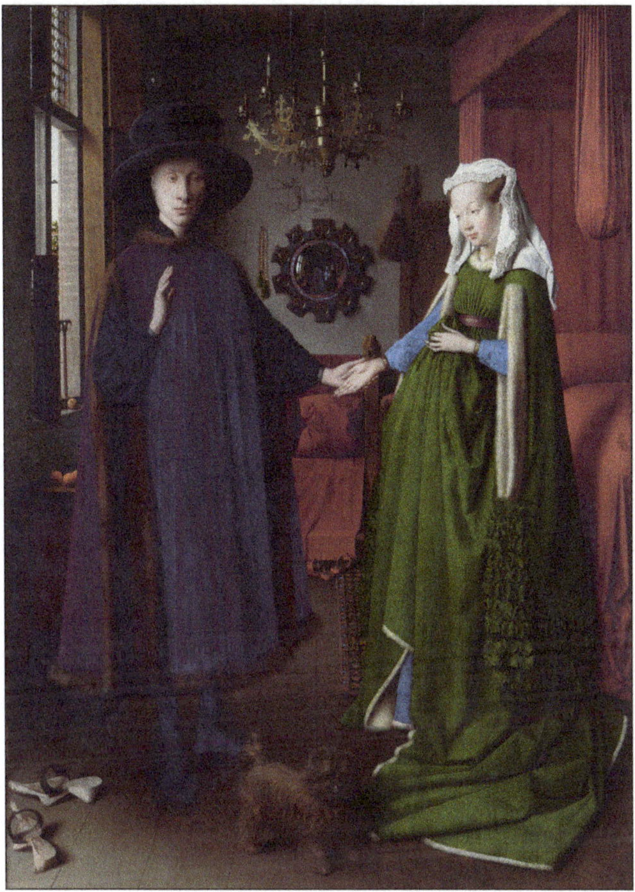

Fig. 8.17 - *The Arnolfini Portrait* (1434) by Van Eyck shows a variety of different textures in the couple's clothes and surroundings.

There are an incredible number of different textures: hard, soft, rough, smooth, wet, dry, prickly, flaky, rocky, scaly, woven, fluffy, bumpy, slick, jagged, and so on. Each one takes practice to capture realistically; however, getting the texture right is very important in realistic artwork. For example, notice the wide variety of textures in Van Eyck's *Arnolfini Portrait* (figure 8.17), like the furry edge of the man's cloak and the shiny hard chandelier.

Texture is one area where it really makes a difference to intentionally learn from others, rather than learning from trial and error. You can learn from others in live classes, books, tutorials, and videos. After studying a specific texture, practice the skill of creating that texture. In chapter 21, Drawing Drills for Seeing Value, I outline a useful exercise to create a texture grid for practice and reference.

COMBINING THE SEVEN ELEMENTS OF ART

All visual art involves some, if not all, of these tools we call the elements of art. Once you've practiced each separately, you'll find you can use them even more expertly together.

Except for introducing line before shape, you can teach these in any order. Introduce and discuss the elements of art as you come across them in your art projects. Most projects already include all or most of these elements. So, if you look for them, you'll find them. To improve your students' art skills, you can focus on one or two elements of art in each lesson. For example, in our *Painting in Tones like O'Keeffe* lesson plan (available for sale on my website), we focus on creating a wide variety of values by painting a flower using tints and shades of only one color (a monochromatic color scheme). In our *Lines and Shapes in Prehistoric Art* lesson plan, we focus on drawing lines and shapes in order to create basic animal figures.

Any time you introduce a new medium, try to experiment with each of the elements of art. For example, when I recently bought a new set of markers, I had a lot of fun experimenting: I drew different kinds of lines, testing how much I could control the thickness of the line and how hard it was to make several identical lines in a row. Next, I created some experimental shapes, testing the look of different straight or curved shapes. I sketched an oval and used crosshatch marks to try to make it look three-dimensional. I tested the marker's ability to cover a large space in an even application of color. Then I made a value scale, coloring over the same spot multiple times for darker areas. I tried out all the colors and tested their ability to blend together. Lastly, I created the appearance of different textures. In something as simple as experimenting with new markers, we can see how all the elements of art come together.

CHAPTER SUMMARY

- The seven elements of art are the tools we use to create art, or the things we look for when observing in order to create art. They are: line, shape, form, space, value, color, and texture.
- Teach the elements of art in all your art lessons, referring to your elements of art poster and reviewing what each term means.

9

ART GRAMMAR: COMPOSITION AND THE PRINCIPLES OF DESIGN

The next component of art grammar is the seven principles of design. 'Design' is sometimes used to mean 'usefulness' in engineering, but in art we define 'design' as how the artist arranges their work of art to create their intended visual outcome. The seven principles of design are the ways the elements of art are used to create a desired effect. Together, they create the 'composition' of the work of art.

- **Principles of Design**: the ways the elements of art are used to create a desired effect in a work of art
- **Composition:** the arrangement of the elements of art in a work of art, using the principles of design

THE PRINCIPLES OF DESIGN

When we're talking about the principles of design, we generally do *not* refer to the principles as present or absent. Instead, we often discuss how and where the artist used the principle, how strong or weak it is, and the effect it has on the artwork.

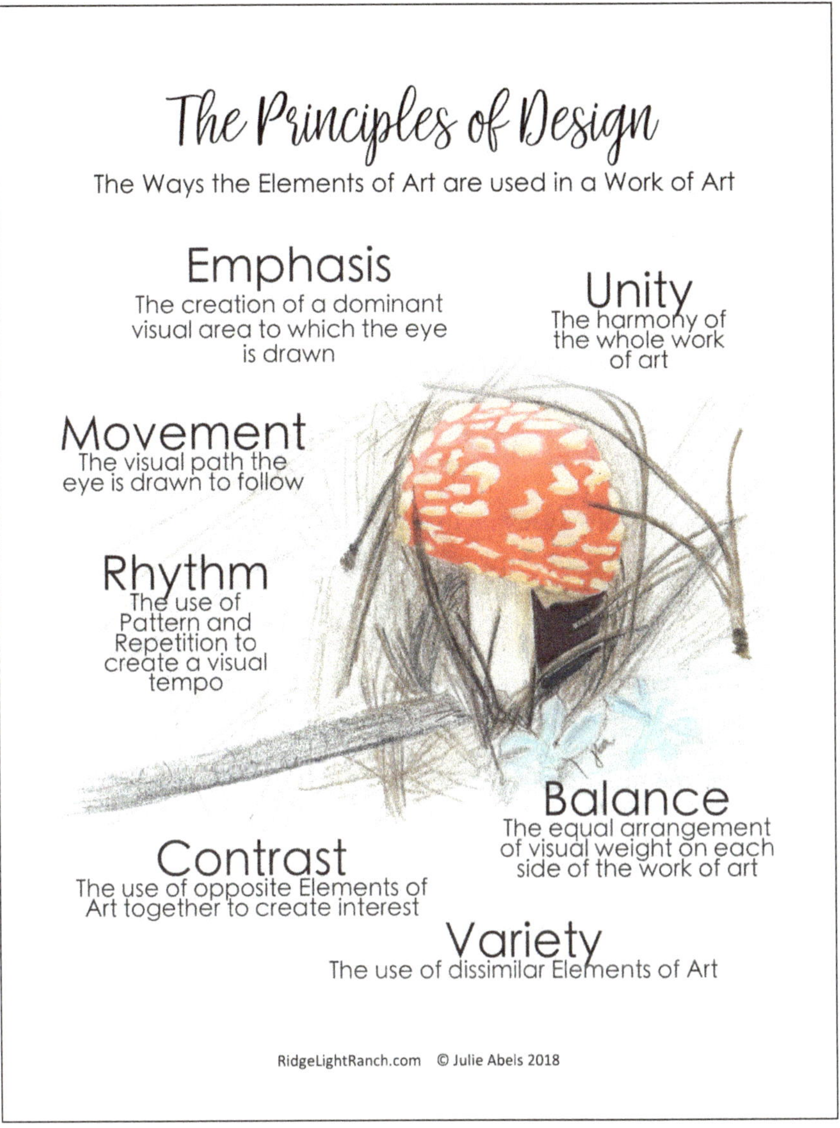

Fig. 9.1 - This poster will help your students remember the principles of design. (Download it for free, as explained earlier.)

Many people assume art is usually created spontaneously without any planning or design beforehand, but that's actually very rare. Most artists carefully plan a masterpiece by first creating many sketches, then creating one or more practice paintings before beginning to work on the final surface. Artists use the principles of design, sometimes consciously and sometimes subconsciously, to plan and design the end result.

The Principles of Design (figure 9.1) are:

- Emphasis
- Movement
- Rhythm
- Contrast
- Variety
- Balance
- Unity

This chapter will introduce you to the principles that artists use to design the composition of their artworks. However, the study of composition can be an extensive topic. Learn the ideas and 'rules' presented here, but also know that most great artists bend and even break the rules frequently. The trick is to know the rules well enough that you know when and how to break them!

Emphasis: the creation of a dominant visual area to which the eye is drawn

The area of emphasis is sometimes called the 'focal point' or 'center of interest.' Having an emphasis in a work of art gives the eye and mind a place to stop and rest. Interestingly, almost everyone's eye will tend to rest on the same focal point or center of interest. In other words, the emphasis is usually consistent from viewer to viewer. For example, in Leonardo da Vinci's painting, *The Last Supper* (figure 9.2), the eye goes to the center where Jesus is the focal point.

Emphasis is created using the elements of art and other principles of design. For example, a contrasting color, texture, or shape can draw the eye and create a focal point.

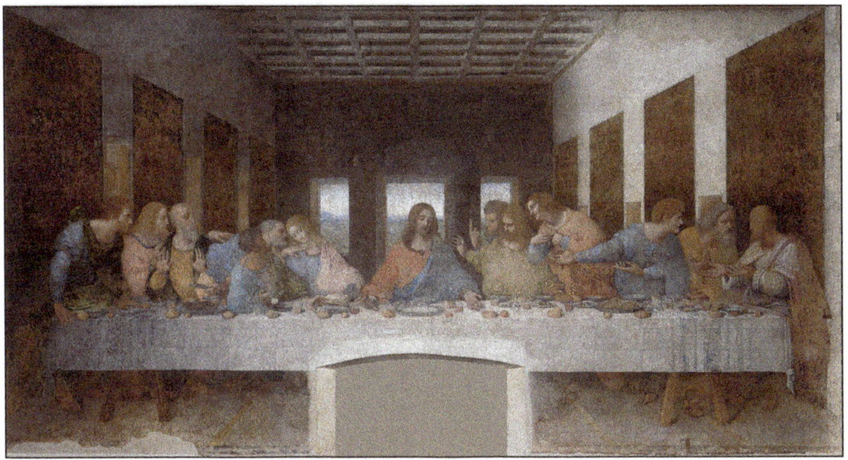

Fig. 9.2 - Jesus is the clear focal point of Leonardo da Vinci's 1498 painting, *The Last Supper*.

Emphasis is also influenced by the overall structure of composition. For example, when using a triangular composition, the focal point will most naturally be at one point of a triangle. Similarly, when using a composition of radiating lines, the focal point will be whatever all the lines are pointing to.

The 'Rule of Thirds' is a popular compositional guide that shows the artist where to place the focal point for an eye-pleasing, asymmetrical work of art. In this design, the canvas is divided into thirds vertically and horizontally. The focal point is then placed at one of the four intersections of the grid (figure 9.3).

The popularity of different patterns of emphasis tends to rise and fall with the different historical art periods (see chapter 12 for more information about art history). For example, Renaissance art, like da Vinci's *The Last Supper* (figure 9.2), often has a centered focal point while Baroque art usually has an off-center focal point.

Be aware that not all art has a focal point—think of a *Where's Waldo* book (yes, I call those art!). Your eye roams around the page, never resting in one place for long. Other art may have a weak or disputed focal point. For example, there is no clear focal point in Claude Monet's painting, *The Four Trees* (figure 9.4). Likewise, Grandma Moses' paintings are similar in that most of them don't have a clear focal point either.

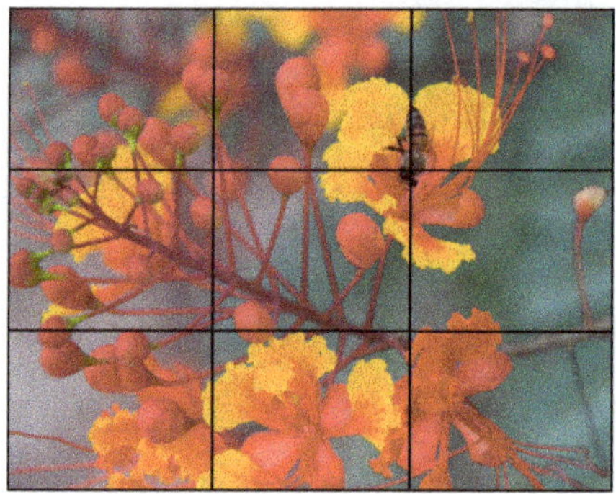

Fig. 9.3 - To use the Rule of Thirds, divide the picture into thirds and place the focal point (the bee in this image) at an intersection of a horizontal and a vertical line.

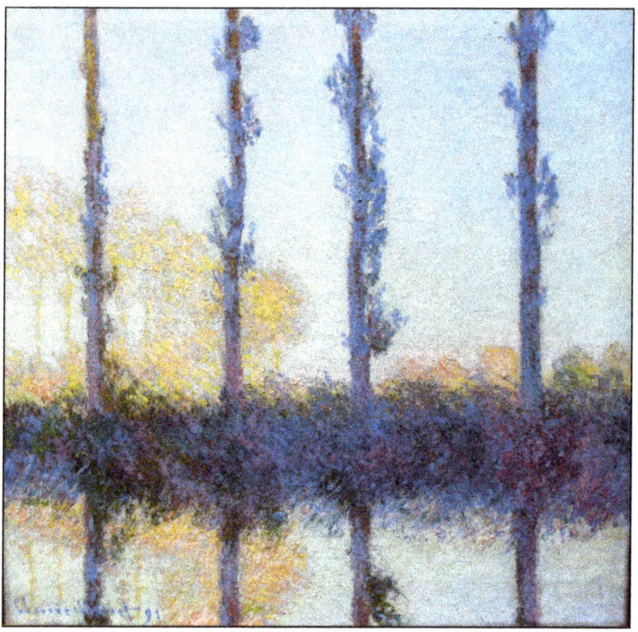

Fig. 9.4 - Claude Monet's 1891 painting, *The Four Trees*, is an example of a weak or disputed focal point.

Movement: the visual path the eye is drawn to follow

Movement is how the eye moves through the composition, eventually resting at the point of emphasis. Movement can be created with lines, colors, shapes, rhythm, and contrast.

Researchers have done studies about how the eye moves when looking at works of art, and the pattern is very predictable. Our eyes tend to move through a visual work of art in the same direction we read—left to right for English and top to bottom. Therefore, creating art that follows that pattern will feel orderly and calm, while having an unexpected direction of movement (e.g. right to left) can make the art feel more exciting and unpredictable. In Winslow Homer's 1872 painting, *Snap the Whip* (figure 9.5), the heads of the boys form a line that the eye follows from left to right, giving a strength and orderliness to an otherwise chaotic school yard game.

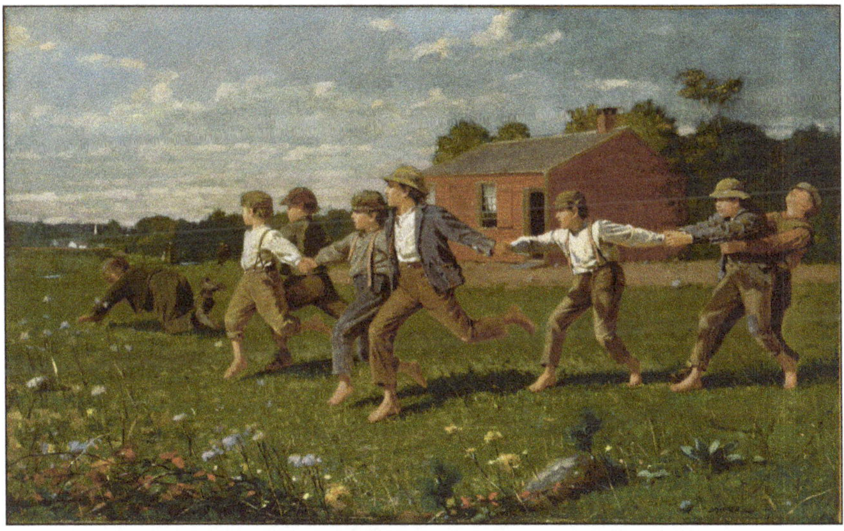

Fig 9.5 - Winslow Homer's 1872 painting, *Snap the Whip*, shows both kinds of movement: a visual path for the eye to follow and the sense that the subjects are moving.

Sometimes the principle of 'movement' is also used to refer to a sense of action that an artist conveys. For example, in the same Homer painting,

Snap the Whip (figure 9.5), the viewer gets the feeling from the stance of the figures that the boys are in the middle of running and pulling on each other.

Rhythm: the use of pattern or repetition to create a visual tempo

Pattern and repetition are very similar and are sometimes used interchangeably. However, pattern is defined as repeating, *predictable, identical* elements of art while repetition is defined as recurring *similar* elements of art.

So, stripes could create a *pattern* when they are repeating identical lines, while plaid uses *repetition* because the lines vary in thickness and color. As with most art terms, don't spend all your time deciding if some part of a work of art should be called 'pattern' or 'repetition.' Instead, spend your time thinking about the effect it has on the whole work of art.

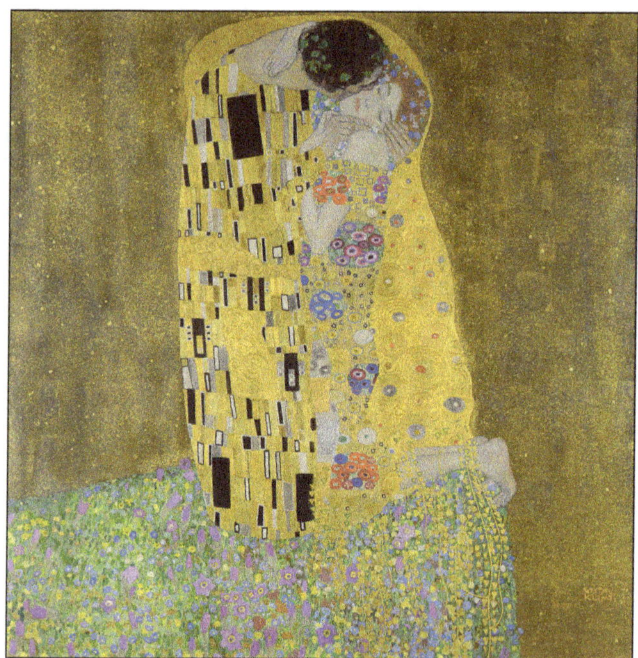

Fig. 9.6 - *The Kiss* (1908) by Gustav Klimt is an example of rhythm using repeating colors and shapes.

Rhythm, whether from pattern or repetition, can create a feeling of cohesiveness, predictability, and order, while a lack of rhythm gives a more energizing or busy look.

You can see examples of rhythm in the repeating shapes and colors of Gustav Klimt's *The Kiss* (figure 9.6). You can see a different type of rhythm in the pointillism (painting with dots of unmixed paint) of George Seurat's painting, *A Sunday on LaGran de Jatte* (figure 9.7).

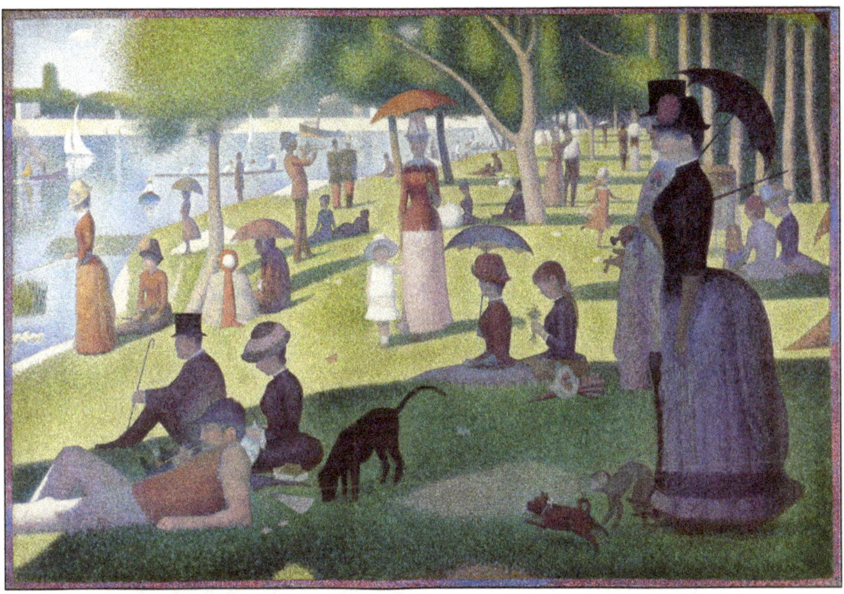

Fig. 9.7 - In *A Sunday on LaGran de Jatte* (1884), Georges Seurat creates rhythm with his pointillism technique.

Contrast: the use of opposite elements of art together to create interest

Contrast can be created with any of the elements of art: thick vs. thin lines, large vs. small shapes, light vs. dark value, rough vs. smooth texture, complementary colors, etc.

You may have noticed that the definition of 'contrast' makes it sound like we're comparing one element to another element. However, contrast is typically between opposite *expressions* of a single element of art, like the previous examples. Occasionally an artist will create contrast between two elements of art. For example, M. C. Escher creates contrast between 'shape' and 'form' in his famous 1948 lithograph, *Drawing Hands* and in his 1943 Lithograph, *Reptiles*. Since the definition of 'contrast' above is similar to most other art instruction, we'll keep using it, but we'll keep this nuance in mind.

All art has some kind of contrast, or our eyes wouldn't be able to detect its presence. For example, our eyes wouldn't be able to see a black canvas on a black wall in a black room. However, the amount of contrast creates different visual effects. A low amount of contrast gives a simple, calming visual effect. A high amount of contrast creates a feeling of edginess or chaos. We typically say a piece of art 'has contrast' when it has high contrast.

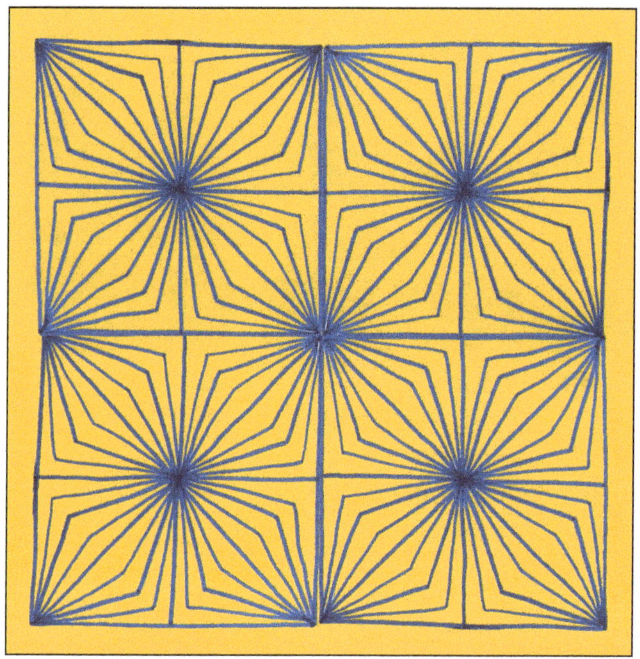

Fig. 9.8 - This Op Art inspired drawing called *In A Daze*, by Julie Abels, makes use of contrast to heighten the effect of energy and movement in the lines.

For example, Op Art (figure 9.8) makes use of both rhythm and contrast to heighten the sense of energy and movement in the lines.

Often artists use contrast to draw our attention to the point of emphasis (the focal point), as we saw in *Washington Crosses the Delaware* (figure 4.5), shown in chapter 4. Compare that painting to *Whistler's Mother* (figure 9.9) and notice how the lower contrast creates a still and quiet effect.

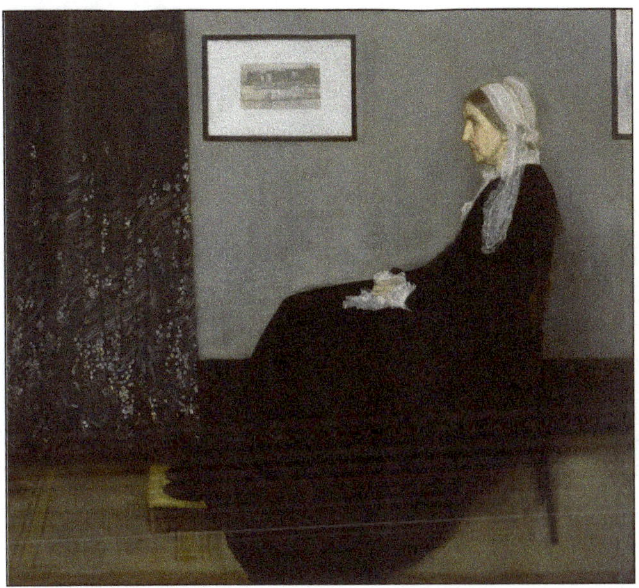

Fig. 9.9 - Whistler's *Arrangement in Grey and Black No. 1* (1871), also known as *Whistler's Mother*, is a good example of low contrast. While there are both black and white in the painting, there are no bright colors.

Variety: the use of dissimilar elements of art

While contrast uses opposite elements of art, variety uses dissimilar elements of art. For example, in Rousseau's painting, *Surprised* (figure 9.10), there's a variety of shapes and colors in the plants. Including variety in a work of art creates interest without the feeling of chaos that high contrast brings. Most artists will combine variety with rhythm to add interest. Variety has such a soft effect that it exists to some degree in all art.

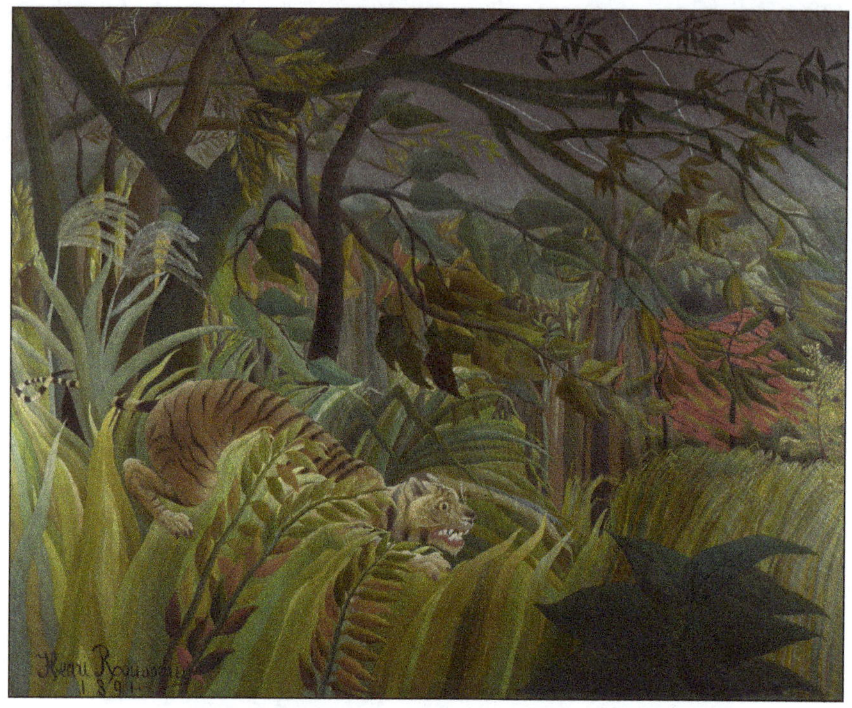

Fig. 9.10 - In Henri Rousseau's 1891 painting, *Surprised* (also called *Tiger in a Tropical Storm*), you can see a variety of shapes and colors.

Balance: the equal arrangement of visual weight on each side of the work of art

Size, color, texture, and contrast can all play a role in balance. We talk about the weight of an object metaphorically, calling something visually 'heavy' or 'light.' Because the eye is accustomed to a balance affected by gravity, we look at balance vertically, comparing left to right. We also tend to expect the bottom of a visual work of art to look heavier than the top, so it doesn't feel top-heavy.

Art is usually either balanced or unbalanced. An unbalanced work of art can give the viewer an unstable feeling. For example, in *Nighthawks* (figure 9.11) by Edward Hopper, the unbalanced composition gives viewers an uneasy feeling.

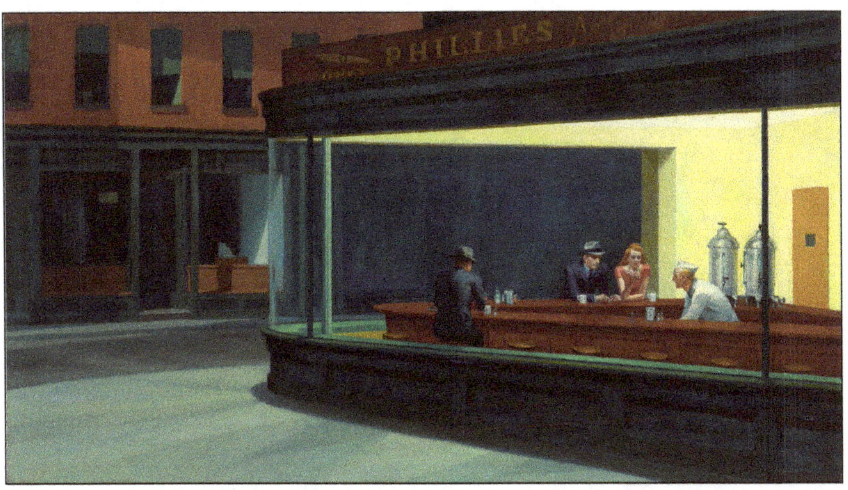

Fig. 9.11 - The unbalanced composition in *Nighthawks* (1942) by Edward Hopper gives viewers an uneasy, off-balanced feel, as if something in the scene was amiss.

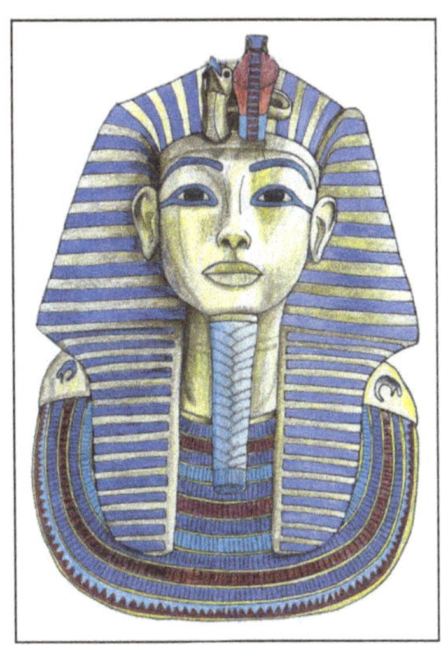

Fig. 9.12 - Julie's drawing of King Tutankhamen's mask, created around 1323 BC, is approximately symmetrical.

Balanced art is either symmetrical, approximately symmetrical, or asymmetrical. Symmetrical artwork is the same on each side of a central axis, typically vertical, but sometimes horizontal, or radial (arranged around a center). Approximately symmetrical artwork is almost the same on each side of a central vertical axis. For example, King Tut's mask (figure 9.12) is approximately symmetrical but not perfectly symmetrical.

Asymmetrical artwork is NOT the same on each side, but it is still balanced. For example, one large item on one side might be balanced by several small items on the other side. You can see this in Botticelli's 1486 painting, *Birth of Venus* (figure 9.13), where the two overlapping figures on the left are balanced by one figure with a flowing bright fabric on the right. The two sides are different but have equal visual weight.

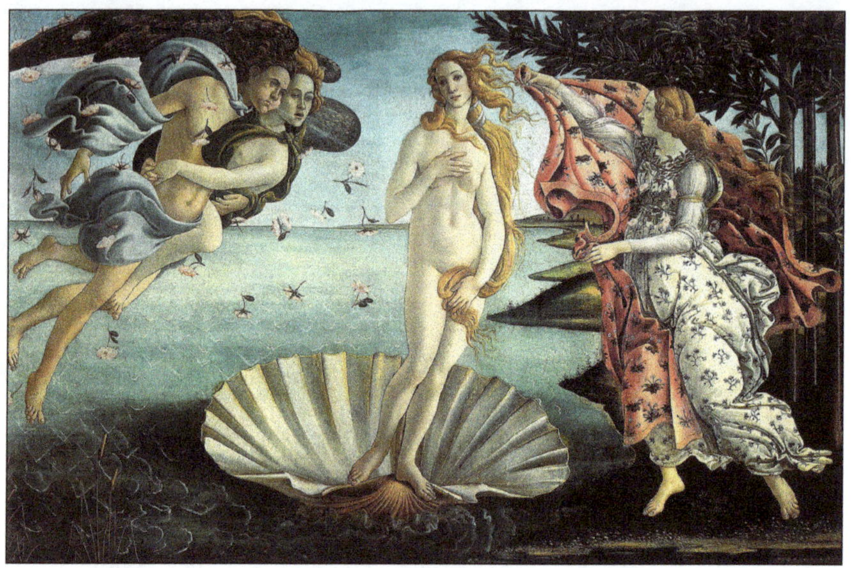

Fig. 9.13 - The *Birth of Venus* (1486), by Botticelli, is balanced even though it is asymmetrical.

Unity: the harmony of the whole work of art

Unity is a look of completeness: an artwork in which everything looks like it belongs. Rhythm is key in creating unity because elements that are repeated rarely look out of place.

Most famous works of art are visually pleasing because they have a strong sense of unity. For example, *Starry Night* (figure 9.14) shows beautiful unity with repeating colors, brush strokes, and curving lines.

However, not all art has unity. For example, sometimes an artist wants their art to feel more like cacophony than harmony. In this case, the artist will add elements that don't seem to belong, preventing unity. For example, in *The Third of May* (figure 9.15), Goya painted one man dressed in a white shirt, while everyone else is in dark clothes. The man looks a little out of place, drawing the viewer's attention to this as the focal point of the painting.

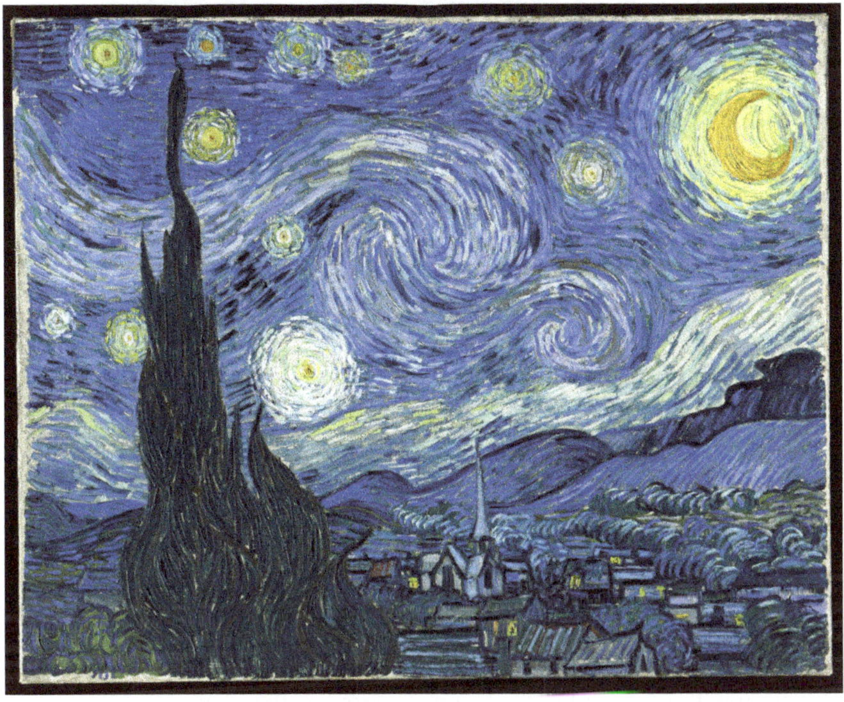

Fig. 9.14 - Vincent van Gogh's *Starry Night* (1889) shows unity. The repeating brush strokes, colors, and shapes tie each element together.

Unity can be subjective and difficult to articulate at times, but don't let that keep you and your students from thinking about the unity in artwork. Ask yourselves, "Does it seem like everything belongs or is there something in this artwork that appears out of place?" If so, why or how does it appear out of place and how does this affect the whole work of art?

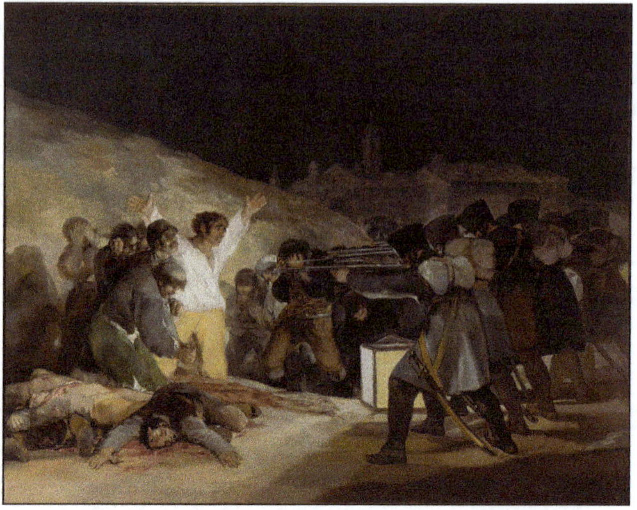

Fig. 9.15 - In Goya's painting, *The Third of May* (1814), the man in the white shirt stands out against the otherwise dark background. The white shirt doesn't seem to belong in this picture, draws your attention. The lack of unity creates the focal point. The man in the white shirt appears innocent, contrasting with the dark horrors of war.

COMPOSITIONAL STRUCTURES

Artists use the principles of design to arrange the elements of art in an eye-pleasing manner. We call the arrangement, the composition. There are a limitless number of different compositions you could use to create a work of art. So, to simplify the study of composition, we categorize the most common compositions into 'compositional structures.'

Artists frequently start off with one or more of the common compositional structures to arrange the elements of art they are using. Then the artist will tweak it, using what they know about the principles of design, to create the visual effect they seek.

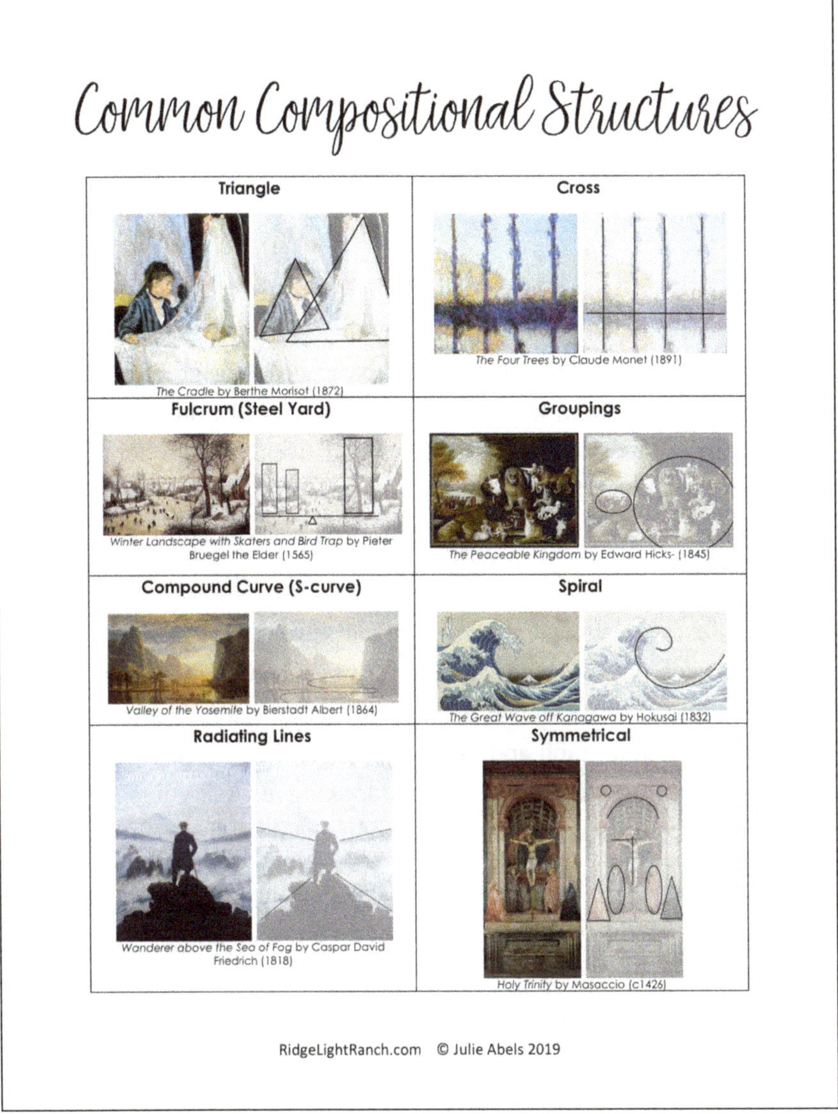

Fig. 9.16 - This poster will help your students remember the most common compositional structures.

The most common compositional structures (figure 9.16) include:

- Triangle
- Cross

- Radiating lines
- Groupings
- Compound curve (also called S-curve)
- Spiral
- Fulcrum (also called Steel yard)
- Symmetrical

In the grammar layer of learning art, we teach students each principle of design and the most common compositional structures. We encourage them to copy famous compositions and try out each principle of design to get to know it better. In the dialectic layer, students experiment by creating art with various compositions and tweaking the compositional structures based on what they know about the principles of design. In the rhetoric layer they use the principles to create a composition for a masterpiece.

Look for examples of the compositional structures and principles of design in everyday life and consider how each principle contributes to those examples. Notice the curb appeal of a house, trends in architecture, or a beautiful photograph and observe the effect each principle of design has on your feelings about what you're looking at. Ask yourself if any of the common compositional structures are present in what you see.

The more often you practice seeing and noticing these principles, the more natural it will become. Then, when you're creating a work of art, you'll be able to consider each principle of design as you plan the artwork so you can create the effect you desire.

CHAPTER SUMMARY

- The principles of design are the ways the elements of art are used in a work of art to create a desired effect.

- The principles of design are emphasis, movement, rhythm, contrast, unity, balance, and variety.
- Common compositional structures combine the elements of art according to the principles of design is an eye-pleasing manner.
- Some common compositional structures are the triangle, cross, radiating lines, groupings, compound curve, spiral, fulcrum, and symmetrical.

10

ART GRAMMAR: MEDIA AND SKILLS

Artists often use the word 'medium' synonymously with the word 'technique.' However, outside of the art room, the word 'technique' is sometimes used synonymously with the word 'skill.' Therefore, I try not to use the word 'technique' at all.

MEDIA

Media (plural for 'medium') are the materials you're using to make art. Some of the most common media are pencil (graphite), charcoal, ink, watercolor, acrylic, oils, pastels, fiber, clay, collage, and mosaic. It's good to give your students a chance to work with each different medium over the course of their school years.

There are pros and cons to each medium, so it's good to experiment with different media. Each medium requires unique skills, so plan on taking time to learn each one. You can experiment on a new medium, but a book, class, or video about that specific medium will make the learning much faster.

When teaching a variety of media, some art teachers like to do a "Media Sampler," using a new medium each week. There are pros and cons to this: New media can be very exciting, different students will naturally take to different media, and a little exposure can help overcome the fear of a medium you've never tried. However, changing media each week also means that students never have enough time to really learn any one medium, art teachers have to purchase more supplies, and some students will be frustrated at never becoming proficient at any one medium. I prefer to balance a variety of media with repetition of one medium.

Tips for Trying a New Medium:

- Do several projects with one medium. (Later you can try doing one project with several media. Limit the variables in your experiment!)
- Look for a book, class, or video about THAT medium to speed up the learning curve.
- When starting a new medium, have students trace a starting image. This way students can focus on the skill of that one medium instead of focusing on how to draw that particular subject.

SKILLS

Just like when learning music or sports, the best way to learn a new art skill is to drill it; do it over and over again. This is why I try to focus on a specific set of skills with each art lesson I write. In Part Three of this book, I'll share all my favorite art skill drills and exercises with you.

Some skills are general and can carry over from one medium to another. 'Seeing' is by far the most important visual art skill. It's fundamental and carries over to all kinds of visual arts—even abstract art. Other skills, like learning the methods of creating perspective and depth, carry over in a general sense.

Some skills are multifaceted; they are actually several skills in one. For example, linear perspective, human proportions (ideal versus actual), and complex shading with reflected light or soft light are all comprised of multiple skills. These ideas should be broken down so students can learn them one piece at a time. We'll discuss each of these in more depth in Part Three of this book.

Some skills are medium specific, meaning they're only applicable to that one medium. For example, blending two colors is a little different with each medium, and the skills required for carving wood will be different than the skills required for carving marble.

FOCUS ON QUANTITY AND QUALITY WILL COME

One of the great things about drills is that they help combat the perfectionist mindset that says, "Every piece must be a masterpiece." We need intentional practice, not masterpiece-making, to improve on a skill. This has been shown over and over again in different studies by a variety of experts.

For example, in the book *Atomic Habits*, James Clear tells the story of Jerry Uelsmann's experiment with his University of Florida photography students. Uelsmann divided his class in half and told half the students they would be graded on sheer quantity of photos they took that semester, while the other half would be graded on the quality of one photo they submitted for the whole semester. In the end, all of the highest quality photos came from the half of the class focused on quantity.

In Malcom Gladwell's book, *Outliers*, he explains the 10,000 Hour Rule discovered by Anders Ericsson. The idea is that, in order to master something, we need a lot of deliberate, mindful practice—intentional practice that strives to imitate the desired result.

Lastly, the Equal Odds Rule, as explained by James Clear in his short book, *Mastering Creativity*, describes how we rarely know when the work we're doing will be great and when it will be mediocre. So, we need to show up over and over again and keep creating.

Walt Stanchfield summed it up well when he said, "We all have 10,000 bad drawings in us. The sooner we get them out the better."

~

CHAPTER SUMMARY

- Media are the materials you use to make art.
- Balance the variety of media you introduce with the repetition of one medium.
- Art skills are best learned by repeating specific drills and LOTS of practice.

11

ART GRAMMAR: THE PURPOSES AND GENRES OF ART

The purposes and genres of art, art history, and art appreciation all work together as we consider the art others have created.

THE PURPOSES OF ART

There are many different purposes or roles of art, including:

- Expression
- Social/Cultural
- Functional
- Persuasive
- Political
- Historical
- Educational
- Scientific
- Spiritual/Religious

Some students may be under the impression that the only purpose of art is to be something pretty on the wall. So, it's important to teach students the fact that there *are* different purposes for art and that there may be multiple purposes for a single work of art. Talking about all the different reasons we create art, and what the primary purpose for a specific piece of art might be, will help students expand their definition of 'art.' It also helps us appreciate all types of art from all types of cultures.

Let's take a closer look at each of these purposes

Expression

This purpose is most popular in modern art. Jackson Pollock's paintings are excellent examples. Pollock once said, "The modern artist is working with space and time, and expressing his feelings rather than illustrating." When the purpose of art is expression, typically the action of creating the art is more important to the artist that the product itself.

Social/Cultural

Recording and celebrating culture is at the heart of this purpose. It often includes scenes of everyday life or important cultural events.

Functional

Functional art always serves a practical function in addition to being art. Some examples of this are decorated dish-ware, hand-carved soap, or hand-made instruments. Sometimes the art is used for its functional purpose, and sometimes it's set aside to preserve the artwork.

Persuasive

The idea of persuasive art is to convince the viewer of something. We hope the artist is leading the viewer toward truth, goodness, and beauty, but that's not always the case.

Political

Political artwork usually makes a statement about or interpretation of current events, politicians, or the issues of the day. Often, it's not particularly pleasant to look at.

Much of the artwork in the Dada movement was political in nature, made in reaction to the horrors of WWI and the increasingly materialistic culture.

Historical

This purpose spans a wide variety of art and time periods. It includes everything from Neoclassical art depicting a past war to court reporter sketches. While the art will always include the artist's interpretation of the event to some degree, the main goal of the historical purpose is to record the event like a historian.

Educational

Educational artwork can appear anywhere, not just in books. It includes any art with the primary purpose of communicating facts to the viewer. Again, the art always reflects a worldview in its representation of the details, but the focus should be on the facts.

Scientific

Scientific illustrations and similar kinds of art are used for recording observations. They are also frequently used for educational purposes, but the primary reason for them is recording what the scientist sees.

Spiritual/Religious

Artwork that is created for a spiritual or religious purpose is primarily made as an act of worship. For example, Fra Angelico, an early Renaissance artist who wept each time he painted the crucifixion, once said, "He who does Christ's work must stay with Christ always." This art is often also used for education or historical purposes as well.

THE HIERARCHY OF GENRES

The Hierarchy of Genres came from the Italian Renaissance and was formalized and taught in art academies starting in the 1600s. The idea was that some subject matters were more noble than others. As many categorizations in art, there can be overlap and one painting can fit into several genres. The Hierarchy of Genres, in order from most noble to least noble:

1. Historical
2. Portrait
3. Lifestyle
4. Landscape
5. Animal
6. Still Life

Let's look at each of those in more depth:

1. Historical

Paintings in the historical genre include religious, historical, and allegorical subject matter. A typical example of this is Giotto's *Raising of Lazarus* (figure 11.1).

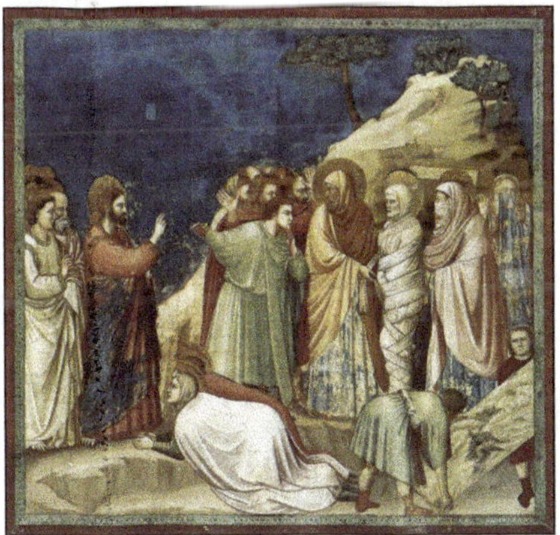

Fig. 11.1 - *Raising of Lazarus* (1306) is a great example of a historical painting created by the 'Father of Renaissance Art,' Giotto di Bondone. It's part of his *Life of Christ* series in the Arena Chapel.

2. Portrait

This genre includes paintings of a group of people or an individual. The people are usually posed in a way to capture their personality, profession, status, and/or distinguishing features. This genre also includes self-portraits. One of the most famous portraits is the *Mona Lisa* (figure 11.2) by Leonardo di Vinci.

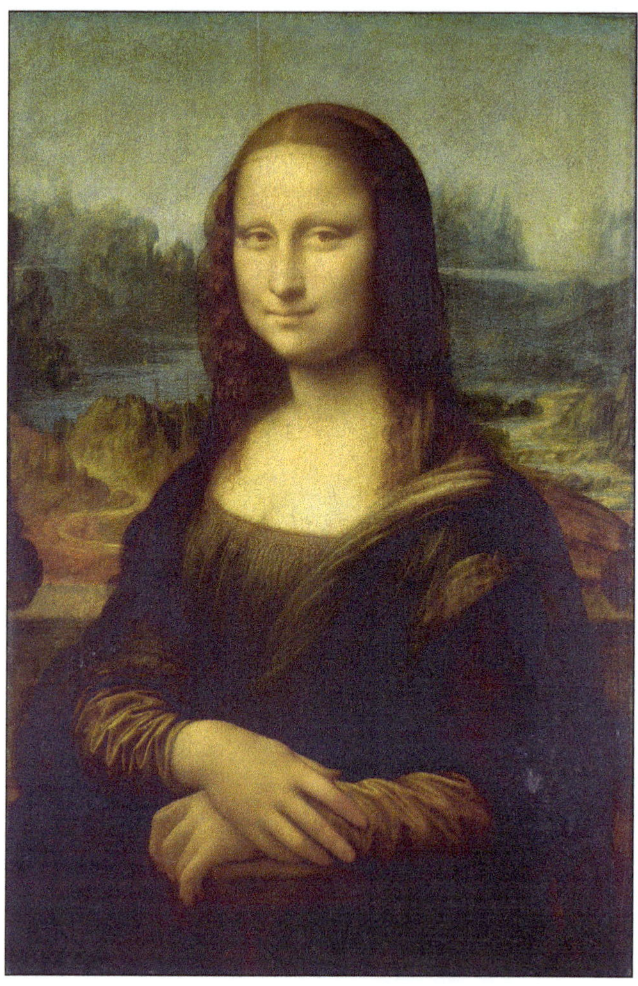

Fig. 11.2 - The *Mona Lisa* (1503) by Leonardo da Vinci is one of the most famous portraits ever painted.

3. Lifestyle

The lifestyle genre includes scenes of everyday life and usually includes people doing their normal activities. Confusingly, lifestyle painting is sometimes referred to as "genre" painting. Like most Impressionists, Berthe Morisot focused on the lifestyle genre, as seen in *The Cradle* (figure 11.3).

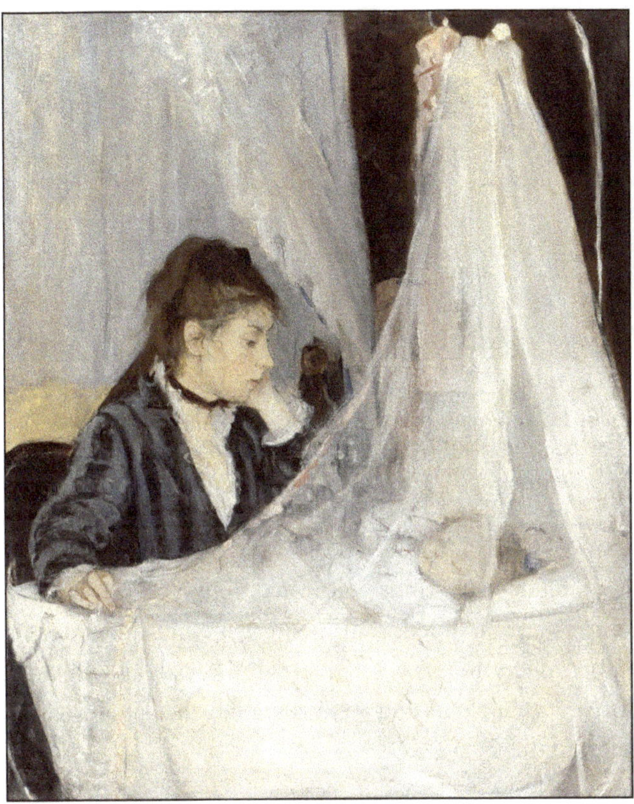

Fig. 11.3 - *The Cradle* (1872) by Berthe Morisot is a great example of the lifestyle genre. It shows a mom, on an average day, checking in on her sleeping infant.

4. Landscape

Paintings in the landscape genre are usually a scenic view. They often may or may not have people in them. *The Grand Canyon of the Yellowstone* (figure 11.4) by Thomas Moran is a great example of a landscape painting.

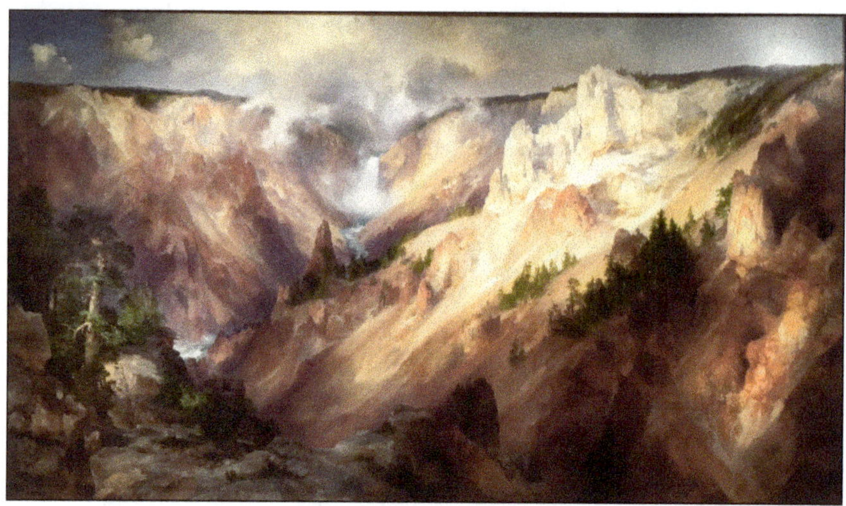

Fig. 11.4 - Thomas Moran, along with all the Hudson River School painters, was famous for his dramatic sweeping landscape paintings like this one called *The Grand Canyon of the Yellowstone* (1872).

5. Animal

This genre includes paintings with an animal as the focal point. The animal genre is not included in all genre lists, but it has been a common subject matter since the time of cave paintings. John James Audubon is famous for his many painting of birds, like this painting, *Ivory Billed Woodpecker* (figure 11.5).

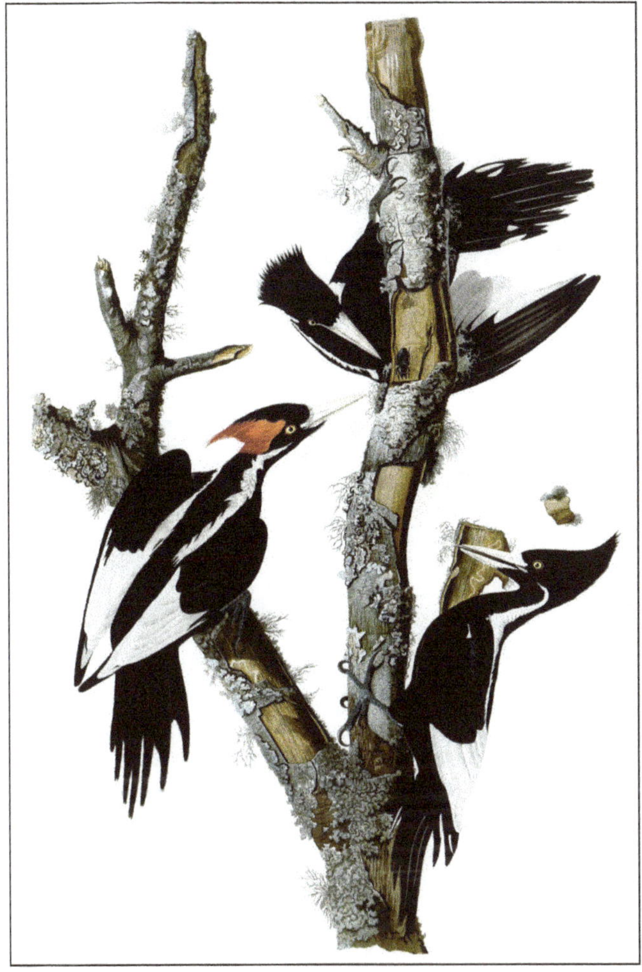

Fig. 11.5 - This painting by John James Audubon, called *Ivory Billed Woodpecker* (c.1825), is a good example of an animal painting.

6. Still Life

Paintings in the still life genre show an arrangement of household objects or everyday items. A great example of a still life is Cezanne's painting, *The Basket of Apples* (figure 11.6).

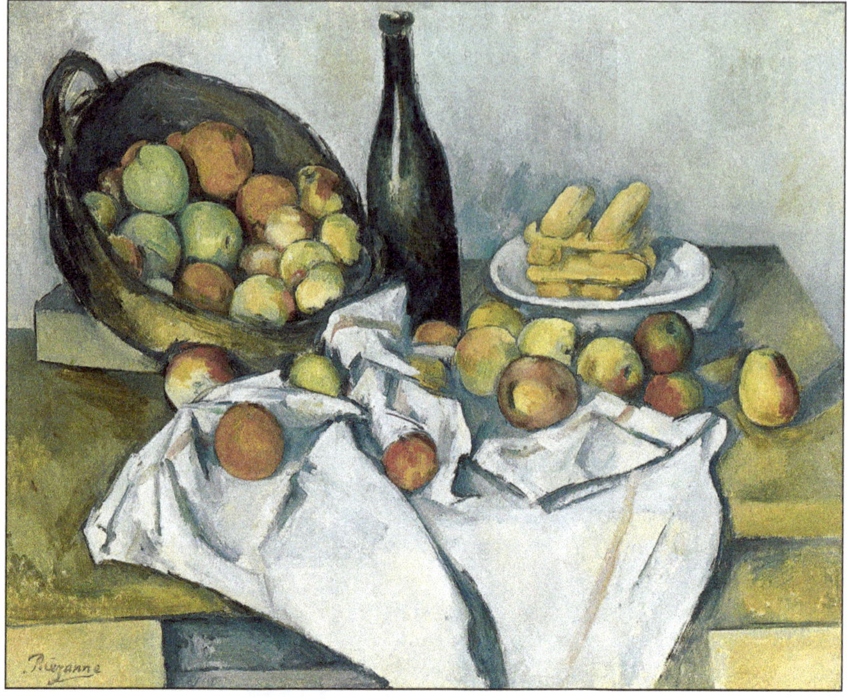

Fig. 11.6 - Paul Cezanne is a well-known still life artist. His 1895 painting, *The Basket of Apples*, is a typical example of his still life art.

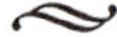

The Modern art world has largely rejected the idea that some genres of paintings are more noble than others, but the Hierarchy of Genres was the dominate way of thinking for most of our history, and we can see its effect on the art created. For example, this bit of history helps explain why we don't see a lot of animal or still life paintings from the Renaissance!

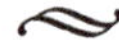

CHAPTER SUMMARY

- The purposes of art help us expand our definition of art and understand the many roles of art.
- The Hierarchy of Genres, developed in the Renaissance period, prioritized certain subject matters over others.

12

ART GRAMMAR: ART HISTORY & ART APPRECIATION

There's so much we can learn within the realm of Art History. To begin with, it is important to realize that culture affects art AND art affects culture. Start by teaching your students this very important concept. Next, explain to your students that there are different periods of art history and each period has some defining characteristics and often contains several movements. The following definitions of 'art period' and 'art movement' provide a framework for the basics of Art History. Then, in the deeper parts of the grammar layer, you can guide your students in memorizing the defining characteristics of each overarching art period and the approximate time periods they occurred in.

- Art Period: a longer block of time encompassing many different artists and their works of visual art, music, theater, and literature. An art period usually includes several art movements with a shared focus or style. Artists and their works of art are usually grouped into an art period by art historians after the period has come and gone.
- Art Movement: a collection of artists and their works of art with a common philosophy or goal, technique, style, or time period.

Many movements formed a club with a manifesto, a spokesperson, and an exclusive art show.

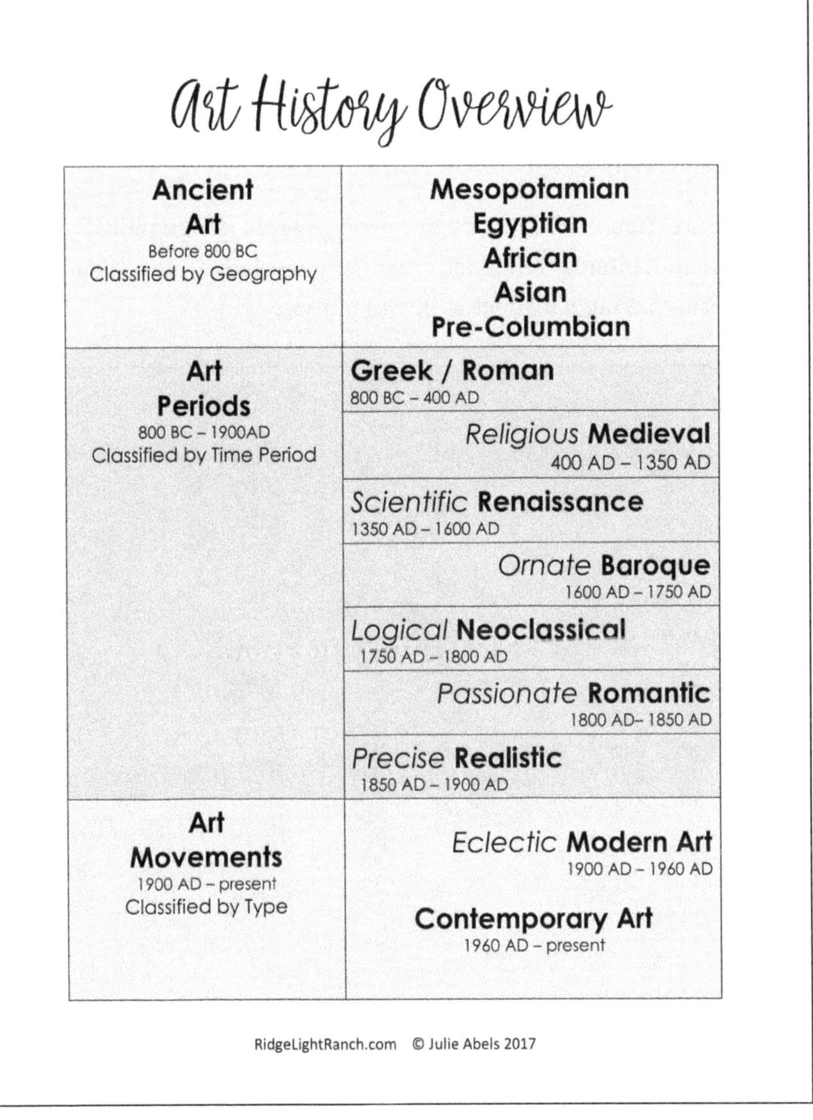

Fig. 12.1 - This art history poster will help students establish a framework for the rest of their art history studies.

This art history overview chart (figure 12.1) is a great tool to help your students internalize the order of the periods, their most basic characteristics, and some approximate dates. As explained in the front matter, a printable version of this poster is included in your free Art Teacher Kit!

When you're moving through different periods of art history, be sure to explain the deeper overarching themes of each period to your students.

ANCIENT ART

Ancient art (figure 12.2) tends to be categorized geographically because the diverse cultures remained relatively secluded, resulting in each culture's art having a distinct look and purpose.

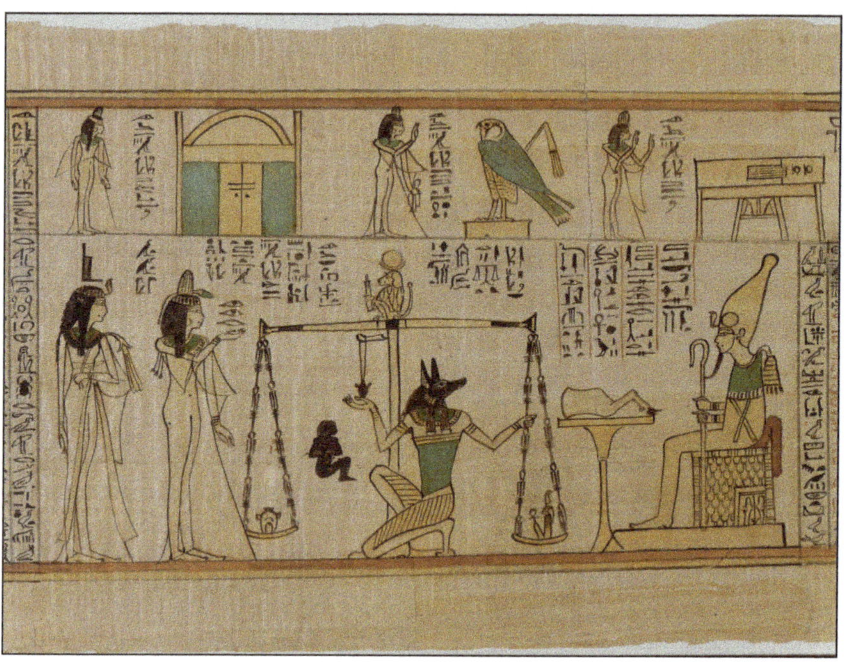

Fig. 12.2 - *The Book of Coming Forth by Day*, also known as *The Book of the Dead*, was written on scrolls as early as 1500 BC and buried with wealthy Egyptians. It is a great example of ancient art.

CLASSICAL ART (C.800 BC – C.400 AD)

The classical art of the Greek and Roman empires focused on beauty, virtue, and harmony. While Greek art mainly revolved around their gods and religion and Roman art usually had a historical focus, the two were still quite similar.

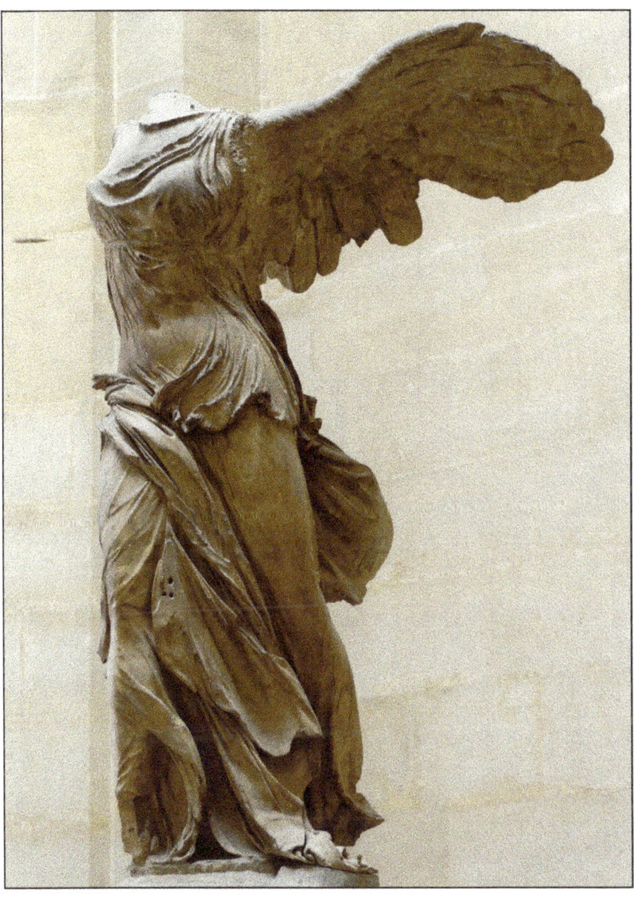

Fig. 12.3 - *The Nike of Samothrace* (also called the *Winged Victory of Samothrace*) (c. 190 BC), is a three-dimensional sculpture from the Hellenistic period of Ancient Greece and is a great example of the traditional definition of form.

Most Greek and Roman art showcases the human form as well as the ideal proportions of the golden ratio. Greek and Roman art includes paintings, mosaics, vases, sculptures (figure 12.3), and architecture.

MEDIEVAL ART (C.400 AD – C.1350 AD)

Medieval European art includes paintings, mosaics, architecture, tapestries, and illuminated manuscripts (figure 12.4). Religious and mythological art was created, mostly for churches since the Catholic church was the center of most of the power and funding.

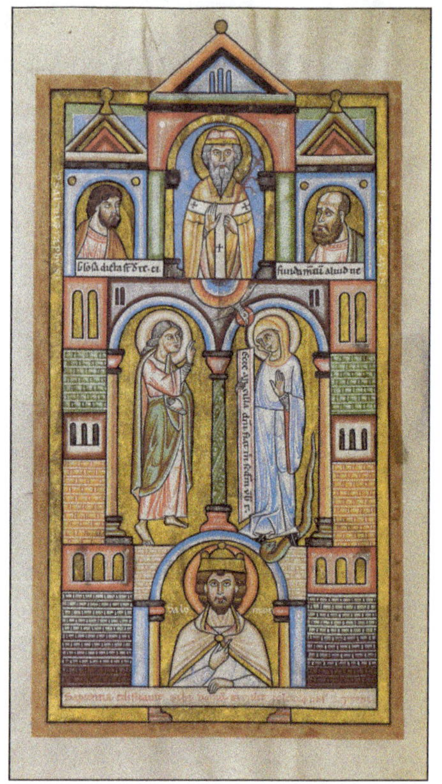

Fig. 12.4 - This painting, called *The Annunciation*, is from The Stammheim Missal, an illuminated manuscript from c.1170 is a great example of Medieval art.

RENAISSANCE PERIOD (C.1350 AD – C.1600 AD)

Renaissance period artists used realistic linear perspective and classical ideals to realistically depict nature and beauty, as seen in Michelangelo's statue called *David* (figure 12.5).

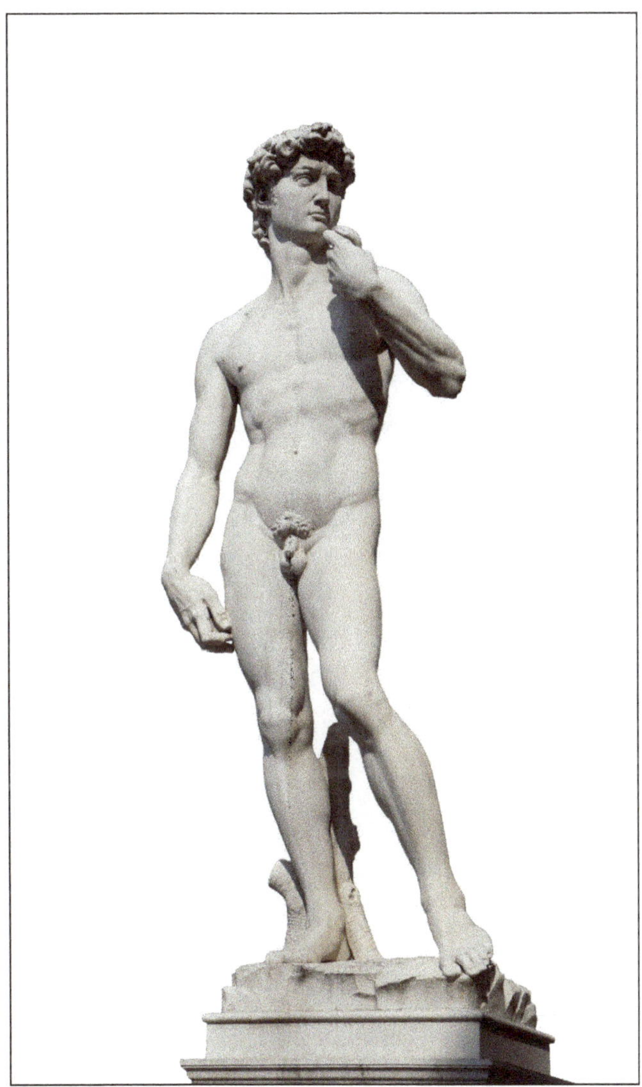

Fig. 12.5 - Michelangelo's marble statue, *David* (1504), is an excellent example of Renaissance art.

There are too many artists from the Renaissance to name, but some of the best-known ones were Giotto, Masaccio, Botticelli, Leonardo da Vinci, Michelangelo, Raphael, Titan, Jan Van Eyck, and Albrecht Durer.

BAROQUE PERIOD (C.1600 AD – C.1750 AD)

The Baroque period generated highly ornate, embellished and dramatic depictions of important events including royalty or religious stories. Artists focused on using deep colors, lots of details, movement, and a high contrast of light and dark, as seen in Rembrandt's *The Night Watch* (figure 12.6).

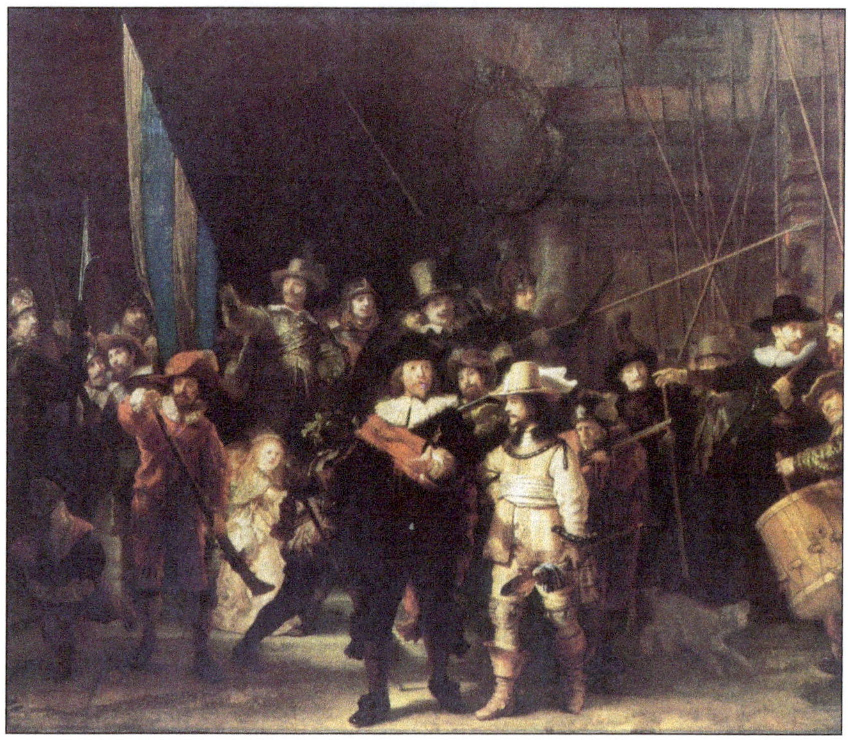

Fig. 12.6 - *The Night Watch* (1642) by Rembrandt is a great example of a Baroque painting.

Artists like Diego Velazquez, Johannes Vermeer, Peter Paul Rubens,

Anthony van Dyck, Rembrandt, and Caravaggio are some of the best-known Baroque artists.

NEOCLASSICAL PERIOD (C.1750 AD – C.1800 AD)

The Neoclassical period saw a return to the Greek and Roman ideas of logic and reason. David's *The Oath of the Horatii* is a great example (figure 12.7).

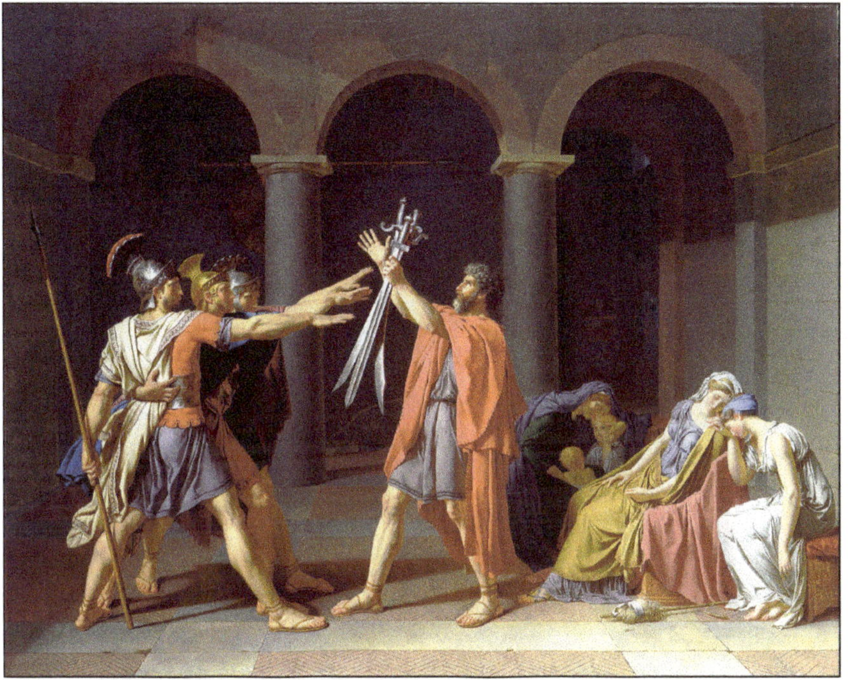

Fig. 12.7 - *The Oath of the Horatii* (1784) by Jacques-Louis David is an excellent example of Neoclassical art.

Artists like James Stuart, Jacques Louis David, Jean-Auguste-Dominique Ingres, and John Singleton Copley are some of the best-known Neoclassical artists.

ROMANTIC PERIOD (C.1800 AD – C.1850 AD)

In the Romantic period, artists honored nature, individualism, intuition, and emotion. The period was an idyllic and dramatic reaction to the artists' dislike of the Neoclassical movement, the Industrial Revolution, and the Age of Enlightenment. A great example of this period is *The Wanderer Above the Sea of Fog* by Caspar David Friedrich (figure 12.8).

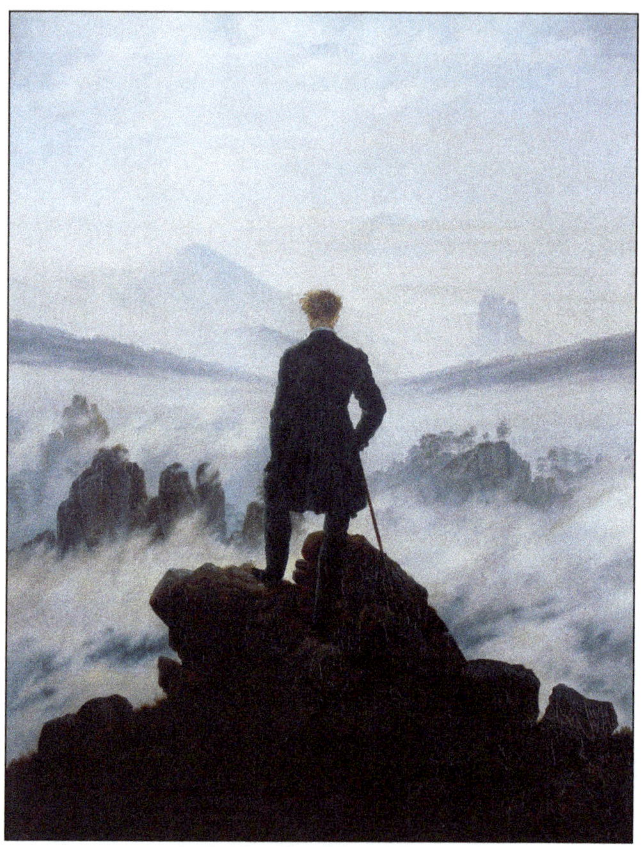

Fig. 12.8 - Caspar David Friedrich's 1817 painting, *The Wanderer Above the Sea of Fog*, is an example of a typical piece of Romantic era art.

Artists like Thomas Cole, Albert Bierstadt, Frederic Edwin Church, Casper David Fredrick, Eugène Delacroix, John William Waterhouse, and Théodore Géricault are some of the best-known Romantic period artists.

REALISTIC PERIOD (C.1850 AD – C.1900 AD)

During the Realistic period, artists tried to represent their subjects truthfully and accurately. The movement was a reaction against Romanticism and the Industrial Revolution and it focused on everyday life, even the unpleasant parts of life. The *Portrait of Madame X* (figure 12.9) is an example of this period.

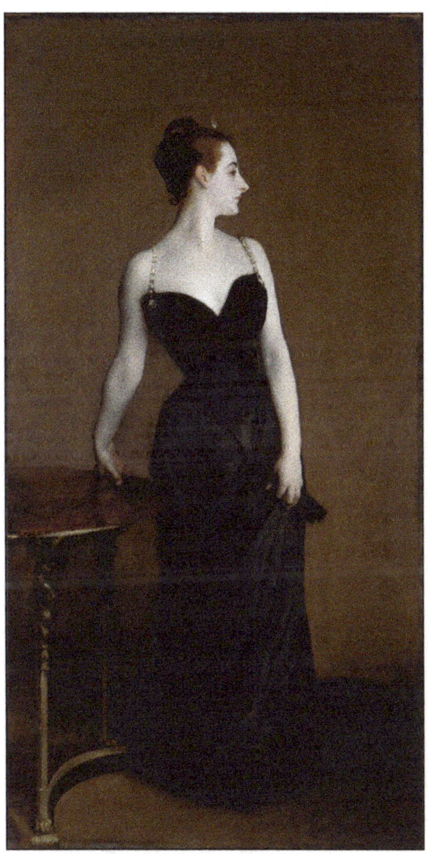

Fig. 12.9 - The *Portrait of Madame X*, by John Singer Sargent in 1884, is a typical example of art from the short Realistic period of the late 1800s.

Artists like Winslow Homer, James McNeill Whistler, John Singer Sargent, Grant Wood, and Norman Rockwell are some of the best-known Realistic artists.

MODERN PERIOD (C.1900 AD – C.1960 AD)

The Modern art period is based on a belief in progress and idealism. It assumed principles could be used to explain reality. Modernist artists focus on techniques and processes instead of a limited group of subjects. *The Scream* (figure 12.10) is a famous example of modern art.

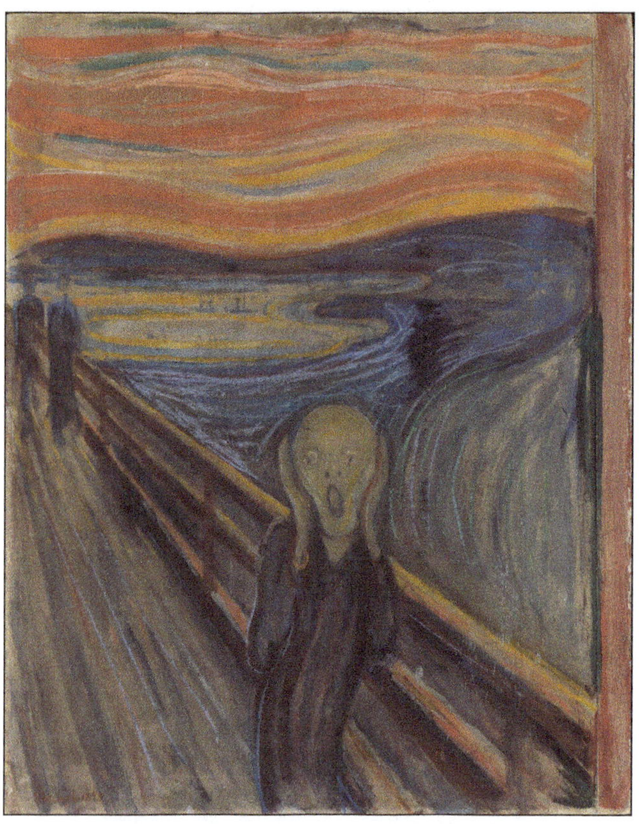

Fig. 12.10 - *The Scream* (1893), by Edvard Munch, is a good example of an Expressionist painting.

Unlike previous art periods, which had mostly unifying characteristics, this art period includes many diverse art movements:

- Pierre-Auguste Renoir, Claude Monet, Mary Casset, Edward Degas, Berthe Morisot, and Edouard Manet are some of the best-known Impressionist artists.
- Jackson Pollock, Edvard Munch, and Wassily Kandinsky are some of the best-known Expressionist artists.
- Pablo Picasso and Vincent van Gogh are some of the best-known Post-Impressionist artists.
- Andy Warhol and Roy Lichtenstein are some of the best-known Pop Art artists.
- George Seurat and Paul Signac are some of the best-known Pointillism artists.

CONTEMPORARY PERIOD (C.1960 AD – PRESENT)

The Contemporary period is still revealing itself. Until we have the perspective of history, we won't fully know what attributes and ideals best characterize the art of our time. It appears the themes will be related to cynicism and rejection of the Modern period's concepts of progress and clarity.

At RidgeLightRanch.com/Art-Periods-and-Movements/, you'll find this same list of art periods, but you'll also find all the art movements within each period and similar brief descriptions of each.

ART APPRECIATION

Art appreciation is all about looking at, thinking about, and asking questions about works of art. We tend to use all the other components of art grammar here.

Art appreciation starts in the grammar layer of learning as we look at art and notice the details of a work of art with our students. While students are young, we just want to let them talk about what they see. There are no right or wrong answers. Students don't have to defend their statements or draw specific conclusions, as they would in the dialectic layer.

Here are some example questions you can ask in the grammar stage to help students notice details in a work of art:

- What's the first thing you see?
- What else do you see?
- What details do you notice?
- What story is this art telling?
- What questions do you have about this artwork?
- Where do you see the seven elements of art or the principles of design in this artwork?
- Does this artwork remind you of anything else?
- How is this art similar to other art we've looked at?
- How is this art different from other art we've looked at?
- When was this work of art created? What else was happening in the world?
- What can we learn from this about the artist's culture?
- What do you feel when you look at this piece of art?
- What do you think the artist was feeling when he/she created this?
- Do you like this work of art? Why or why not?

As you plan out different art projects, it's a good idea to combine art purposes, art periods, and art appreciation by picking out an art period and looking at (appreciating) art from that period. Discuss that artwork's purpose and genre and then create some art like it. Over the years, try to sample art from each purpose, genre, and period.

VOCABULARY

Now that you're familiar with what content to teach in the grammar layer of art, we're ready to learn about the dialectic layer of art. However, before we move on, I want to say a few words about words.

Words are more important than we tend to assume. Agreeing upon definitions of words allows us to communicate effectively with each other. Because of this we need to learn art vocabulary as well. You'll find a short glossary of basic art terms at the end of this book and a longer glossary on my website at RidgeLightRanch.com/Art-Glossary/. Use it to introduce two or three related art terms into each of your art lessons. There's no need to introduce the words in a particular order. Just teach them as you use them. As you introduce words to your students, check them off. You'll be amazed at how many words you and your students know by the end of just one year!

CHAPTER SUMMARY

- Art historians break art history into manageable chunks called art periods.
- In art appreciation we look at, ask questions about, and think about great works of art.

13

THE DIALECTIC LAYER

In the dialectic layer of education, we are primarily training the brain to think and reason. It's only through wrestling with ideas that students can arrive at a rich and nuanced understanding of a topic. The riches are in the wrestling! We teach students to grapple with each topic by asking questions, having deep discussions, and experimenting.

To help us ask quality questions and begin deep discussions, we use the five common topics: definition, comparison, relationship, circumstance, and testimony/evidence (figure 13.1).

The 'five common topics' is a comprehensive structure for learning how to interact with a topic and stimulate good questions. Originating with the ancient Greeks, it has been developed and refined over the years. As explained by Leigh Bortins in her book, *The Question,* the five common topics are:

- **Definition:** What does this mean? What does it not mean? In the grammar layer we memorized many definitions, but here we are going beyond a succinct definition and discussing what the topic is and is not. The purpose is to wrestle with the ideas, not to have a definition written in stone.

- **Comparison:** What is this similar to? What is it different from? To what degree is it similar or different? This is sometimes called 'compare and contrast.'
- **Relationship:** Is this caused by something else? What could cause it? Why does it exist? What effects can it have? What typically comes before or after it? What are its contraries (things that belong to the same category and cannot both be true, but can both be false)? What would contradict this (one must be valid and the other invalid)?
- **Circumstance:** When thinking about this topic, what circumstances surround it? What sort of things are possible or impossible in that circumstance? What must have happened or must later happen in this circumstance?
- **Testimony:** What do the experts say about this? What do the amateurs say about this? Is there any quantitative evidence about this from research and experiments? Are there any laws, precedents, or common sayings we should consider?

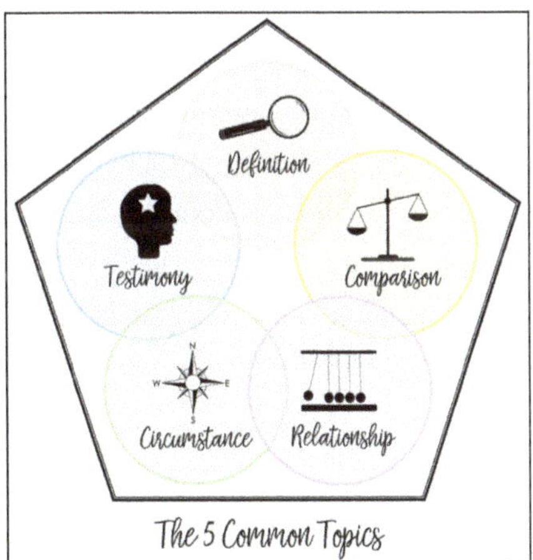

Fig. 13.1 - The 'five common topics' provide a structure to help us ask good questions, stimulate discussion, and learn about a subject.

The point of these questions is to create deep thought and discussion. So, as you use them with any subject, don't get hung up trying to figure out which of the five common topics your question falls under. There can be a little overlap and that's okay.

In chapter 14 I'll apply each of the five common topics to art and give you examples of how to use them in *art creation* with your students who are in the dialectic layer of learning.

In chapter 15 I'll connect the dialectic layer to *art appreciation* and walk you through a sample set of questions you could ask about a specific work of art.

ARE QUESTIONS ONLY ALLOWED IN THE DIALECTIC LAYER?

No! Questions are encouraged no matter what layer of learning your students are working in. However, questions in the grammar stage look different from questions in the dialectic stage. In the grammar stage, questions are fueled by a desire for facts and information. Students usually accept the answers as facts and move on to their next request for more information.

However, in the dialectic stage, students want to debate and argue. They're wrestling with ideas and testing answers, trying to prove them wrong or insufficient. So, in the dialectic stage, we focus on teaching students which questions to ask and how to ask them politely. We train them to approach a subject logically and participate in discussions with the end goal of gaining understanding (not just winning the argument).

CONVERSATIONS, NOT UGLY CONFRONTATIONS

In the dialectic layer, we also invest time training our students to be respectful during discussions and giving them tools to help them not take disagreements personally. Many people feel like a good-hearted discussion can turn into an ugly confrontation, so they avoid it. This stifles discussion and leaves us without the insight that conversations can provide. We want to train our students to value civil discussion as a means to understanding.

Start training your students early to have calm, polite, thoughtful discussions. Establish ground rules for your discussions like:

- Be humble and love your neighbor.
- Listen, ask questions, and seek to understand the other person.
- Look for terms that you may be defining differently than the other person.
- Be respectful when you disagree.
- Never attack a person. Instead focus on the subject being discussed.
- If you start to lose control of your emotions or feel attacked, tell the other person you need to take a break from the discussion.

The best way to learn these skills is to practice on topics that aren't as important to you and that you aren't personally or emotionally invested in. Keep in mind that, even as adults, we may have to teach *ourselves* all of this prior to being able to pass it on to our students.

Some students will resist these conversations because they're not yet comfortable with ambiguity. We don't always know the answers to all the questions we ask in the dialectic layer of learning. However, there's still a lot of learning that can take place in these discussions, even if they don't end with a clean conclusion. We'll learn more about the world around us if we ask questions and dream up some potential answers. Some students will love the process of thinking through hypotheticals, and others will resist it. Encourage all your students to participate in the discussion as an exercise in training the brain to think.

THE IMPORTANCE OF GREAT BOOKS

I mentioned the importance of stories in the grammar layer, but stories also help us process some of the hardest questions in the dialectic layer by taking difficult academic questions and placing them in a real-world situation, even if the story itself is fiction. For instance, in *The Scarlet Letter* by Nathaniel Hawthorne, students are faced with questions about sin in society, judgment, and forgiveness. Stories give us a way to talk about these elements with compassion for specific characters.

WHEN TO LAYER ON DIALECTIC LEARNING

As we prepare to engage in dialectic learning, it's important to consider when it's time to start layering some dialectic activities on top of the grammar of art with your students. I suggest you wait for three things:

1. Wait until your students have learned some grammar about the subject, but don't wait for 100% mastery—that's not even possible! If you've introduced your students to the grammar in the art grammar chapters in this book (chapters 7-12), that's plenty of art grammar. If you and your students aren't familiar with all the grammar here, you may still be ready to add the dialectic layer as long as you have a foundation of some art grammar. More grammar will create a richer dialectic learning experience, but it's not necessary.
2. Wait until your students are developmentally ready. It's really hard to give an age, but nine or ten years old is probably the average age a student is ready to begin dialectic learning. The younger the student, the more grammar they need before they're ready for a dialectic activity. The more passionate a student is about a subject, the more they'll learn about it, so they may be ready for dialectic wrestling at an earlier age. Look for signs that your student is interested in analytical thinking, debating, and wrestling with concepts that include ambiguity.
3. Wait until you and your students have time and patience to enjoy the process. You really don't want to rush through a dialectic activity because its primary purpose is to get the brain thinking and train the brain to reason.

~

Now that you understand the basics of the dialectic layer of education, let's examine what art creation looks like in the dialectic layer.

~

CHAPTER SUMMARY

- In the dialectic layer of education, we train our students' brains to think and reason using stories, conversations, and questions.
- High-quality questions are generated from the five common topics: definition, comparison, relationship, circumstance, and testimony/evidence.
- When compared to the grammar layer, students in the dialectic layer will often debate answers to the questions.
- You'll know it's time to incorporate dialectic learning once the student has a foundation of grammar, is developmentally ready, and has time to spend in discussion.
- Most people will need to learn the art of calm and polite discussions in order to effectively use the five common topics.
- Be sure to keep reading quality literature to enhance students' understanding of hard topics.

14

ART CREATION IN DIALECTIC

Since art creation and art appreciation are separate activities with separate goals, I address them independently in this book. This allows us to fully understand how the classical model of education applies to each one. However, it's good to integrate them together when teaching art. In my art lesson plans I often include a short segment of art appreciation before a related art creation project. The integration makes both components more memorable for students.

We'll look at art creation in the dialectic layer in this chapter and art appreciation in the next chapter. However, before we jump into art creation, recall that the dialectic layer of learning is questioning, analyzing, discussing, experimenting, and learning to enjoy this wrestling. In art, this means students will need time to tinker around with different subjects and media. Students may need extra time to learn to enjoy the process.

As with many subjects, reluctant students often find a love for art only after they have been exposed to it several times. Help students persevere by frequently teaching your students art, but don't force them to work on art for longer than thirty minutes at a time if they want to quit. Many short art classes are more likely to encourage a reluctant art student than a solid week of nothing but art.

As homeschoolers, we have a distinct advantage of being able to get out our art supplies, teach a short lesson, and then allow our reluctant students to work on their art for a short time while our more enthusiastic students can spend a few hours on their art. If you don't have this freedom, consider planning some different activities for early finishers and open your art room after school or during lunch for those who want to come back and wrestle with art some more.

As we look at the dialectic layer in art creation, we'll consider both the subject we're creating and the media we're using. Here are some ways to include each of the five common topics in art creation.

1. DEFINITION IN ART CREATION

Start by looking at and thinking about your subject—what do you plan your artwork to be about? What are the key components of your subject that make it recognizable as your subject? For example, if you were trying to draw a donkey (figure 14.1), what about a donkey makes it look like a donkey (white nose, big eyes, large ears, etc.)?

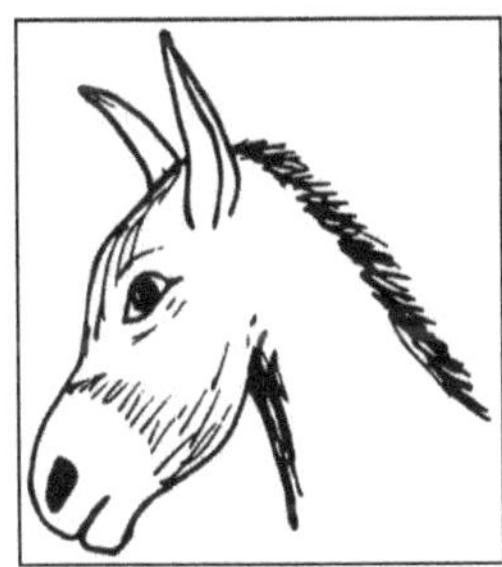

Fig. 14.1 - This simple sketch is clearly of a donkey because of the simple features that differentiate it from a horse.

Now think about the medium you're using. What is it made of? For example, watercolor paint is made from pigments and filler. Some pigments are dye-based and some are mineral-based. These will behave differently on the paper. Watercolor paper generally has more cotton in it than other paper, allowing it to absorb water without buckling. Knowing the supplies you're using will help you decide what sort of art you want to create.

2. COMPARISON IN ART CREATION

We'll start again with the subject—how is this subject different from others?

For example, how is a donkey different from a horse? One possible answer is that donkeys have shorter legs, a shorter face, less mane, a straighter back, and a shorter tail. To what degree are the horse and donkey different? How much shorter is the tail of the donkey compared to a horse?

You'll find these are great questions to ask when you're drawing a plant or animal for some sort of scientific observation because you'll notice more details when you're drawing the subject of your observation. For example, you might ask how the shape, base, tip, and edge of the leaves of one plant differ from another.

Now think again about your medium. How is this medium different from others? For example, how are my three different homemade clays similar and different from each other? Some possible answers are that one is stickier than the others, another is very grainy, and one takes longer to dry than the others. Perhaps one is easier to manipulate, but more expensive than the others.

As another example, how are my Faber Castel watercolor pencils different from my Prismacolor pencils (figure 14.2)? The Faber Castel pencils have more pigment in them, while the Prismacolor watercolor pencils are waxier. This allows me to create different effects with each one.

Researching and formulating the answers to these questions helps students understand the subject better, even if they never articulate their answer to someone else! I also use questions like these when I'm in an art store asking the clerk about a specific brand of art medium.

3. RELATIONSHIP IN ART CREATION

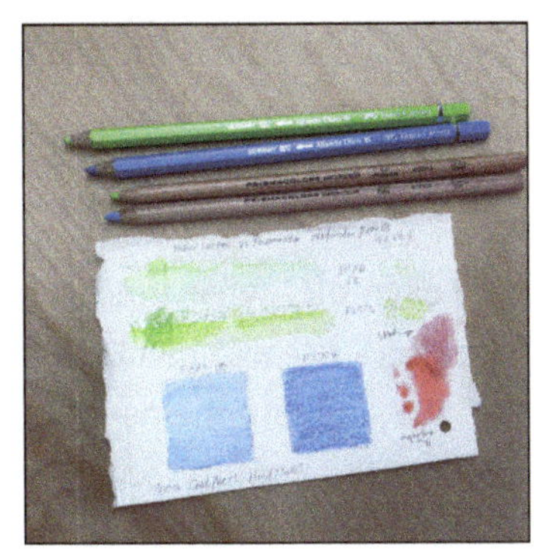

Fig. 14.2 - Comparing two different brands of watercolor pencils allows me to learn more about both of them and know when I want to use each brand.

Remember from chapter 13 that relationship is where we ask questions about cause and effect, before and after, and contraries and contradictions.

When drawing, 'relationship' includes proper proportions. When I'm drawing a donkey, I need to understand how long to draw the legs in relation to the body and the neck. If one donkey has shorter legs than another, I should ask why. Is this a malnourished donkey? A different breed of donkey? A younger donkey?

Relationship also includes perspective. We use all the methods of perspective (as explained in chapter 23) to create depth so the viewer knows the spatial relationship between two subjects in our artwork. How could you use each method to achieve the look you want?

You could also ask yourself what effect certain colors will have on your end result. What does your culture typically associate with each color? What effect does each color have on each other? Think about the principles of design and determine what elements of art you want to use to achieve your desired result. For example, if you want a busy chaotic feel, use a lot of variety of color and texture. If you're trying to calm your artwork down, choose to limit your color palette and have a lot of repetition in color and texture.

When learning about different media, ask questions like: What would be the effect of using more water or a different brand of paint? What happens when we dab wet paint with a paper towel? What's the effect of putting salt, sand, or chalk in the watercolor paint?

4. CIRCUMSTANCE IN ART CREATION

In the 'circumstance' topic, we ask ourselves questions about the subject's circumstance and the possibility of that circumstance.

For example, what time period is our art depicting? Did you know that Grandma Moses, painting in the mid-1920s, was very careful to never include modern items like power lines or telephone poles when she painted the country scenes of her childhood in the late 1800s? She was looking at the current land for inspiration, but she had to keep asking herself what the circumstance would have been in the era she was depicting. This kind of attention to detail is part of what caused people to identify with Grandma Moses and love her artwork.

We should also ask ourselves if we're depicting the subject in a nearly impossible pose. Some of my favorite photos of animals show the animals doing silly things. However, I've found they're extra hard to draw because the viewer's brain keeps trying to figure out what's going on. It will always be easier to draw something in a very normal position and surrounding.

Now, think about your medium. What will happen if we try this same medium in a new circumstance, like on different paper or in a different ambient temperature? Paints perform differently in different temperatures and levels of humidity.

Also ask what is possible with this medium. What's impossible? For example, is it possible to rehydrate clay? (Yes, for many clays it is!) Is it possible to give the impression of color in a fully black and white medium like pen and ink? (Yes, by creating shades of gray with stippling and cross hatching, our eyes will interpret certain shades as being representative of color.)

5. TESTIMONY IN ART CREATION

Testimony reminds us to always consult with experts and learn what they can teach us about a subject. We connect with experts through books, videos, or live classes about how to draw certain subjects or how to use certain media. For example, in a class I attended about drawing plants, I learned an amazing amount about what to focus on when identifying and drawing plants.

Concerning media, you might ask if there are any laws about disposal. Is there any data available about this medium's safety? Will I need to travel to dispose of it properly? How quickly will this paint dry? Does this 'dry time' vary when working inside or outside? What about the lightfastness (how resistant the medium is to fading when exposed to light over long periods of time)? Sometimes you can find data on the product online. For example, there may be opacity ratings for different brands and types of paint, which tell you how much you'll be able to see through a single layer of the medium. You can also ask the employees at your local art store (the kind of store where the students in art school purchase their art supplies). They are often very familiar with all the media they sell and they're a wealth of information!

Now let's discover art appreciation in the dialectic layer of art education.

CHAPTER SUMMARY

- In the dialectic layer of art creation, ask and answer questions generated by the five common topics about your subject and the medium you're using in order to gain a deeper understanding of the subject and medium.

15

ART APPRECIATION IN DIALECTIC

In addition to art creation, we can also ask dialectic questions in art appreciation. Pull out a work of art (famous or personal) and start with the same questions you used in the grammar layer of learning (chapter 12). Then dig deeper by asking questions from each of the five common topics. Don't feel like you need to ask *all* these questions for each piece of art. Instead pick and choose a few that fit the subject best.

1. DEFINITION IN ART APPRECIATION

What is the main focal point of this work of art? What genre of art is this (Historical, Portrait, Lifestyle, Landscape, Animal, or Still Life)? Or is it instead abstract or scientific? What media was used to create this artwork?

You can also go wide and ask questions about art in general with questions like: What is art? What is not art? To what category does art belong? What else is in that group? When is a work of art abstract? When is it not abstract? According to tradition, a work of art is usually considered abstract when the artist was not intending to represent reality, but since we don't always know the artist's intentions, what's another definition we could use?

Alternatively, you can dig deep into each of the elements of art and the principles of design by asking questions like: What is a shape? What is not a shape? To what group of things does this shape belong? What else belongs to that group? How is this shape different from those things? Can a shape be broken into pieces? If so, what are those pieces? What makes a shape a shape?

2. COMPARISON IN ART APPRECIATION

Compare and contrast two works of art using the grammar you know. You can compare two works by the same artist or two works by different artists. How are they similar? How are they different? What's the effect of these differences on the art's purpose, appearance, and appeal? If you choose two works of art from different time periods or different cultures, you can use these questions to learn more about those two periods or cultures.

Compare and contrast two parts of a single work of art. How is one area or subject treated differently than the other? Are the colors lighter or darker? Warmer or cooler? More saturated or more washed out? Is one subject painted with precise detail while another is blurred?

3. RELATIONSHIP IN ART APPRECIATION

How do different elements/principles/components relate to each other? Generally, what effect does each of these have on the work of art? If you wanted to achieve a certain mood or feeling in a work of art, which elements and principles would you need to use to create it? Are there any elements or principles that cannot co-exist?

What might have caused the artist to want to create his or her art this way? Is the art a result of a particular life-event or a national event? What seems to be the main point or purpose of this art—why did the artist create it? What must the artist believe about the world since he/she created this work of art?

Remember to encourage your students to take part in these discussions, even though we don't know the answers for certain. The goal of these questions is to go deeper with our art appreciation by causing us to think in many different ways as we reflect on the work of art.

This is another great time to bring in history and culture. What might have been the consequences of this piece of art in the time period it was created? Did this style of art affect the culture of that day, or vice versa? How does it affect people today? Does the art glorify God and His creation? What effect does this art have on you?

What's the relationship between this work of art and other subjects like science, history, politics, and so forth?

4. CIRCUMSTANCE IN ART APPRECIATION

We can discuss 'circumstance' from several different angles:

- **Historical:** When was this artwork created? What was going on in history when this piece was made? How did that circumstance enable the artist? Would this kind of art have been possible or likely in another culture or era?
- **Personal:** What was going on in this person's life when this piece was made? How did this affect the art he/she created?
- **Geographical:** What geography surrounded the artist? How might the surrounding landscapes have influenced the artist's work?
- **Philosophical:** What were the prevailing philosophies and theologies at that time? How did they influence the art of the time? (Nancy Pearcey covers this beautifully in her book, *Saving Leonardo.*)

5. TESTIMONY IN ART APPRECIATION

In testimony we turn to experts in the field and look at what they say about the work of art. How would experts answer some of our previous questions? What do they say about this work? Do the experts all agree? What biases may your chosen experts have? Do you agree with the experts?

Next, we look at the quantitative data. Do we know for sure when this art was created or what media was used? How much is it valued at? How is this value determined? Do the experts all agree?

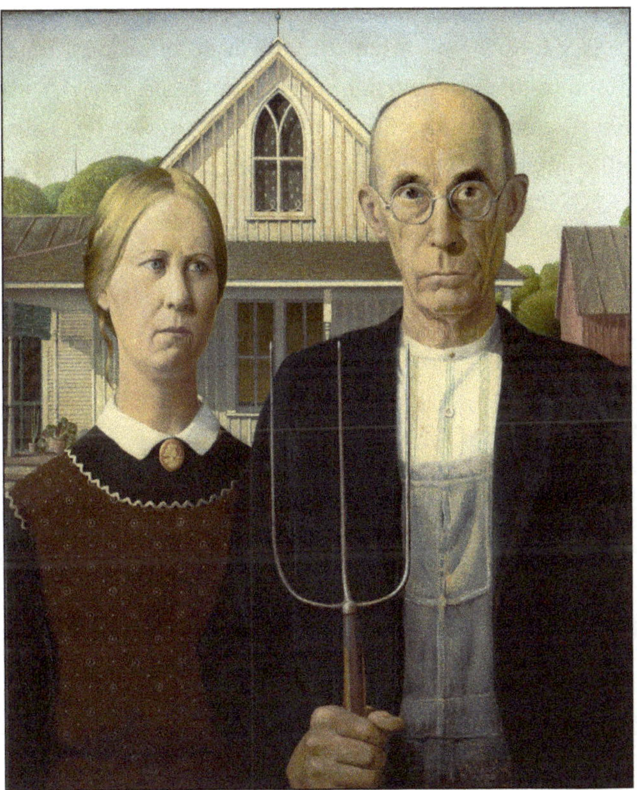

Fig. 15.1 - Grant Wood's *American Gothic* (1930) is a great example of a painting that's taken on a life of its own in our culture.

In addition to consulting experts, we also look at what our culture, as a whole, thinks of the artwork. Has it gained cultural connotations? For example, when the Impressionists first started showing their art to the public, the experts thought it looked mundane, unfinished, and unimpressive. However, the public liked the look and the subject matter. Another example is *American Gothic* (figure 15.1) by Grant Wood, which was originally supposed to hold up rural farmers as hard-working heroes. But now the painting has taken on a life of its own, constantly being remade with different characters

DIALECTIC ART APPRECIATION EXAMPLE

To help you see how you might use all these questions, here are some grammar and dialectic questions you could ask specifically as you discuss *The Oxbow* (figure 15.2) by Thomas Cole. I've also included some sample answers though many are open to debate.

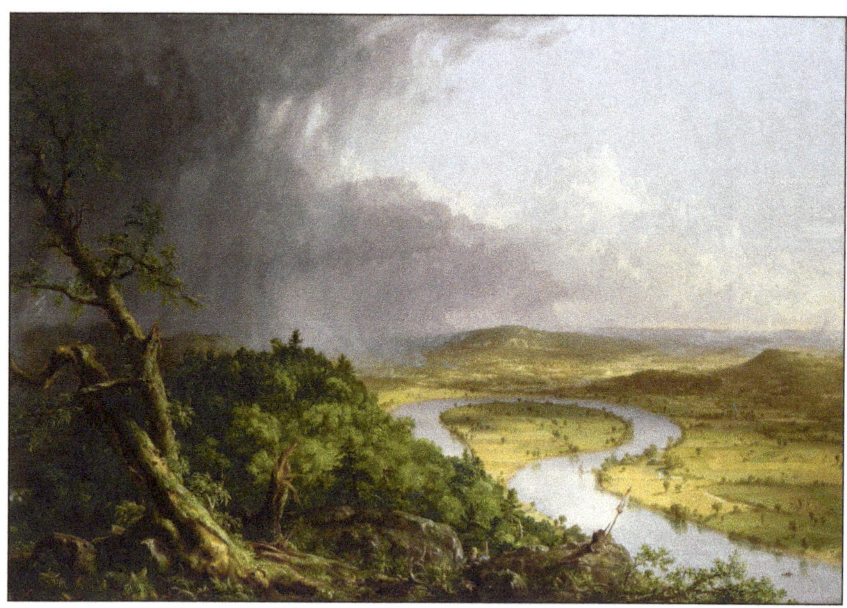

Fig. 15.2 - *The Oxbow* (1836) by Thomas Cole

- Who created this work of art? *Thomas Cole.*

- When/Where did the artist live? *Eastern America in 1801-1848.*
- When was this artwork created? *1836.*
- What else was going on in history at that time? *American Expansion and Manifest Destiny. (Discuss what this means.)*
- What media was used to create this artwork? *Oil on Canvas.*
- What genre of art is this? *Landscape (which, according to the Renaissance Hierarchy of Genres, was a less noble subject, but Cole is elevating it to something worthwhile here).*
- What is the main focal point of this work of art? *The river.*
- What else do you notice in the painting? *There is a dead or dying tree on the left, farm fields, and houses on the right.* What might those represent to Cole?
- Does this artwork appear to be realistic or abstract? *Realistic.*
- Does this art belong to a particular movement or period? *Romantic.*
- What do we know about the Romantic Movement? How would you define it? *An art movement in which artists honored nature, individualism, intuition, and emotion. The movement was an idyllic and dramatic reaction to the artists' dislike of the Neo-Classical period, the Industrial Revolution, and the Age of Enlightenment.*
- What other artists belonged to this movement? *Friederich, Turner, Gericault, Delacroix, Constable, Bierstadt, Church, Bingham. If you aren't yet familiar with any of the other artists of the movement, skip this question.*
- Did this artist identify himself as a particular type of artist? *He was part of a group of artists who called themselves the Hudson River School. They liked to paint within the themes of discovery, exploration, and settlement.*
- Where do we see lines and shapes in this artwork? How do they affect the look of the painting? *The line of the river is striking. The edge of the green hill/cliff seems to lead the eye to the storm.*
- What values (lights and darks) and colors do we see in this painting? How do they affect the look of the painting? *The left*

side is dark and stormy with cool colors while the right side is light and clear with warm colors, creating a sharp contrast.

- What might have caused the artist to want to create his or her art this way? *Cole seems to be drawing attention to the differences between the calm, settled farmland and the wild, stormy wilderness.*
- What seems to be the main point or purpose of this art—why did the artist create it? *The purpose seems to be to display the contrast between the wild and settled lands.*
- What must the artist believe about the world since he/she created this work of art? *He might believe that America's expansion into the frontier is scary or necessary, good for the country or bad for the country. Answers will vary.*
- Compare this painting to another painting. What are the similarities and differences?
- What do experts say about this painting? *Most experts agree that Cole, like many in the U.S. at the time, believed America had a Manifest Destiny—that it was ordained by God to settle the westward territory. The right (east) side of the painting shows order, calm, and productivity, while the left (west) side shows chaos and unproductivity. This painting displays the benefits of America following through with its destiny to tame the wild land, as the artist believes she should.*

I hope you'll start incorporating these dialectic methods of art creation and art appreciation in your homeschool soon. They produce a deeper investigation of art and a more thorough understanding of art than any other means. Next, we'll cover the rhetoric layer, and then in part three, I'll give you the practical tools and exercises I use to teach students.

~

CHAPTER SUMMARY

- In the dialectic layer of art appreciation, students ask and answer questions generated by the five common topics about famous works of art.
- These discussions help stimulate discussion and lead to a more thorough understanding of art.

16

THE RHETORIC LAYER

To review, the grammar layer of learning is absorbing information and the dialectic layer is asking questions and analyzing. This brings us to the rhetoric layer, which is presenting and defending conclusions. Rhetoric is the use of grammar (knowledge) and dialectic (understanding) to express wisdom, truth, and beauty.

We want to allow plenty of time in the dialectic stage, but we don't want to stay there forever. We often need a rhetorical (application) goal to look toward, even if it's small. Remember that the rhetoric layer of learning is all about training the brain to express truth.

CULTURE CLASHES

We should pause here and address the fact that our modern culture does not use the word 'rhetoric' the same way it is used in classical education circles. These days, the word rhetoric implies manipulation and propaganda. Historically, however, rhetoric was not such a negative word. Rhetoric was supposed to be Truth-serving, not self-serving.

Leigh Bortins, in her book *The Conversation*, defines rhetoric as "the use of knowledge and understanding to perceive wisdom, pursue virtue, and proclaim truth." The knowledge is the information we gathered in the grammar layer. The understanding is the thoughts we processed in the dialectic layer. In the rhetoric layer of learning, we're using both the knowledge and the understanding to bring truth, goodness, and beauty into the world.

Another point of confusion that arises when we discuss the rhetoric layer of learning is understanding that it's a layer of *learning* at all. We tend to think of rhetoric activities like writing books, teaching classes, giving speeches, and inventing new products as the *result* of learning. From a classical education perspective, these activities are both a display of past learning *and* an act of learning. A rhetoric activity can be a culmination of learning, but it's also an activity that inspires us to return to the dialectic and grammar layers to fill in the holes of our understanding.

Lastly, in our modern culture we tend to assume that this third layer of the Trivium should be reserved for certain people; we want only experts to teach, only professionals to lead, and only the certified to perform. But who are the experts? Who are the professionals? Those who have completed a standardized test, filled out their applications, and received the government's stamp of approval? We all know the ability to pass a test is never a good indicator of intelligence, skill, or experience. Personally, some of my favorite teachers have been people with no credentials whatsoever.

Additionally, most truly great ideas have come from those who were outside of the entrenched establishment created by tests and certifications. Think of all the world-changers who never had a college degree, like Bill Gates, Steve Jobs, Michael Dell, Richard Branson, Jane Goodall,[1] John D. Rockefeller, and Henry Ford. In fact, in 2016, CNBC reported that 30% of the world's billionaires didn't even have a bachelor's degree.[2]

We shortchange ourselves as a society if we are only willing to listen to those who have jumped through the hoops the current gatekeepers have created.

We also shortchange ourselves if we never step up to create, teach, or lead because we haven't reached 'expert' status. There's a tremendous amount of learning that takes place in these rhetorical activities. If you've ever taught a class, you know the teacher always learns more from teaching than any student learns from listening or doing.

Be brave! Step up and model the rhetoric layer of learning for your students. Don't wait until you feel like you know it all, because you never will. Teach what you know! You'll be amazed at how much you learn and how much you're able to pass on to your students.

In the rhetoric layer of learning, we use a set of five steps called the five canons of rhetoric to bring truth, goodness, and beauty into the world. I'll explain each of these in general first. Then, in the next chapter I'll explain how they apply to art.

THE FIVE CANONS OF RHETORIC ARE:

- **Invention:** What should be communicated? This is really the grammar and dialectic layers of learning all wrapped up into one tidy word. In this step, the student researches and wrestles with ideas, using the five common topics, until they decide what truth they want to express.
- **Arrangement:** In what order should it be communicated? In this step, the student takes all their ideas and decides what structure to organize them in. (Chronological? Topical? Big picture followed by the details?) The student is figuring out the best order to present it in so the reader will understand the key ideas.
- **Elocution:** How should it be said? This step is all about style. The student must decide if he/she wants to use an allegory or just report straight facts. Should the facts include data or anecdotal evidence? Should it be said casually or formally?
- **Memory:** What role will memory play? In Ancient Greece, this

step was when students memorized their whole speech. However, now we tend to ask ourselves, "How much of my speech do I need to memorize?" (Will I have cue cards? PowerPoint slides? A teleprompter?) This is also where modern students may stop to consider what main piece of information they want the recipient to remember, and how to make it memorable.

- **Delivery:** How should this truth be presented? Now we come to the last step, which is determining the way the material is presented. If Elocution and Delivery seem the same, think of Elocution as what you do in speech-writing-mode while Delivery uses the set of skills you practice in every speech. If they are giving a presentation, students should decide how to dress, what mannerisms they will use, where in the speech they should vary their speed or volume, etc. If instead students are writing papers, Delivery is where they decide what font, spacing, and margins are appropriate, if they need a cover page, or if their paper needs a special kind of binding.

In all these steps the students must focus on their intended audience because the answers vary widely depending on who the audience is.

Now, how does this relate to art? We'll explore that question in the next chapter.

CHAPTER SUMMARY

- The rhetoric layer of learning is the use of grammar (knowledge) and dialectic (understanding) to express wisdom, truth, and beauty.

- We use the five canons of rhetoric to plan our expression:
- Invention: What should be said?
- Arrangement: In what order should it be said?
- Elocution: How should it be said?
- Memory: What role will memory play?
- Delivery: How should it be presented?

17

ART IN RHETORIC

In the rhetoric layer of learning art, we create expressive works of art, speak/write convincingly about art-related topics, and teach these same things. Of course, we continue to use all three layers of learning as we go. It's important to note that it's not just a few talented people who get to participate in the rhetoric layers of art. We can all dabble in this third layer of learning and experience its benefits.

It's also good to remember that the delineation between the dialectic and rhetoric layers doesn't need to be clearly labeled. For example, let's say you were tinkering around with a new medium doing all the dialectic things but then realized you had created something beautiful! Was that dialectic or rhetoric? It's both! It all counts as learning and you don't need to classify it as only dialectic or only rhetoric. Let the structure of the Trivium work *for* you and help you—don't let it limit you! Many of the ideas and questions here still apply, even if you didn't plan your transition between the layers of learning. You can get to 'rhetoric' in multiple ways. It all counts.

What does it look like as we use the five canons of rhetoric in both art creation and art appreciation? Again, we'll start with art creation and then look at art appreciation.

ART CREATION IN THE RHETORIC STAGE

Creating visual art can be a beautiful way to express your ideas and communicate with others. Here are some ways to include each of the five canons of rhetoric in art creation.

1. Invention in Art Creation

Work through all the same questions we generated when using the five common topics for dialectic art creation in chapter 14. Then ask yourself, what is the purpose of this art? What does it need to accomplish? Why am I creating it? Who is my audience?

If my goal is to create a cute Christmas ornament, then I can do a quick sketch, go over it with ink, and add color all in the space of an hour or two. If I'm being commissioned to paint a twenty-foot mural, I'll need to plan more and know what my patron wants to see.

If I'm teaching a class on art, leading my students through art creation, I should ask myself what grammar I want to include. How much information can I include in one art lesson without overwhelming my students?

2. Arrangement in Art Creation

In visual art, this is when we plan the composition of the artwork. What will be the focal point, and where should it go? What other subjects do I want to include, and where will they go? How will I display the background and make it all look how I want it to, using the methods of perspective?

For example, if I'm creating a botanical illustration for a plant identification book, like the one in figure 17.1, what's the best layout for that format? Will it need a white background? How can I show each part of the plant and also indicate the relative size of each portion? If I'm drawing it for my nature journal, what's the best way to lay it out? If the artwork will be hung on a wall, would a more dramatic painting with depth be better suited?

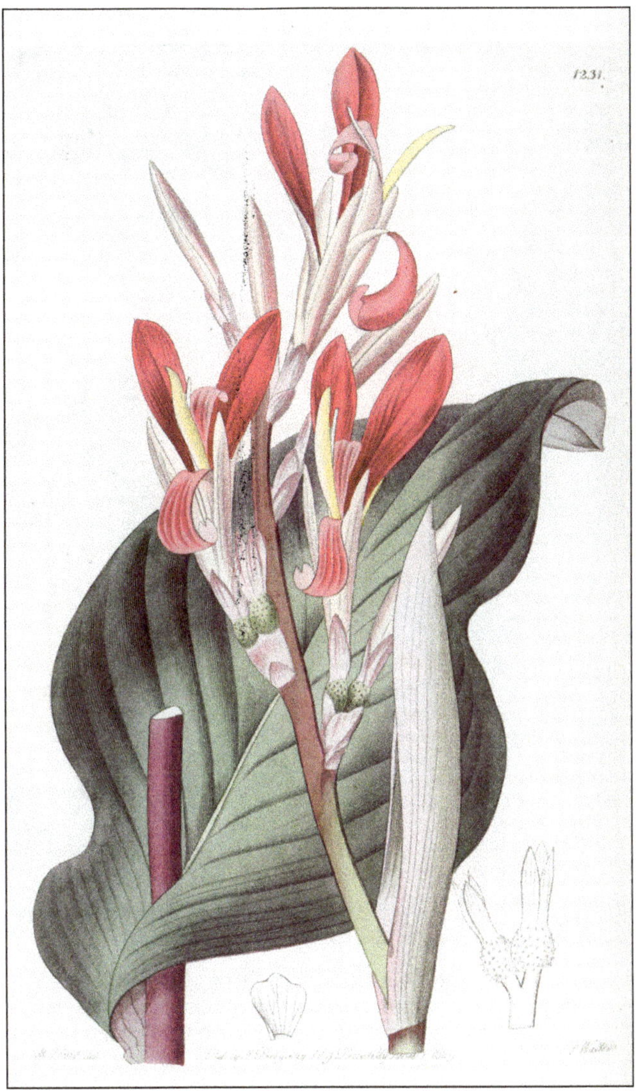

Fig 17.1 - This *Canna indica* botanical from *The Botanical Register* (1829) by Edwards and Lindley was arranged and composed based on the purpose of cataloging the plant and showing all its identifiable features.

If instead of creating a botanical, I'm creating a bold painting designed to capture the attention of a passerby, I might create something more like Georgia O'Keeffe's *Red Canna* (figure 17.2).

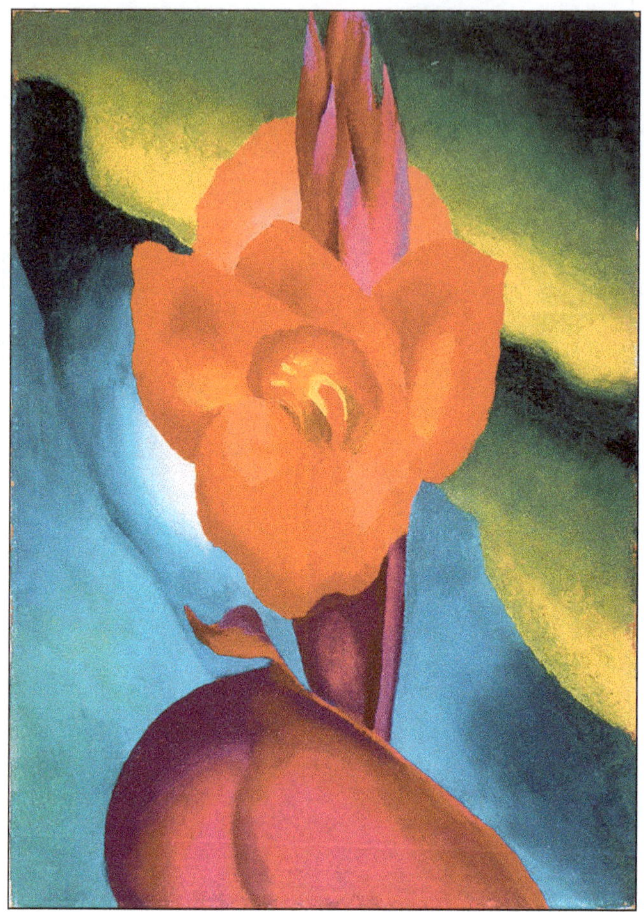

Fig. 17.2 - *Red Canna* (1924) by Georgia O'Keeffe was designed to capture the attention of busy New Yorkers and help them see what she saw in the flowers.

3. Elocution in Art Creation

In elocution, we ask ourselves questions like this: What medium would be best for this art project? Some styles are easier to achieve in some media. For example, it can be challenging to get the same intensely saturated colors with watercolor that you can get with acrylics. In the same way, blending is easy with chalk pastels but nearly impossible with traditional ink pen.

Where will the final art be stored and what weather will it be exposed to? This will greatly influence the medium you choose to use. Artwork that will be displayed outside by the ocean will be exposed to salty, humid air, while artwork that will be in the snow will be exposed to freezing and thawing. Artwork hung in a kitchen or bathroom will be exposed to more humidity than artwork hung in a bedroom or family room.

Should this work of art be detailed or stylized? Realistic or abstract? What colors will best convey my message? Do I want to include some visual metaphors in my artwork?

4. Memory in Art Creation

For the memory step, we ask ourselves: Will I need to draw from memory, or will I have a model available? Do I have some photographs I can sketch from? Can I gain permission to draw from the photos if I don't own the copyright?

What will make this work of art memorable to my audience? For example, if I'm sketching quick visuals to help my students remember some science grammar, drawing my subject a little silly might make it more memorable than a sketch that is realistic.

Do I remember any other works of art that could inspire my creation?

5. Delivery in Art Creation

For delivery, we might ask if our work of art needs to be framed or preserved in some way after it's finished. How should it be displayed or delivered to my audience? Do I need to write a few sentences about the art to hang alongside it in a professional gallery or for display on my website?

Can you see how the five common topics help us systematically plan and, in doing so, free up our minds to create? They help us avoid costly mistakes and problems that might arise from a lack of planning. This allows us to create freely.

Now that we see how the five canons of rhetoric apply to art creation, let's look at how they apply to art appreciation.

ART APPRECIATION IN THE RHETORIC STAGE

In the rhetoric layer of art appreciation, we want to communicate the ideas generated from our dialectic discussions. This could be done in a podcast, video, live presentation about art in general, an elevator pitch about your own art, or a book about an artist. Here are some ways to include each of the five canons of rhetoric in art appreciation.

1. Invention in Art Appreciation

What do I want to say about this art or artist? What point am I trying to make? Who is my audience and what do they already know about the subject? Which pieces of art do I want to show my audience?

2. Arrangement in Art Appreciation

In what order should I present this all information? If I'm talking about a particular artist, does it make sense to talk about the artist's upbringing or his/her impact on culture first? What organization will make the most sense to my audience? If I'm writing a book, how will I arrange the visual art alongside the text of the book?

3. Elocution in Art Appreciation

Does my audience expect something casual or formal? Do I want to write/speak in first, second, or third person? Should I include humorous stories or elegant prose? Is this the sort of thing my audience will consume all in one sitting, or will I deliver it to them in parts?

What's the best way to make this point? Is it a presentation, a movie, a blog post, a book, or something else? What style of visuals do I want to include? If copyright will be a problem, what type of visuals can I use that will still convey the point?

What is the easiest and most convenient way for my audience to hear this? At what grade level do I want the text of my speech or writing to be? Sometimes we use simpler language so it's less work to understand, even though our audience is capable of understanding something written at a higher grade level.

4. Memory in Art Appreciation

If I'm giving a live presentation, will I memorize my presentation or use notes? If I'm recording a video or podcast, will I speak from an outline or script?

What will make this point/presentation memorable to my audience? Should I encourage them to take notes? Do I want to provide an outline to my audience so they can follow along?

5. Delivery in Art Appreciation

What attire and body language will be appropriate? Do I want my clothing to help my audience relate to me as their equal, or see me as an authority on the subject?

If I'm writing a blog post or book, how much white space will I include? Do I want title headings and words in bold to make it easier for my readers to quickly get the gist of what I'm saying?

You may be thinking to yourself that you don't plan to give a presentation about art any time soon, but art really does play an important role in everyday life. Now that you know so much about art, you can teach it to your students! You'll also find that, with your newfound knowledge of art, situations will pop up where you have something art-related to say. Art can be a great conversation starter!

Now you have a solid foundational understanding of art and how to use the classical model of education to teach art. I hope you're excited and ready to learn how to easily do this in your classroom or at your dining room table. In Part Three of this book I'm going to give you many examples and drills you can use as you are introducing art grammar, dialectically wrestling with art, and rhetorically creating and discussing art.

CHAPTER SUMMARY

- We use the five canons of rhetoric (invention, arrangement, elocution, memory, and delivery) to plan and prepare for art creation and art appreciation.

III

PRACTICAL WAYS TO TEACH ART

18

PLANNING ART PROJECTS

Now that you understand the classical model and you know what to include in each layer of learning, you'll need to consider what this looks like on a practical level in a homeschool classroom.

This part of the book is filled with projects and exercises you can do at home or in a classroom. I suggest you read through this section, referring back to Part Two of the book as needed. Then pick out some projects to do together. The sequence of activities is usually not important, but I'll mention prerequisites when they occur.

I also want to point out that these art projects have been stripped of their subject integration components to give you maximum flexibility. I want you to be able to see exactly how an art project teaches the grammar of art without any extras in the way to muddy the field. Then you can incorporate them into a complete art lesson for your students.

PLANNING YOUR ART LESSONS

Let's start with a look at the overall structure of an art lesson plan. When

I create an art lesson plan to share with other teachers, I combine three main components:

- non-art subject matter, like history or science
- art grammar
- an art project

First, I pick the non-art subject matter theme. For example, I might pick seashells, the Civil War, or a specific historical artist. This will become the subject integration component, which, as you know, is very important in the classical model of education. When I create an art lesson plan specifically to go along with some other unit in our homeschool, the theme is already established.

I do my research and write notes on the topic. Then, I condense my notes into a five-minute script for teachers to read to their students. (I love it when teachers make this piece their own, but I like to provide a script to make it easier.)

Next, I ask myself dialectic questions about the non-art subject matter theme in order to pick one or two pieces of art grammar that will integrate well. (Review chapter 13, The Dialectic Layer, for ideas on what questions to ask.) These one or two pieces of art grammar will be the focus of the art basics section of my lesson. I plan a quick script about that component of art grammar (which will look suspiciously similar to the text in the art grammar chapters of this book) for the teacher to read aloud to his/her students.

Finally, I pick an art medium and design a project (which will look suspiciously similar to one or more of the practical art drills, exercises, or tricks in this part of this book).

Now, can you see how you're fully equipped to teach art? You have all the art grammar you need in Part Two of this book, and I'm giving you a bunch of projects to choose from here in Part Three!

On my website, RidgeLightRanch.com, I sell art lesson plans with the non-art subject matter (like history or science) integrated with the art grammar and the art project. While many people decide to continue taking advantage of my affordable and time-saving lesson plans, once you grasp all this you'll be able to create your own art lessons to integrate with any subject! I'd love to hear how you use your newfound knowledge of art! (Refer to the last page of this book for how to best connect with me!)

ART TEACHER MINDSETS

As you learn about the different practical ways to teach art, I ask you to try to maintain these art teacher mindsets.

1. Art Takes Practice

I've said this before, but it bears repeating because it's so contrary to our modern view of art creation. There's an extremely small number of natural artists who can draw what they see without having to practice drawing. Anytime you meet an artist, if you have an opportunity for conversation, ask them if they've always known how to draw or if they had to learn at some point. Ask them how much and how often they practice. I think you'll be surprised how frequently artists practice and how few claim to have any skills they haven't had to work hard to gain. Every single artist I've ever met has worked hard for their skills and continues to practice daily. Encourage your students with the knowledge that they *can* become a very skilled artist with practice.

Some people do seem to gain drawing skills more easily than others. However, these seem to be the people who have developed the right/visual side of their brain and are practiced at seeing what actually exists instead of a left/verbal representational version of reality. So again, it's about practice.

. . .

2. Art is Not a Separate Elective or a Luxury

Treat art as a core part of education, not an optional elective thing on the side. Integrate it into everything and teach the principles in everyday life. Of course, you don't have to do a full art project every day, but when you feel yourself looking at art as a luxury, as our culture usually does, review Part One of this book about all the benefits of art in education. Remind yourself of the purpose of education from chapter 1: "Classical education is the cultivation of wisdom and virtue by nourishing the soul on truth, goodness, and beauty, so that, in Christ, the student is better able to know, glorify, and enjoy God."

Encourage your students to look for art opportunities in their daily work and give extra credit when your students are willing to add some art to their assignments. For example, when writing fiction or non-fiction papers, I offer my students extra credit for an illustration accompanying their paper. When we were studying American history, I had my children draw a few American landmarks (figure 18.1). Review chapter five of this book for more subject integration ideas.

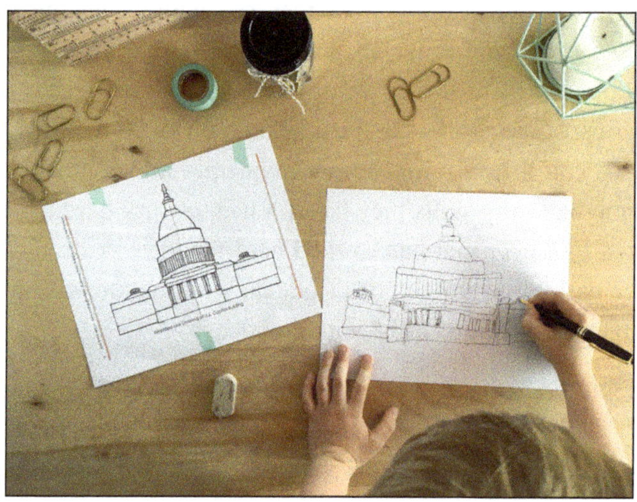

Fig. 18.1 - When studying American History, we did some drawing projects using American landmarks like the Capital Building.

When possible, I incorporate art into all our other subjects and I try NOT to section it out as 'art time.' However, there are occasions when we'll do an art project specifically. For example, around Christmas time, we always make the grandparents something special. These projects are special in their purpose but not in the fact that art supplies are available. My children always have access to art supplies so when they notice a good opportunity for art, they can take it.

3. Art Isn't Optional

I try not to ask my students *if* they like art or want to do art. Instead, I want my students to think of art as another thing they learn in school. No one knows if they will enjoy riding a bike until they learn how and then spend some time actually riding a bike. Art is the same way. We must learn the basic skills and practice them before we know if we like it!

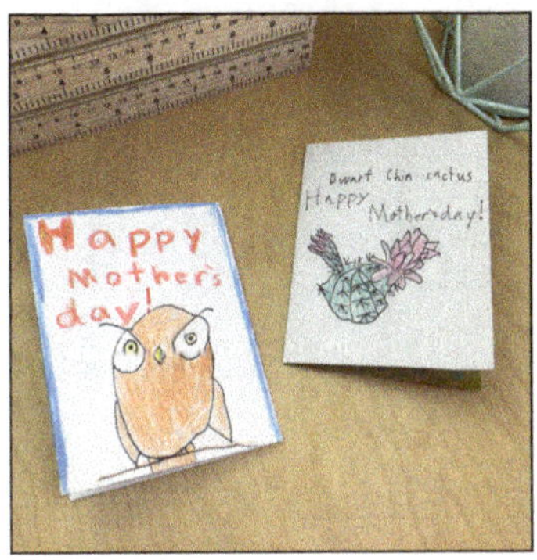

Fig. 18.2 - My kids really don't have a choice as to whether or not they make Mother's Day cards for their grandmothers, but they do get to choose how much effort they put into them.

As another example, our family usually makes Mother's Day and Father's Day cards for their grandparents each year. My children can choose how much time and effort they put into them, but they aren't optional. At first, I got some resistance, but over the years my boys have come to enjoy drawing cards and they get better every year (figure 18.2).

On a similar note, you as the parent need to make art a priority. We all make time for what's important to us. You don't have to do art every day, or even every week to gain most of the benefits of art in your child's education. (Of course, if you really want to master the skill, you will need to practice daily.) However, you do need to plan time for art or the whole year can slip by.

4. Plan a Project, Then Be Flexible

When teaching art in any of the three layers of classical education, I always plan a specific project. The alternative of just setting out art media and telling kids to make something will work for some students, but it will paralyze others. Plus, given freedom to draw anything, many students will draw the same subject over and over. Repetition is great, but students also need some variety to increase their skills. A planned assignment or project is a great way to direct and teach students.

Of course, even with the perfect project all planned out, some students will go off on their own and create something entirely different. Since I don't grade art projects, I usually don't say anything to these rogue students. When I take art classes myself, I will often modify the project to something I will enjoy more. I try to stay flexible and balanced between the plan and someone's impromptu idea.

It might help students to learn that professional artists often find having constraints placed on them makes them more creative. For example, artist Jake Parker creates an annual drawing challenge every October called Inktober. In this free international art community event, hundreds of thousands of artists follow Parker's daily prompts, draw something, and post it for others to see. Parker found that the constraint of a prompt, along with the accountability of committing to post a drawing every day, significantly improved his and his followers' skills as artists (figure 18.3).

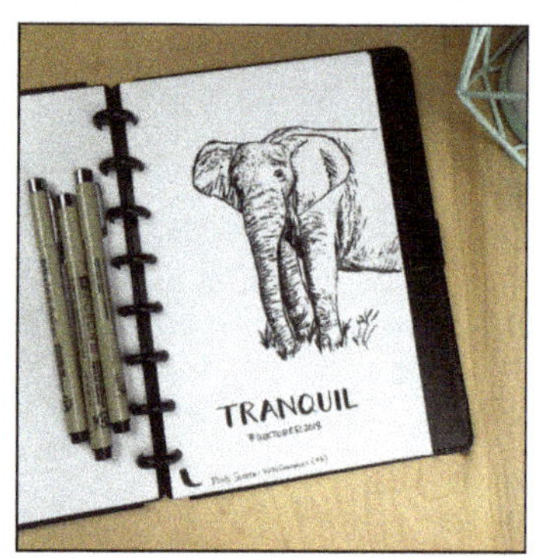

Fig. 18.3 - This elephant sketch of mine came out of the constraints and accountability of the Inktober challenge.

5. Teach and Practice for Gaining Skills, Not Creating Masterpieces

Most art projects are not going to result in a masterpiece. Instead we complete a fun, quick project where we integrate other subjects with art and introduce some art grammar. When students are ready to add on the dialectic layer of learning, you simply layer the dialectic questions on top of the projects.

Consider working up to one masterpiece near the end of a semester of art. Plan out the artwork, create sketches leading up to the final project in the same way you'd outline a paper, and then have a rough draft prior to creating a final draft. Give plenty of time for it and have some extra materials available in case students need to scrap the project and start over once or twice.

CHAPTER SUMMARY

- Plan art lessons to include non-art subject integration content, art basics, and an art creation project. When teaching, keep in mind that art needs practice, integration, planning, intentionality, flexibility, and more practice.

19

PROGRESSION OF DRAWING ACTIVITIES

If you'll be having students draw in the art project you're planning, think about your students' skill level and passion level. Then choose an activity along the progression of drawing activities that matches their level. You'll want to find a drawing activity that is a little challenging but not so hard as to overwhelm the budding artist. If you have a mix of skill levels in your class, you can modify the art project by having some students use one of these activities and others use a different activity.

For any given subject you may be drawing, this is the progression of drawing activities from easiest to hardest:

1. Mindful Tracing
2. Directed Drawing
3. Modeled Drawing
4. Drawing from a Drawing
5. Drawing from a Black and White Photo
6. Drawing from a Color Photo

7. Bonus drawing trick: Grid Drawing
8. Drawing from Life
9. Bonus drawing trick: Using a Picture Plane
10. Drawing from Memory
11. Drawing an Idea

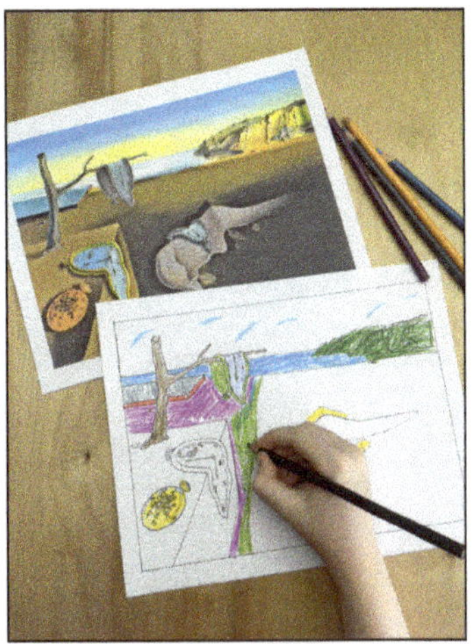

Fig. 19.1 - Coloring isn't exactly drawing, but it's a great pre-drawing activity because it helps students develop fine motor skills.

I first want to mention that if your young students don't know how to hold a pencil yet, coloring may be a better activity than drawing. Coloring has many benefits, including growing children's fine motor skills, which they'll need to start tracing and drawing (figure 19.1).

1. MINDFUL TRACING

This is the simplest type of drawing and I love starting here with all my students. In fact, I love and respect tracing so much that I want to go into a little more depth on it than the other drawing activities.

You probably have already used tracing in your own life and encouraged your children to use it in handwriting practice. We can use these same principles to help children and adults learn to draw. Tracing is fun and it boosts confidence in new art students. Once students learn to trace, they can continue to work on their drawing skills when their teacher isn't available. Not only that, but tracing has been shown to improve other skills like visual spatial skills and fine motor skills. Even after students master basic drawing skills, tracing can still be used to help simplify a complicated work of art or speed up a drawing.

You could use tracing in many different art projects with children, but I really love using it as a time-saver or skill-gap-filler. For example, if I'm trying to condense an art lesson into a thirty-minute time slot, I often use tracing to help the students move along faster. As another example, if my younger students are likely to get frustrated trying to draw something, I'll use tracing to give them a quick win

Tracing Methods

There are several tracing methods you can use in your classrooms, which I explain in more detail on my tracing webpage (RidgeLightRanch.-com/Tracing), but my favorite for a classroom is tracing paper (figure 19.2). It's quick and easy for several students to all work at the same time.

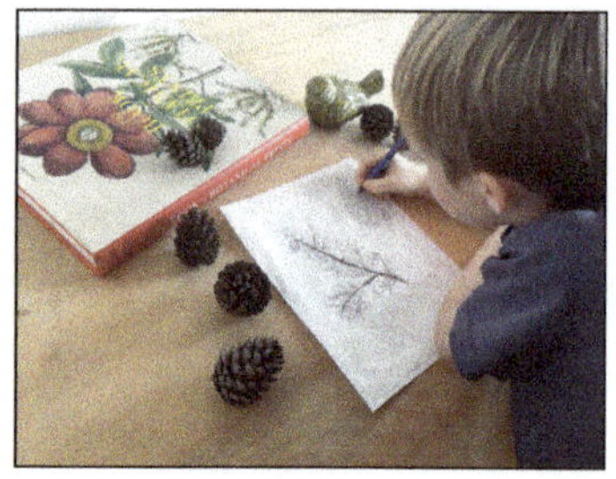

Fig. 19.2 - Tracing paper allows a whole classroom of children to trace an image quickly and easily.

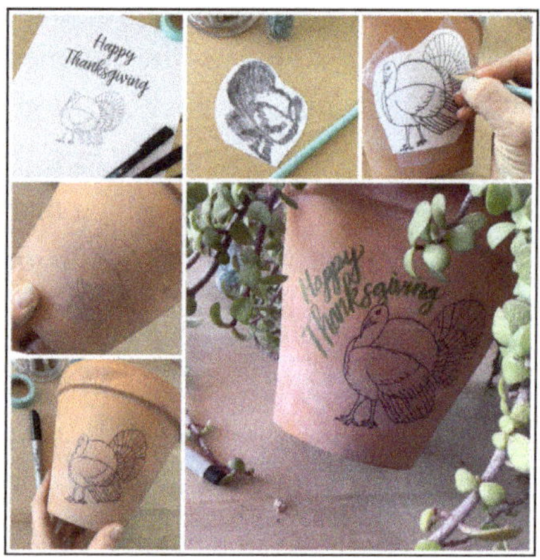

Fig. 19.3 - Layering graphite (pencil 'lead') onto the back of a drawing and then tracing the drawing transfers the graphite to a new surface. This allows you to trace onto an opaque surface, but it takes a little more time.

If we're tracing onto an opaque surface I will usually have the students cover the back of their image with graphite (pencil). Then students lay the image on the opaque surface, image up and graphite down, and then trace the front. The graphite transfers to the new surface nicely (figure 19.3).

At home, my kids use my light pad. It's very simple and makes it possible to trace onto thicker paper (figure 19.4). I keep an up-to-date recommendation for a light pad you can purchase on my tracing webpage (RidgeLightRanch.-com/Tracing).

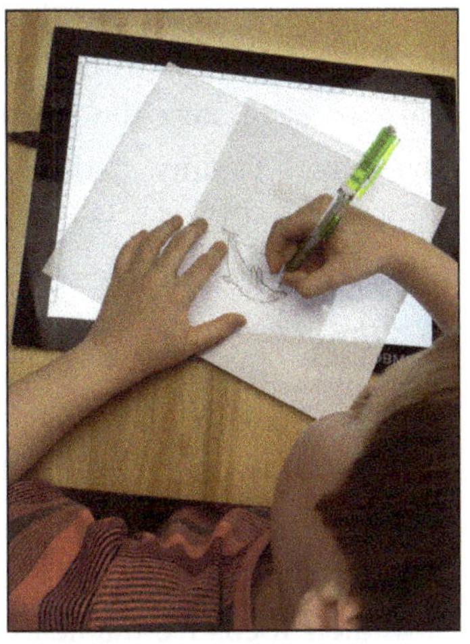

Fig. 19.4 - A light pad makes it easier to trace a drawing onto a thicker piece of paper, but only one student can use it at a time.

Be Mindful When Tracing

The key to getting the most from your tracing is to learn to be mindful while tracing! When you're having students trace, give them the following tips to help them trace mindfully, not mindlessly.

Help your students keep their minds engaged with these questions:

- Is this a curved or straight line?
- Is the line moving closer to the line next to it or farther away?
- At what angle is this line moving? Is it closer to horizontal or closer to vertical?
- How big is this part of my drawing relative to the rest of my drawing? (For example, if you were drawing a face, you might notice how big the eyes are relative to the ears, nose, and mouth.)
- Where is this part of my drawing relative to the rest of my drawing? (For example, if you were drawing a face you might notice where the eyes are relative to the ears and mouth.

Now that we've thoroughly explored tracing, let's turn our attention to some more drawing drills that will help develop your art students.

2. DIRECTED DRAWING

In directed drawing, the teacher instructs the whole class one step at a time. In each step, the teacher explains and models what kinds of lines and shapes to draw and where to draw them. All the students complete each step before the teacher moves on to the next. If your students are old enough to follow directions and they have the hand-eye coordination to draw basic shapes (rectangles, circles, etc.), they can do directed drawing.

If you're drawing on the whiteboard, don't forget to start by drawing a rectangle to represent the edges of your paper so students know how big to draw their shapes. Some students will find it difficult to constantly shift their focus from a nearby piece of paper to a far away whiteboard. If your students are getting frustrated, try getting out a piece of paper and drawing on it right next to them. For some students, this will make all the difference in the world!

You don't have to invent the steps yourself. There are a staggering number of step-by-step drawing guides available. Look for ones that start with basic shapes like circles, rectangles, triangles, and lines (as opposed to organic shapes). I like to look for ones that I can print out on one or two pages so I can take them into class with me (figure 19.5). Younger children will usually enjoy a simplified cartoon image while students around ten years old or older will usually want a more realistic looking image.

Here are a few places to look for step-by-step drawing guides:

- Pinterest: Search for "how to draw ____ step-by-step" (enter the subject you want to draw in place of the blank).
- Google: Search for "how to draw ____ step-by-step" and then click "Images."

- Amazon's Kindle bookstore: Search for "how to draw step-by-step".
- Your local library: Search for drawing books and then see which ones have the steps drawn out.
- Books by Ed Emberley (great for younger students)
- *Draw and Write* books by Carylee Gressman (which also include handwriting practice)
- *Draw Your World* books by Marie Hablitzel (which also include handwriting practice)
- *Draw 50...* books by Lee J. Ames (great for older students)

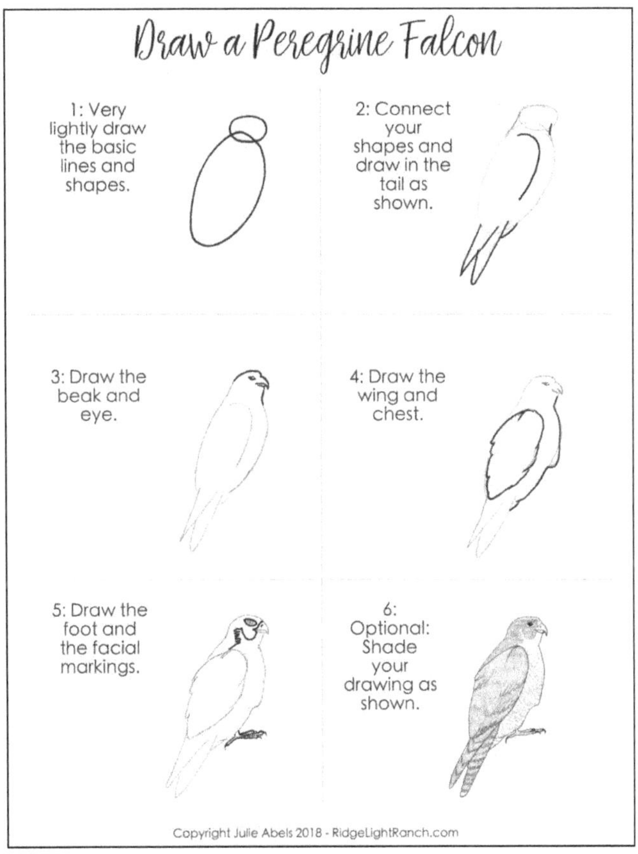

Fig. 19.5 - This is the type of step-by-step instructions used in both directed drawing and modeled drawing.

3. MODELED DRAWING

Modeled drawing can use the same resources listed above for directed drawing. The difference between the two is that in modeled drawing, the teacher shows the whole drawing sequence from white paper to finished picture and then allows the students to draw the item at their own pace, adding detail as desired.

Typically the students will naturally draw the subject in a slightly different order as they are forced to look for and find the basic shapes. Some students will need additional help, while others will enjoy drawing on their own. This drawing exercise seems to work well with a classroom of students with a wide variety of drawing skills.

4. DRAWING FROM A DRAWING

When drawing from a drawing, the teacher shows the students a simple line drawing and walks the students through deciding how to go about drawing the subject. The teacher can ask questions like, "What basic shapes do you see in this drawing? Where do you see curved or straight lines? How big is one section compared to another?"

The difficulty of drawing from a drawing will be proportional to how detailed the reference drawing is. With a very simple line drawing, the student has fewer lines to choose from so it's easier. With more detail, the student has to pick and choose what shapes make up the overall structure of the subject and draw those first.

Drawing from a drawing will also be easier if each student has a copy of the original drawing he/she can mark on. Encourage him/her to look for basic shapes like ovals, rectangles, and triangles. Have each student draw those basic shapes on top of the reference drawing if needed.

5. DRAWING FROM A BLACK AND WHITE PHOTO

Drawing from a black and white photo can be taught in the same way as drawing from a drawing. However, the complexity of a photo is higher than the complexity of a drawing, so it requires students' eyes to do more work when deciding which lines to sketch first and which lines to leave out entirely. The teacher can help walk the students through the process of finding basic shapes, similar to drawing from a drawing.

If the jump from 'drawing from a drawing' to 'drawing from a black and white photo' is too hard, look for an app or computer program that will convert a photo into a sketch. It won't be as simple as a line drawing, but it will be easier to use than a black and white photo. I use Pixelmator on my iMac. It's amazing how much this helps!

6. DRAWING FROM A COLOR PHOTO

Drawing from a color photo is just like drawing from a black and white photo, but now your eyes will have to translate the colors into a gradient of tones. The first few times you do this, you might want to provide both a color photo and a black and white photo. Show the students how areas of color were translated into black and white. It's a surprisingly difficult task that can stump even experienced artists! However, it's very helpful to gain some mastery of this step before you move on to drawing from life.

6B. BONUS DRAWING TRICK: GRID DRAWING

Drawing with a grid, or grid drawing, is a variation of drawing from a drawing or photo. It makes any of those activities a little easier and I frequently use it in the following situations:

- When my reference image is composed of a lot of lines instead of recognizable geometric shapes

- If I'm struggling to get the proportions just right
- If I'm struggling to get the perspective just right
- If I'm significantly enlarging the image, like to paint a mural

I suggest you introduce it to your students in an early art project and remind them they're allowed to use it anytime.

In the previous drawing activities, we encouraged students to look for basic shapes in the subject. The grid drawing method breaks it down further by looking at the basic lines and shapes in a very small section.

How to Draw with a Grid (figure 19.6):

1. Start with a photo or a drawing. Draw a grid of squares onto the image by hand or using computer software. (I use an app named Grid# on my iPhone to do this.)
2. Now draw a proportional grid of squares onto your drawing paper.
3. The squares do not have to be the same size, but you will need the same configuration of squares. So, if you drew a grid of three rows and four columns of squares on your image, you'll need to draw a grid of three rows and four columns of squares on your drawing paper.
4. If you change the size of the squares, you'll change the size of the finished drawing. In fact, this method of drawing is a very common way artists enlarge an image to create a mural!
5. Now draw what is in the upper left square, looking only at that square.
6. Next draw the square below it and so on, drawing one square at a time.

This is such a helpful way to draw that it might deserve a chapter all its own, but it's so simple that it's just not long enough for a whole chapter.

So, I'll have to just *highly* encourage you to try it out. It's so helpful, your students may even feel like they're cheating. Remind them that this is a valuable tool, used by professional artists for hundreds of years. This activity is simply helping the student look at smaller sections so they can *see* more clearly! Even young students can grasp this method and use it beautifully. To make it even easier, have them draw on graph paper so they don't have to draw the initial grid themselves.

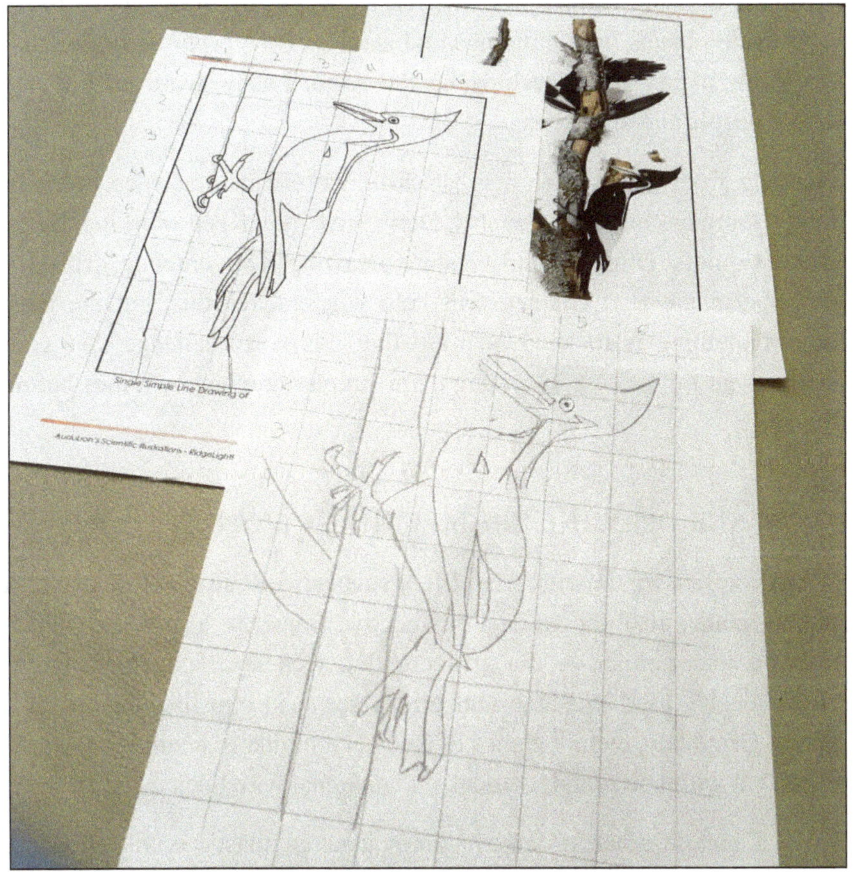

Fig. 19.6 - Drawing a grid over your reference image can make transferring it to your paper much simpler.

7. DRAWING FROM LIFE

There are many factors in drawing from life that make it really difficult. The student must combine all the skills mastered in the previous drawing exercises, while trying not to move, as that would change his/her perspective or angle. Plus, the student has to work fast enough to capture the subject before it moves!

To make drawing from life a little easier, begin by drawing stationary man-made objects, like buildings and statues. Then progress on to landscapes or plants that may blow in the wind. Lastly, work on drawing active people and animals.

Drawing from life is such a great skill. We use it in science journals, travel journals, and cartography. Don't give up! Keep working on it! Blind Contour Drawing and Gesture Drawing, two drawing drills I'll describe in the next chapter, will help you practice this, but the most important thing is to keep in mind that this *is* a challenge. Set your students up for success by giving them simpler drawing activities before this one.

7B. BONUS DRAWING TRICK: USING A PICTURE PLANE

When you first try drawing from life, I suggest you use a picture plane. A picture plane, also known as a perspective frame, or a grid viewfinder, uses an idea similar to the grid drawing technique explained above. However, it's used to frame and grid a scene in real life, instead of a photo. Originally, picture planes looked very similar to a window without glass, but with horizontal, vertical, and diagonal wire lines.

Now, a picture plane usually includes glass or plastic with permanent lines drawn on it and a frame around the outside of it. Sometimes picture planes include just one horizontal and one diagonal line. Other times they have additional lines to help the artist further break down the drawing. You can purchase a lightweight, plastic, durable perspective frame from

Betty Edwards' website, Amazon, or Blick Art Material. Edwards also includes instructions on how to make your own picture plane in her book, *Drawing on the Right Side of the Brain.*

To use a picture plane:

1. Hold the picture plane up in front of you, moving it around until what you want to draw on paper is framed in the picture plane.
2. Using a dry erase or wet erase marker, draw the key lines of your subject directly onto the clear surface of the picture plane.
3. Set the picture plane down on white paper and use it as a reference when drawing your subject.

In her book, Betty Edwards gives several examples of well-known artists from the 1400s through the 1800s, like Leonardo da Vinci, Leone Battista Alberti, Albrecht Durer, Vincent van Gogh, and Hans Holbein, who used picture planes to improve their drawing or to speed up the drawing process long after they had become expert artists. Albrecht Durer included a sketch and explanation of how to use a picture plane in his Renaissance-era book called *Four Books on Measurement* (figure 19.7). Inspired by Durer's picture plane, Vincent Van Gogh created his 'perspective device' and described it in letters he wrote around 1882, complete with sketches showing how it worked (figure 19.8).

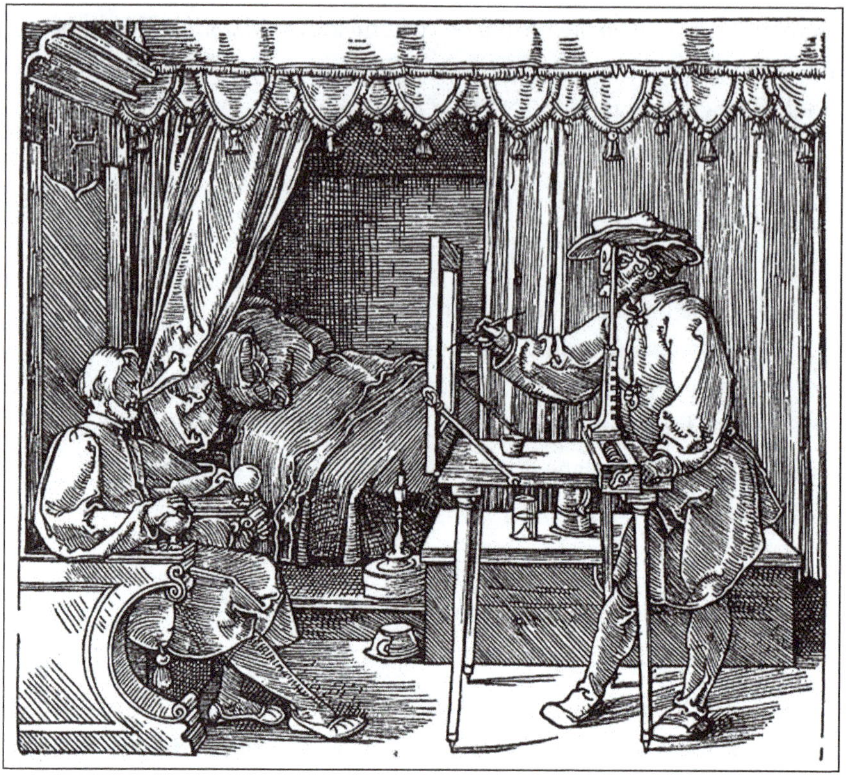

Fig. 19.7 - Albrecht Durer included this image of a picture plane in his 1525 book, *Four Books on Measurement.*

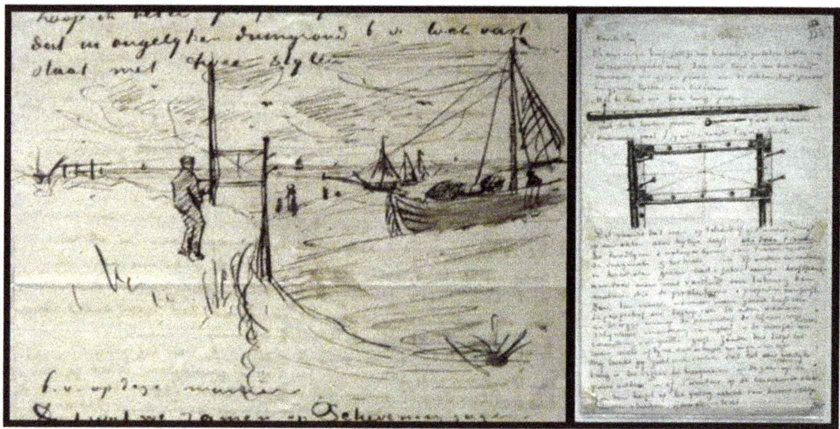

Fig. 19.8 - Vincent Van Gogh included these images of his picture plane in some of the letters he wrote.

8. DRAWING FROM MEMORY

Now we're moving beyond drawing what we see with our eyes to drawing what we see in our mind. This step in our drawing progression is one of the hardest because now we have to see with our memory what we want to draw. It's fascinating to me how often people tell me they can't draw because they tried to draw from memory and couldn't. If only they understood how very advanced this is!

Some people have a photographic memory (or something close to it) so this step isn't as hard for them. However, for those of us who never memorize anything accidentally, the key to drawing from memory is to intentionally memorize what something looks like. The best way to do that is to draw it multiple times. Start with the easier drawing activities in this progression and practice until you can remember how the lines should curve and move. Once you've memorized a subject, you'll be able to draw it from memory.

In addition to being able to draw this favorite thing anywhere and everywhere, there are some other great benefits to learning to draw from memory. First, having this level of comfort with a subject I'm drawing is the only way I've found that I can still draw it while it's moving. When an animal (or person) moves, you either have to remember how it looked or already know how it tends to look when moving.

Second, this level of familiarity is also how we can begin to make up animals or places that don't exist. We're able to pull features from animals or places that do exist and combine them in new and interesting ways. The more information you have stored in your brain, the more creative you can be!

9. DRAWING AN IDEA

We've finally arrived at the peak of our progression of drawing activities: drawing something we've never physically seen, but have in our mind.

This is the hardest step in this progression; not only are we drawing without seeing, but we're also using the muscle of creativity.

Remember from chapter 2 that creativity is simply "the divine ability to imagine new combinations of things." All humans were given this ability when we were created in the image of God, but creativity can be strengthened and refined with intentional use.

In chapter 22, Drills for Strengthening Creativity, I give some fun exercises for strengthening creativity. These types of drawing exercises really get students' minds moving and help them strengthen their creativity muscles. It's good to remember that some of us are not as strong visually and these types of drawing activities may never come easily, and that's okay. Encourage students to bravely do things they aren't necessarily good at—it's the only way to get better at them!

HOW TO USE THIS PROGRESSION IN YOUR CLASSROOM

Now you have a great list of the different ways to draw and an understanding of why some are easier than others. When your students are struggling with drawing, look at the list and help them take one step (or more) back on the progression and try again.

I have a vague memory of an early childhood art experience in which I was trying to draw my dog, an active little black poodle. I didn't have any good photos of her (digital cameras didn't exist yet), and she refused to hold still. I grew so frustrated, I wanted to cry! Instead I quit. It didn't occur to me that I was trying a very advanced drawing activity. Explaining this progression of drawing activities to your students will help them avoid that kind of frustration by giving them tools they can use even when you aren't around.

Now let's look at some different drawing drills you can use in your art classroom as warm-ups, extra credit, or quick skill builders.

~

CHAPTER SUMMARY

- Plan art projects while keeping in mind where the drawing activity falls along the progression of difficulty. Teach your students how to step back from an activity that's too hard to one that's challenging but doable.

20

DRILLS FOR DRAWING

The progression of drawing activities in the previous chapter will help you plan out your art projects, but they aren't the same as drills. A drill is something an artist uses to help develop their skills—not something they typically use to create a masterpiece. Your art students may not initially like these drills because they can feel awkward and often result in ugly drawings. So, warn your students and find a way to get a good laugh at the results. Then reassure your students that each of these drills has been used by many art students to improve their skills. Students don't need to show anyone these drawings or creations, and they don't even have to keep them if they don't want to. However, if they do keep them, they'll get to see their own improvement over time.

We'll start with a set of drills that help improve simple line drawing skills. Then I'll explain some drills that help with seeing value (the light to dark gradient) in chapter 21, and end with some fun drills for exercising creativity in chapter 22.

Drawing skills have 'seeing skills' at their core. Learning to see what is really present in a subject is the most fundamental skill students need to develop in the visual arts. If you stop and think about it, you'll see how each of these drawing drills work to improve the skill of seeing more than anything else. So, while I talk about them in terms of drawing, you'll find they end up helping with all sorts of two- and three-dimensional art media beyond basic drawing.

1. TRACING

In the previous chapter, I presented tracing as a drawing activity. However, tracing can also be used as a drawing drill. It's a great way to get accustomed to a new subject or to draw a tricky perspective. Reference the tracing section in the previous chapter for more info on how to incorporate tracing.

2. REPLICATING LINES

Our second drawing drill is a perfect warm up exercise for any art class. It helps students slow down and activate the visual part of the brain without the stress of trying to make their drawing look like a recognizable subject. The goal is just to replicate a set of lines or shapes (figure 20.1).

To do this drill:

1. Create pairs of small squares. A grid of eight, one-inch squares in two rows of four works well.
2. In one square of each pair, draw some random lines or patterns. Make each square different. Leave the other half of the pair blank.
3. Make some copies and have your students try to perfectly replicate the lines and patterns in the blank squares.

Alternatively, pass out a paper with all the squares left blank. Have the students draw random patterns and lines in one half of the squares and then trade papers with a friend to replicate the lines in the blank squares.

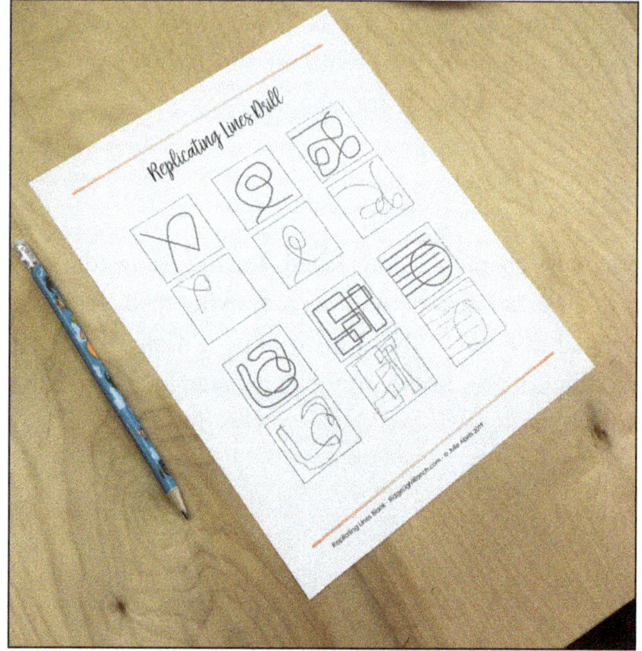

Fig. 20.1 - In this drill, the student simply replicates what is in each box.

3. UPSIDE DOWN DRAWING

Upside down drawing is most effective with students over ten years old who are having trouble transitioning from symbolic drawing to realistic drawing.

I first heard about upside down drawing in Betty Edwards' 1979 book, *Drawing on the Right Side of the Brain.* Since we've been using this drawing method in Classical Conversations, my curiosity led me to find a copy of the book and reread it. Edwards explains that in most people aged ten and older, the dominant left side of the brain handles verbal and rational thoughts while the weaker right side of the brain handles visual and intuitive thoughts. The stronger verbal side filters what the person sees and interprets it verbally, storing the information symbolically. This prevents the weaker visual side from ever really seeing, for example, how the edge of an item twists and turns. Since drawing is more about seeing than it is about drawing, Edwards has discovered several different exercises that help the visual side to become stronger, thereby overriding the editing process and allowing the person to really see.

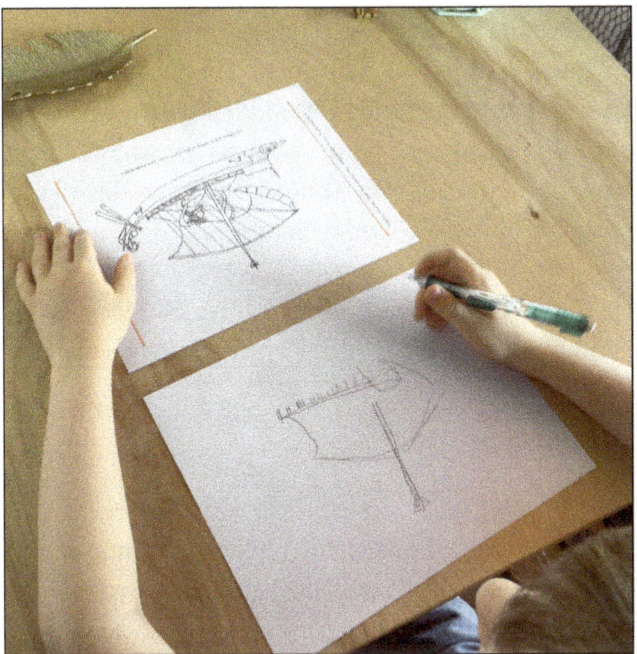

Fig. 20.2 - In this drill, the student turns the reference image upside down and draws it.

One of those exercises is drawing upside down (figure 20.2). The strong verbal side is not very good at instantly recognizing a picture when it is upside down, allowing the weaker visual side an opportunity to look at the lines and shapes as they really are.

- To do this exercise, start with a line drawing (a drawing with just lines—no color and no shading).
- Place the line drawing with the bottom at the top and the top at the bottom. If your line drawing is simple and the subject is easy to identify, even when upside down like this, try covering most of the picture and just revealing a bit of it at a time. Resist the urge to figure out what it is. That urge is your verbal side trying

to name the subject so it can provide you a symbol of the subject! Instead, focus on the lines: Are the lines straight or curved? How are they angled? How much space is there between the lines?

- Draw the whole picture.
- When you finish, try to notice what it felt like to engage your visual side of the brain. This is the ultimate goal of this exercise —learning to engage the right, visual part of your brain on demand. Edwards calls this "R-mode" and says this right-brain mode should always be used with drawing.

We have used this drawing drill in several lesson plans available on my website. Search for 'upside down' at RidgeLightRanch.com to see them.

4. MIRROR/SYMMETRY DRAWING

In this drawing drill, you provide half of a picture or drawing of a symmetrical object and the students replicate the mirror image of the drawing. The student then removes the half drawing and, looking at what he/she just drew, completes the other side of his/her drawing (figure 20.3).

This is a great brain-stretching exercise that helps students focus on the direction of the lines instead of what the object actually is. It can be done as a warmup to help engage the visual/spatial part of the brain, or as a stand-alone lesson. This is also a great opportunity to talk about how balance and symmetry play a role in the principles of design!

We have used this drawing drill in several lesson plans available on my website. Search for "symmetry" at RidgeLightRanch.com to see them.

Betty Edwards does a slightly different version of this in her book, *Drawing on the Right Side of the Brain*, that might also be helpful.

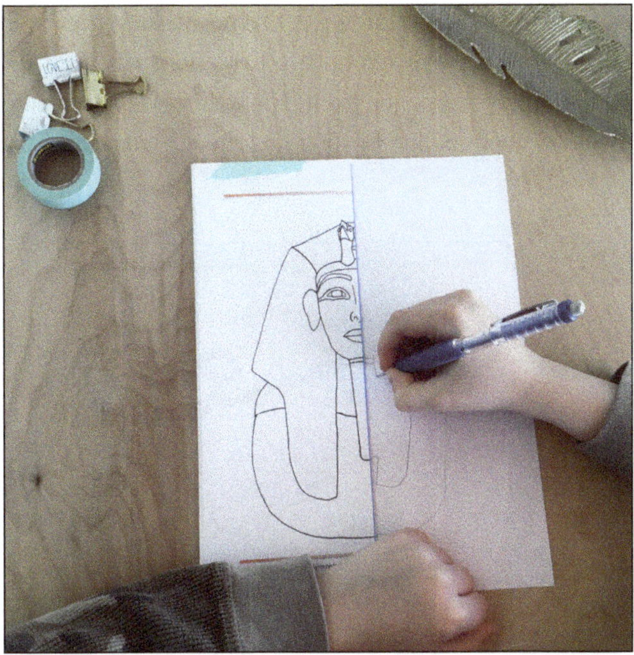

Fig. 20.3 - In this drill, the student looks at one half of a symmetrical drawing and draws the mirror image.

5. NEGATIVE SPACE DRAWING

As explained in chapter 8, negative space is the space around the subject —everything but the subject of the drawing.

In everyday life we tend to look at the objects around us and not the negative space surrounding the objects. It's perfectly normal but when we're trying to draw that object, ignoring the negative space around it is like only gathering half the information. Practice seeing the negative space by looking at objects around you and then focusing on the shape of the background. This will feel strange at first, but your mind will adjust to seeing the negative space.

Since your verbal-left brain does not have simplified icon-type images for these spaces, your right-visual brain will engage and you'll more easily see the actual shapes.

Now have students practice drawing the negative space by placing an object in front of them with interesting negative space (not just a cube). Try a step stool, microscope, or plant. Have them leave a white silhouette of the object on their paper by drawing in the negative space (figure 20.4).

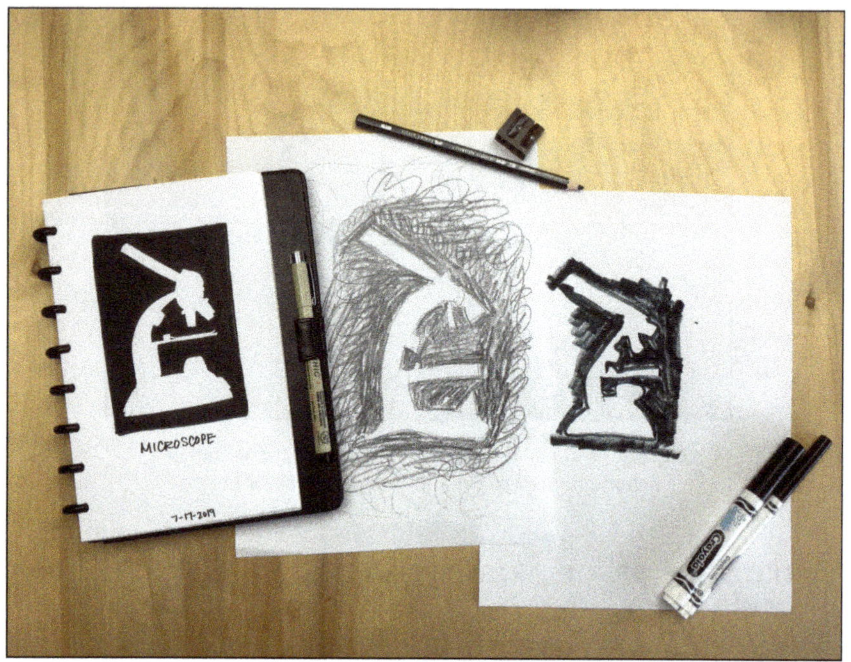

Fig. 20.4 - Focusing on the negative space, as we did in these microscope drawings, can help us draw more accurately.

Again, this is a good warmup drill for engaging the right/visual brain. Be aware that very young students sometimes have trouble understanding the idea of negative space. However, once they understand the concept, they are able t0 complete this drawing drill.

6. BLIND CONTOUR DRAWING

Blind contour drawing was made popular by Kimon Nicolaides in his 1941 book, *The Natural Way to Draw*. In this drawing exercise, the student looks at a still life or model (not a drawing or photo) and slowly draws the outline, or contour, without looking down at his/her paper. Nicolaides says you should imagine your pencil is actually touching the model and tracing its outline. Focus only on the contour of the subject, like you're drawing its silhouette. This exercise usually produces a scribbled mess the first few times—however, it's great for developing the skill of seeing as an artist sees and the results improve dramatically with time (figure 20.5)!

> *"Learning to draw is really a matter of learning to see—to see correctly—and that means a good deal more than merely looking with the eye." —Kimon Nicolaides*

This is a good warmup drill to help intermediate and advanced artists see what's really there instead of what the brain already knows about that subject.

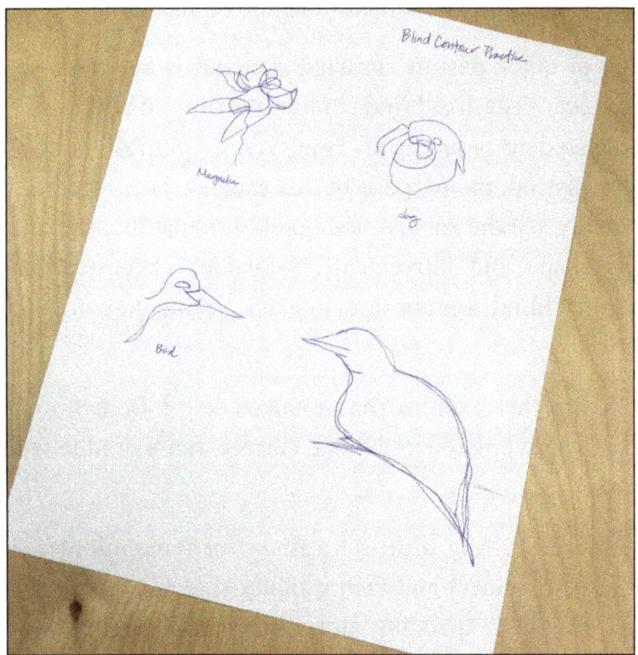

Fig. 20.5 - Blind Contour Drawing feels awkward and produces laughable results at first, but it helps students learn to see, and therefore draw, if they persist!

Many art teachers modify this exercise by allowing students to occasionally look at their paper. However, the effectiveness is lost if the student is frequently looking at the paper.

You might also want to combine this drill with air tracing. This is where you hold your pencil in the air in front of you. Now draw your subject on an imaginary window about half an arm's length away, between you and your subject. Trace the contour in the air first and then do it again with your pencil on paper, without ever taking your eyes off the subject.

7. GESTURE DRAWING

Gesture drawing is another exercise presented in Nicolaides' book, *The Natural Way to Draw*. Like blind contour drawing, it's a drill designed for intermediate and advanced artists. This drill was developed to help students learn to capture the movement and action of human figures, but it also works well on other subjects that move, like animals.

Doing a lot of quick gesture drawing sketches is a great way to study a moving subject. Also, like blind contour drawing, it will rarely produce a drawing the student is proud of. However, its purpose is not to create a work of art. Instead, the purpose of this exercise is to increase the artist's ability to really see the subject and quickly sketch the key lines that will capture its shape and movement. Nicolaides suggested that students should practice blind contour drawing and gesture drawing every day for a full year!

Over the years this exercise has evolved a bit from how Nicolaides described it. Allow me to explain the current, more productive way to do this exercise.

To do a gesture drawing drill, set a timer for three minutes. Look back and forth at your subject and then **quickly** sketch its basic shape (figure 20.6). Be sure you're spending more time looking at the subject than at your paper. Do not start with the contour, and do not draw any details. After the three minutes are up, move on to a new subject. Over time, work to reduce the time you're working on a drawing.

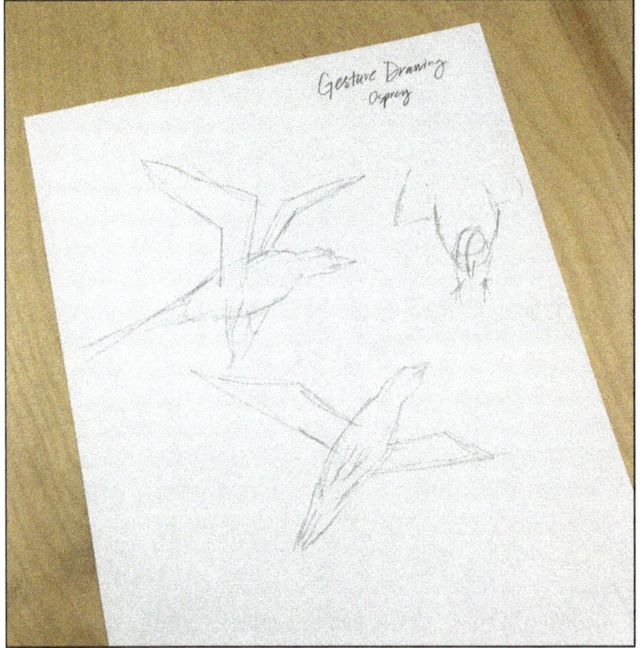

Fig. 20.6 - Even though the results aren't very pretty, gesture drawing helps students learn to capture the overall shape of the subject, especially when the subject is moving.

Remind students that they don't have to show anyone these drawings—they don't even have to keep these drawings. We're training their eyes to see!

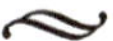

CHAPTER SUMMARY

- Try each of these drawing drills with your students to help them improve their drawing skills: tracing, replicating lines, upside-down drawing, mirror drawing, negative space drawing, blind contour drawing, and gesture drawing.

21

DRILLS FOR SEEING AND CREATING VALUE

These next three drills are exercises to help students learn to see and create value. Remember that value is the light to dark gradient of a color you create by adding white or black. You're developing the skill of seeing how light or dark a color is in life or a photo.

1. CREATE A VALUE SCALE

This exercise can be done with any media and it's a great way to get the feel for a new medium. The goal is to create as many different, distinct values of the medium as you can to help you get the feel for how to create value in works of art.

- Create a rectangle (something about 1 inch x 6 inches works well).
- Apply the medium showing the gradual change from light to dark.

The simplest version of this is done with a basic pencil. Lay down (color in) a heavy layer of graphite (pencil lead) on the dark end. Then create lighter and lighter layers so that you end up with no graphite on the light end. Blend (smear) the graphite with a blending nub, your finger, or a piece of paper towel until you have a smooth gradient from dark to light.

To do this exercise with acrylic paint, mix one color (for example, purple) with varying amounts of black for the dark end of the scale and then a new bit of purple paint with varying amounts of white paint for the light end of the scale (figure 21.1).

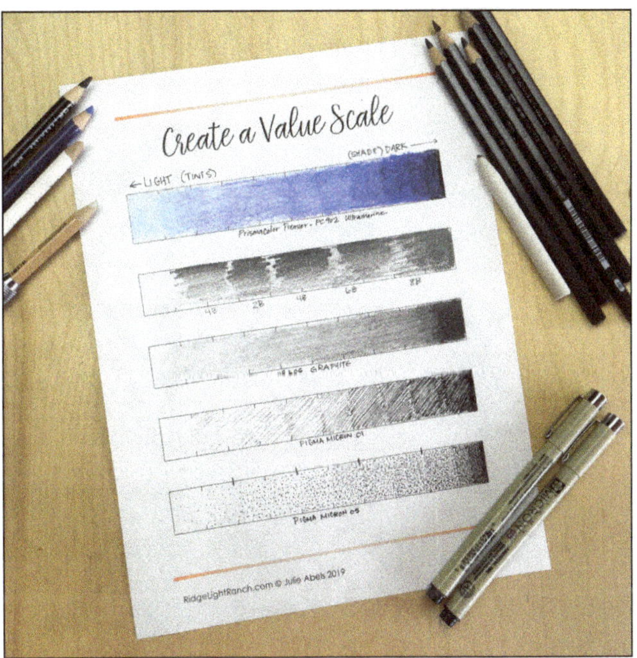

Fig. 21.1 - Creating a value scale helps students learn to see and create value. It's also a great way to get to know a new medium or paper.

This is also a great exercise to complete any time you're working with a new type of paper.

2. TEXTURE SQUARES

This is the best way to learn how to create the illusion of texture in any given medium. To create the illusion of texture we use a combination of lines, shapes, and value, so it's good to save this drill until after your students have created a value scale in the medium you plan to use.

This drill is very similar to the Replicating Lines drill in chapter 20, but this time we're including changes in value and perhaps color, depending on the medium you choose.

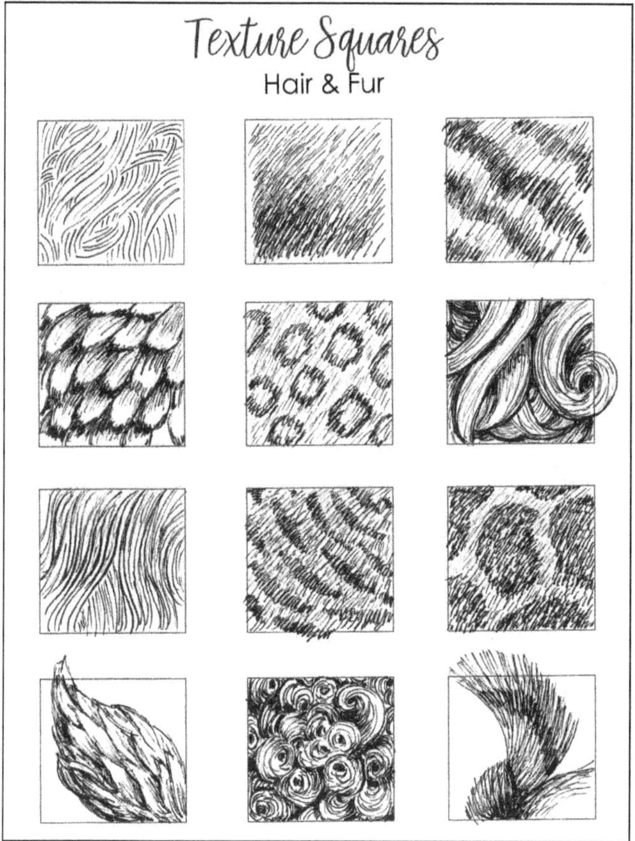

Fig. 21.2 - Creating texture squares helps students gain experience in reproducing texture. Students can refer back to these texture squares later when they're producing a finished work of art.

To do this drill:

1. Create a grid of small squares.
2. Find a book or website about the medium you've chosen and use photos as your sample. Recreate different textures from the sample on your squares (figure 21.2).
3. Notate each square with a texture description, if applicable.

This has the added benefit of being a helpful reference that students can look back to later when they're trying to achieve a certain texture within a work of art.

3. TEXTURE EXPERIMENTS

This is a fun way to experiment with a new medium and get a feel for how it works to create textures. It ends up looking very similar to the texture squares exercise, but it's more experimental in nature.

To do this drill:

1. Create a grid of small squares.
2. Fill each square with a different combination of lines and patterns and with a variety of value.
3. Have students step back and imagine what kind of texture it reminds them of. Label each square with that title. (Students may not have a label for every square.)
4. Keep these squares as a reference for later (figure 21.3).

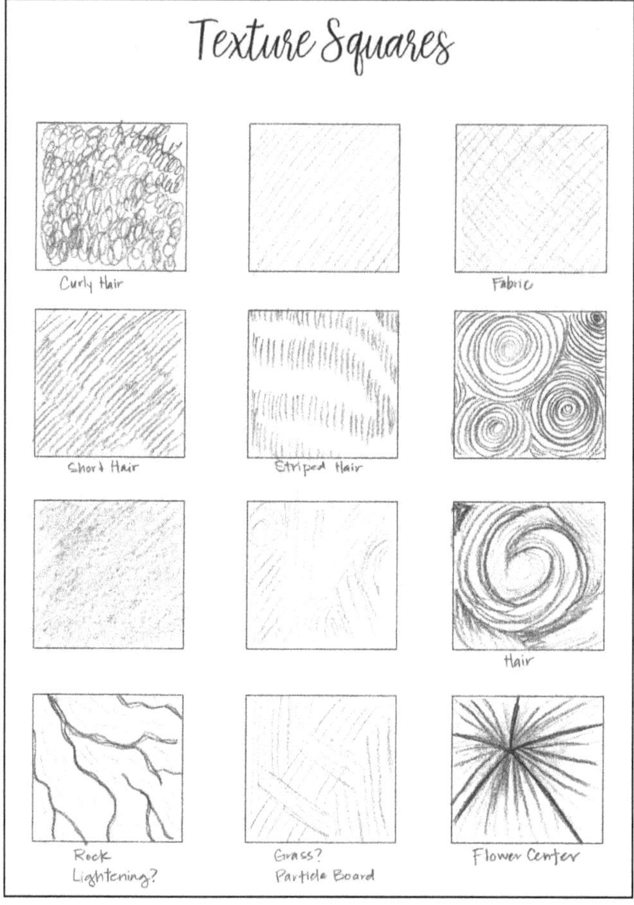

Fig. 21.3 - When students experiment with texture, they gain familiarity with the medium they're using and learn what kinds of lines, shapes, values, patterns, and contrast create the illusion of particular textures.

4. TWO-TONE DRAWING

Once again, we work on the skill of seeing, but this time instead of seeing the outlines or basic shapes of an object, we're training the eyes to see the lights and darks of an object.

In this exercise, students draw using a single thick black marker. Without using cross hatching or other pen-specific shading techniques, have students draw a subject, converting it all to white and black (figure 21.4).

This strange drill can sometimes look like Japanese Notan art, but it exercises the mind in the process of converting color in all different shades to either all dark or all light.

As students progress in their art skills, these value exercises will help equip them for drawing all sorts of different subjects in all sorts of different situations. Let's turn our attention now to drills that help us exercise our creative muscles.

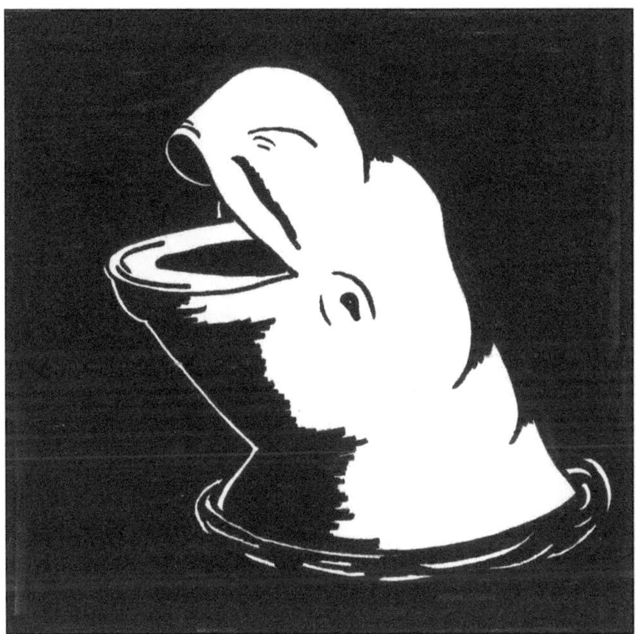

Fig. 21.4 - Creating two-tone drawings, like this Beluga whale, helps students learn to see the dark and light values in life and in their art.

CHAPTER SUMMARY

- Try each of these value drills with your students to help them improve their ability to see a variety of lights and darks: value scale, texture squares, texture experiments, and two-tone drawing.

22

DRILLS FOR STRENGTHENING CREATIVITY

The previous drills helped students increase their ability to draw and see, but these next few exercises will help them strengthen their ability to think and act creatively. As we explained in chapter 2, creativity is the divine ability to imagine new combinations of things, and it's derived from our being made in the image of God. Creativity is like a muscle that atrophies without use but grows stronger when exercised. While all art creation involves some creativity, these exercises are great ways to focus in on creative skills.

1. MODIFY AN INK SPLOTCH

In this simple project, students drip or splash some ink or paint onto paper and then step back and imagine what the splotch could become. The students draw or paint on the paper to turn their splotch into something recognizable (figure 22.1). This is somewhat similar to what kids do when they stare out the window and see giant dragons in the shapes of the clouds.

You can use this as a drill and have students complete it quickly, many times, or you can create a full art project out of it. There are even picture books, like *Beautiful Oops* by Barney Saltzberg, that can help you introduce the idea.

This exercise has the added benefit of helping students learn how to turn an "oops" into something great in their other works of art.

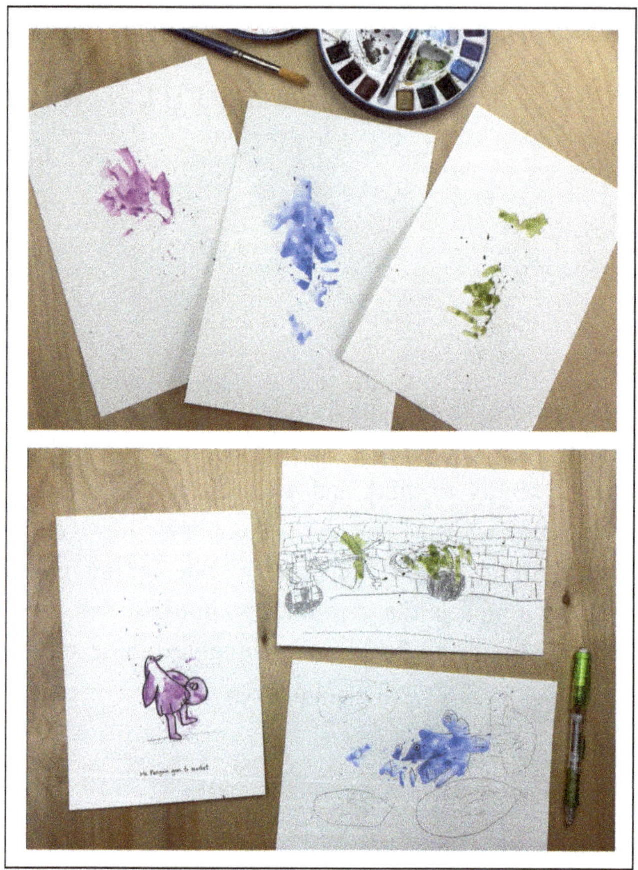

Fig. 22.1 - Converting a random ink splotch into something else is a great exercise in creativity.

2. DISTORT A SUBJECT

In this exercise, students draw a normal object, but distorted. You could tell your students to make it extra long (figure 22.2), imagine what it would look like twisted, or what it might look like if you were looking through curved or faceted glass.

Many famous artists, like Dali, Picasso, and MC Escher have used this to create well-known works of art, so this is a project that can go along well with the study of one of those artists. The results are often very interesting, and the exercise has great value in stretching our students' brains and strengthening their creativity.

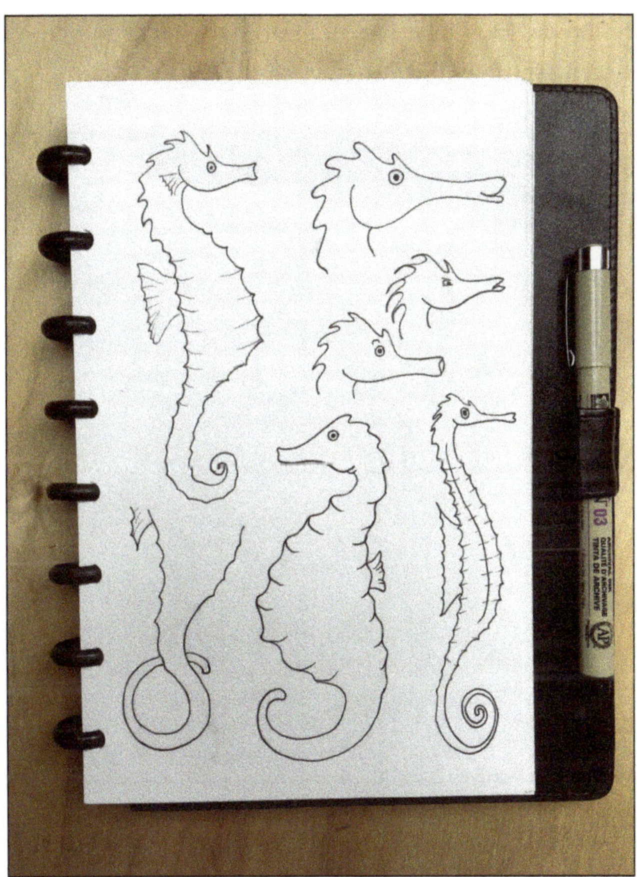

Fig. 22.2 - Distorting a subject, like this seahorse, helps stretch the imagination and hone drawing skills.

3. DRAW A NEW ANGLE

This is a more advanced exercise that helps students grow creatively. It also helps students grow the skill of 'drawing from an idea,' which as we discovered in the Progression of Drawing Activities in chapter 19, is one of the hardest drawing activities.

For this activity pick a subject your students have drawn many times and ask them to draw it in a new position or from an angle they haven't previously drawn. Don't be too strict about what they may or may not have ever seen—just get them to start imagining.

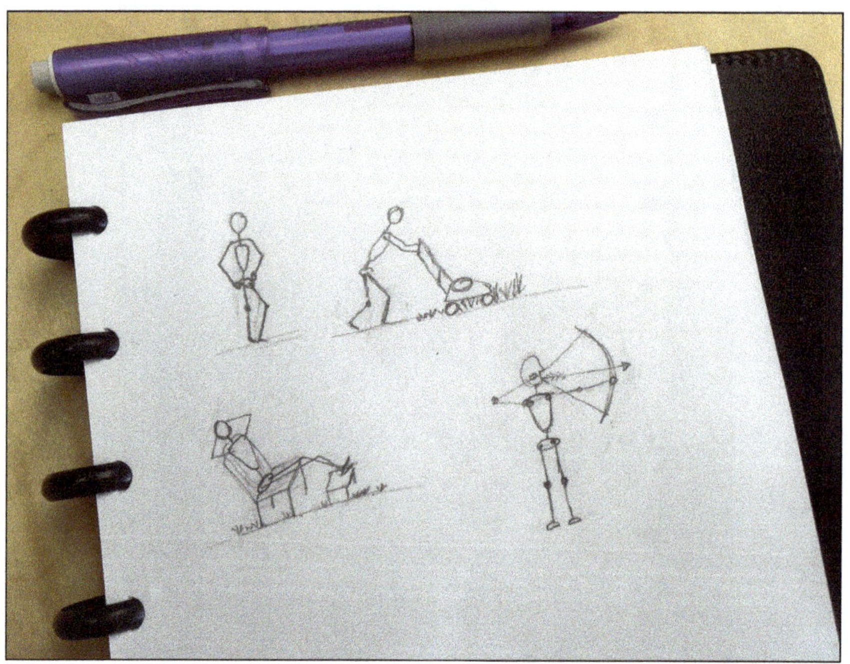

Fig. 22.3 - Imagining what an object would look like in a new position helps exercise creativity and encourages students to pay more attention to what they see in everyday life.

For example, if they've drawn people before—even stick people—have them imagine what it might look like to see someone mow the lawn. Yes, they've seen someone mowing the lawn before, but they've probably never watched the activity with their artist eye. What angle are the arms and legs at? Is the whole body tilted forward a little from the effort of pushing the mower? What angle would the head be at? Will the hair be blowing in the wind? How will the clothing be twisted—where will all the folds be? Now have the students try to draw the stick person mowing the lawn (figure 22.3).

4. INVENT AN ANIMAL

This is an intermediate to advanced project that students typically enjoy after they've had a chance to draw plenty of animals. It's also a fun way to practice the skill of drawing an idea.

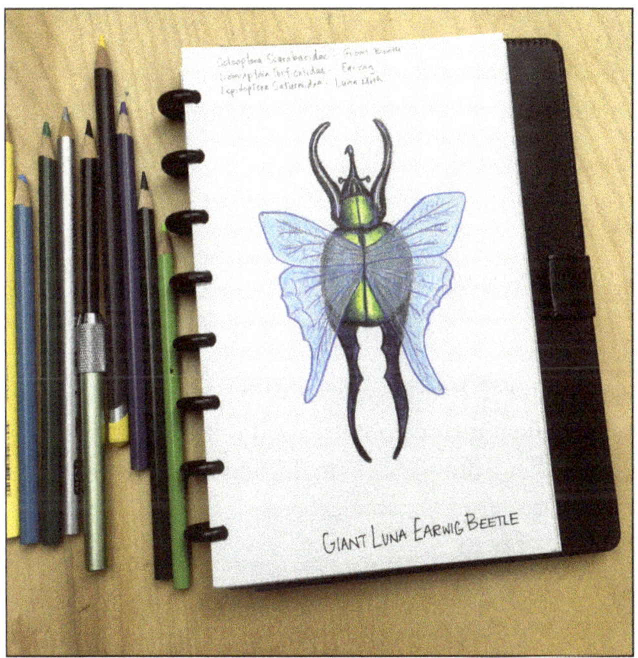

Fig. 22.4 - Inventing a new insect, like this "Giant Luna Earwig Beetle" from pieces and parts of real insects, helps students think outside the box and exercise their creative muscles.

For this exercise, ask the students to think of several different animal traits and combine them in funny and strange ways. For example, they could start with something like a dog, but give it a horn like a rhino and wings like a bat. This is even easier to do with insects (figure 22.4).

With repetition, their made-up animals will get stranger and stranger. They'll look less like something you know, and more like a whole new kind of animal.

All these drawing, value, and creativity drills can be used independently or within an art project. Try them out yourself and plan ways to use them with your students. Pick one, use it many times, and point out to your students how their drawing skills are improving.

Now, for the last chapter in our Art Creation section, I want to explain the basic methods of creating perspective in art.

CHAPTER SUMMARY

- Try each of these creativity drills with your students to help them strengthen their creative muscles: modify an ink splotch, distort a subject, draw a new angle, and invent an animal.

23

THE METHODS OF PERSPECTIVE

Many parents tell me their own drawings look like a three-year-old drew them. Learning to draw with perspective is one of the easiest ways to change that!

Once we understand how to look at a subject and see its basic shapes, we'll want to create a work of art in which the subject is shown within a realistic space. This means we'll need to know how to create the illusion of depth using one or more of the methods of perspective.

One of the skills that beginning artists struggle with most is creating the illusion of three-dimensional depth or perspective in their two-dimensional art. Even though they don't know it, this is often the main thing that makes their art look 'off' or 'childish.'

Once your students understand these methods of perspective, they will have the ability to add a new level of sophistication to their art no matter what media they're using.

Remember from chapter 8 that form is the three dimensions of an object that take up physical space, and space is the area around and within the subject.

The methods of perspective are ways to create the illusion of form in a work of art. We use the methods of perspective within the space of a work of art to give the illusion of form. In other words, the methods of perspective give two-dimensional artwork a feeling of three-dimensional depth. This depth makes our art look more realistic and generally 'makes sense' to our eyes. Depth also makes a work of art more interesting to the human eye.

I want to give you a brief overview of each of the methods of perspective (figure 23.1) because they're so helpful in drawing and painting:

1. Overlap
2. Size
3. Horizontal placement
4. Value
5. Color
6. Degree of detail
7. Linear perspective
8. ...Bonus: Foreshortening

Learning about each of these methods is really just a way to articulate what we actually see. Artists with a natural talent for drawing already use these methods often without realizing it. As someone who is strongly left-brained and analytical, I find it very helpful to dissect each method and look for examples. Then when I'm drawing or painting, I'm much quicker to see the perspective method at work and use it accurately in my own drawing. Or, as is often the case, I'm faster at figuring out why I don't like what I've created and how to change it into something I like!

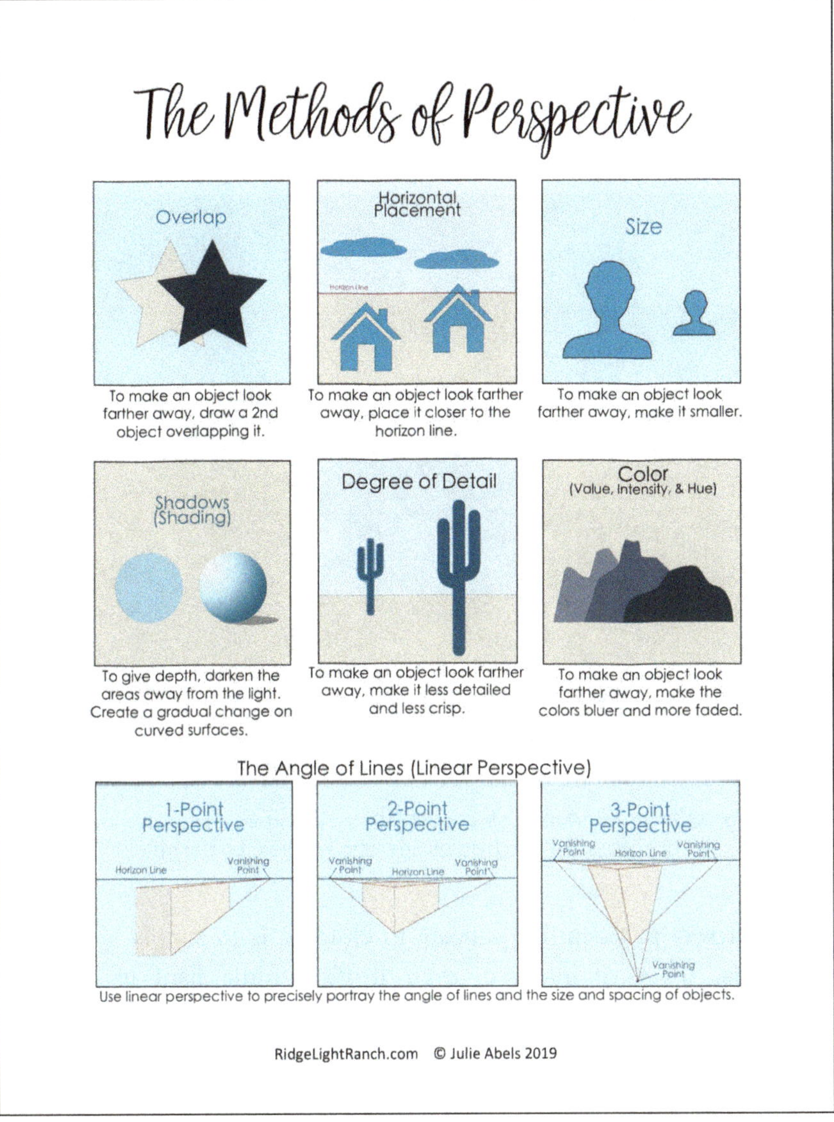

Fig. 23.1 - This poster can help students remember the different ways they can create the illusion of depth in their art.

1. OVERLAP

This one is probably the simplest and most intuitive method for creating depth. A solid (opaque) object blocks the viewer from seeing what is behind it. So, you can draw two identical overlapping shapes and the one in front will naturally appear closer. You can see this at work in Gericault's famous painting, *The Raft of Medusa* (figure 23.2). The people overlap each other, creating the illusion of depth.

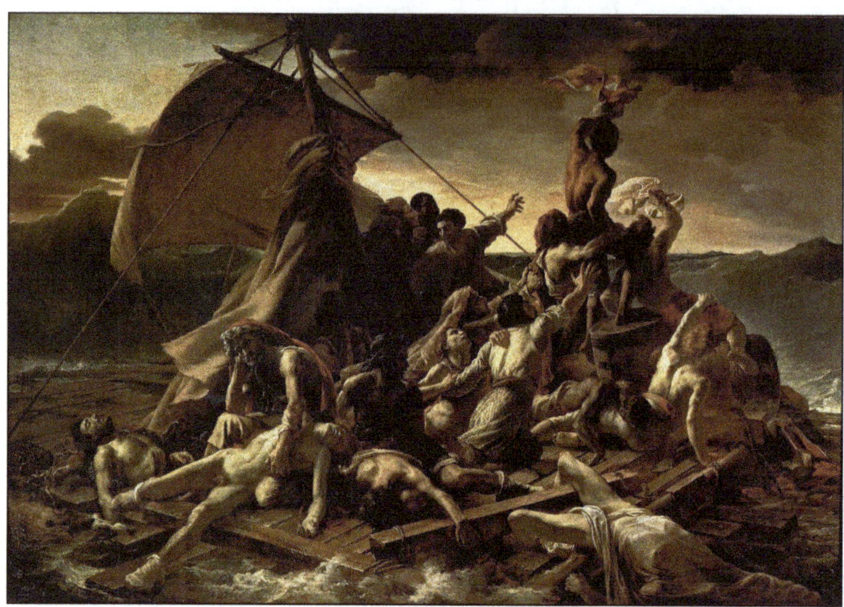

Fig. 23.2 - In *The Raft of Medusa* (1819) by Theodore Gericault, simple overlap is used to help us see who is where on the raft.

The best way to teach this concept to children is to simply show them examples. It's very intuitive, even if it's a little hard to articulate sometimes.

2. HORIZONTAL PLACEMENT

In my experience, this one is NOT intuitive at first. However, once you 'get it,' it seems obvious and you see it everywhere. Let's start by defining a new term:

- **Horizon line:** the horizontal (side to side) line where the sky meets the land or water. (It's sometimes called 'eye level,' and it's affected by the viewer's height when looking at a scene.)

Many budding artists learn to draw an object higher up if it's farther away, but that only works if the object is on the ground. What about items in the sky, like clouds or the tops of buildings? Anything above eye level will appear lower the farther away it is. Instead of teaching kids to draw something farther away higher on the paper, teach them to draw it closer to the horizon line. You'd be surprised how many four-year-olds will quickly understand this because it matches what they see so well.

You can see horizontal placement at work in Cole's painting, *The Voyage of Life- Childhood* (figure 23.3). Notice the cliff in the upper-middle of the painting. The farther away part is lower on the paper, closer to the horizon line.

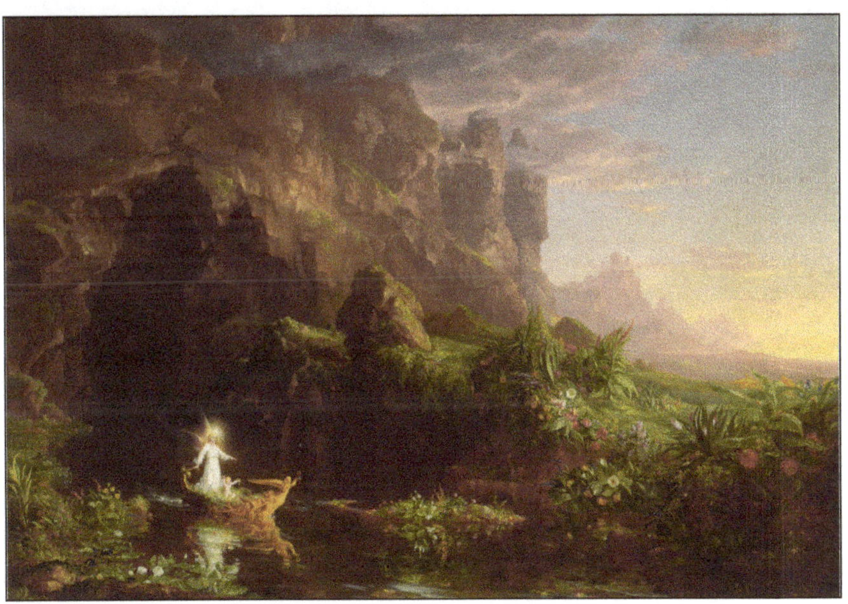

Fig. 23.3 - In *The Voyage of Life- Childhood* (1842), Thomas Cole correctly uses horizontal placement to make the top of the cliff look farther away on the right. Notice how the cliff face on the left side of the painting is higher up on the paper the closer it is.

3. SIZE

This is simply the fact that objects appear smaller the farther away they are. It's most important that this is accurate with items that are actually the same size. For example, since trees are all different heights, you can fudge on them a little. However, if you're drawing a series of semi-trucks, which are always the same height, it will be more important you have the size diminish accurately. So, to make an object look farther away, make it smaller.

While this is one of the most obvious and frequently used methods of perspective, it's rarely used alone. It's almost always used along with one or more other methods.

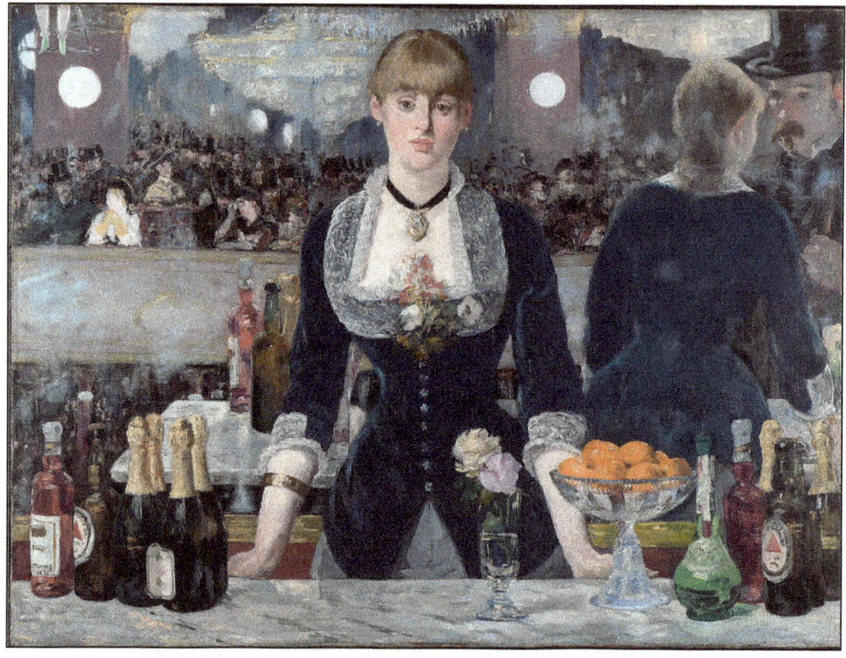

Fig. 23.4 - In his painting, *A Bar at the Folies-Bergere* (1882), Edouard Manet paints the people in the mirror in the background very small to indicate how far away they are.

You can see size in play in Manet's painting, *A Bar at the Folies-Bergere* (figure 23.4). The people in the background are drastically smaller making them look very far away.

4. SHADING IN SHADOWS

This method is NOT about how far away your subject is from you. Instead, it is about light and what part of your subject is facing the light. Just like objects can block you from seeing other objects (overlap), they can also block or redirect the light. That's how shadows are created. Using shading to create value in our art gives us the illusion of depth as it shows the effect of light and shadows on the shapes present.

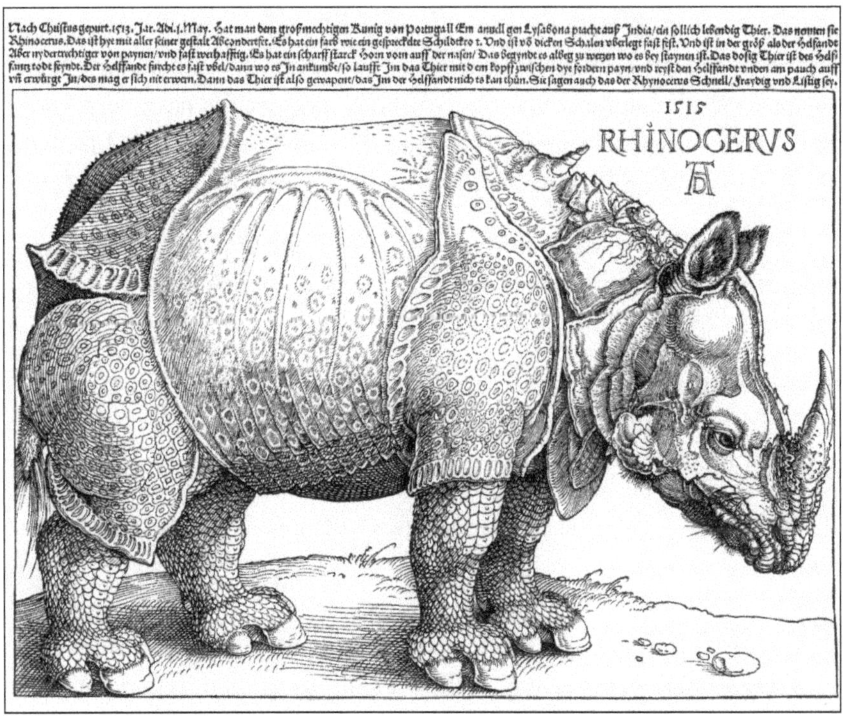

Fig. 23.5 - In his 1515 woodcut, Albrecht Durer uses shading to give his Rhinoceros a rounded, three-dimensional appearance.

Usually, the side of your subject that is farther away from the light will be darker and cooler (green, blue, and purple) in color. The side of the subject that is closer to the light will be brighter, lighter, and warmer (red, orange, and yellow) in color.

A curved surface will show a gradual transition from light to dark. This is called a value gradient. A flat surface will show a fairly consistent value, with changes in value only occurring where there is overlap or an edge. Objects also usually cast a shadow onto other objects as they block light.

You can see how shading adds shape and depth in Durer's Rhinoceros (figure 23.5). The horn, legs, and other parts of the body have a rounded three-dimensional look due to the shading.

5. THE ANGLE OF LINES (LINEAR PERSPECTIVE)

Linear perspective is fairly well known in a general sense, but not very well understood. The more casual types of linear perspective have been known and used by artists for thousands of years. However, it wasn't until 1420 that the Renaissance artist Brunelleschi was able to formalize linear perspective.

Other Renaissance artists used his methods of linear perspective to create beautiful depth in their paintings like Masaccio's painting, *Holy Trinity* (figure 23.6).

Since using linear perspective is a multi-step process, this book only covers it generally. Linear perspective is used to precisely portray the angle of lines and the size and spacing of objects.

There are at least four types of linear perspective. I'll explain each briefly:

- **Casual Perspective**: used in casual sketching—no ruler needed
- **One-Point Perspective**: used as a simplification of two-point perspective. In one-point perspective, there is one vanishing point and there are horizontal, vertical, and diagonal lines. It is the simplest form of linear perspective.
- **Two-Point Perspective**: used in most realistic drawings. In two-

point perspective, there are two vanishing points and there are vertical and diagonal lines.

- **Three-Point Perspective**: used for drawing from an extreme perspective (when eye level is very low or very high or when the viewer is looking up high or down low). In three-point perspective, there are three vanishing points and only diagonal lines.

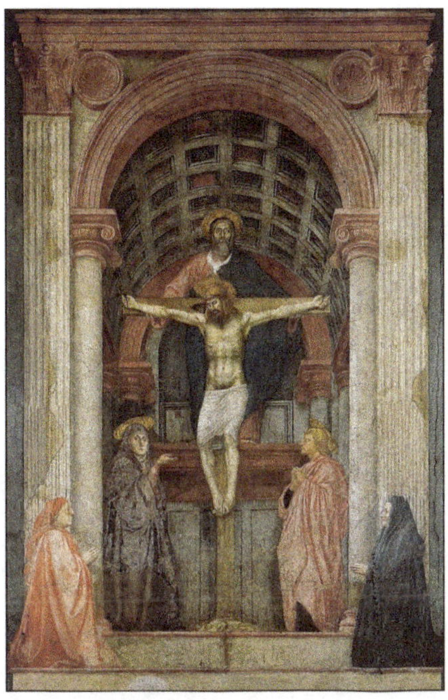

Fig. 23.6 - Renaissance artist Masaccio did an excellent job of using linear perspective in this painting, called *Holy Trinity* (1427).

6. DEGREE OF DETAIL

Now we're getting fancy! I tend to think of these next two methods (Degree of Detail and Color) as more nuanced. When I teach the methods of perspective, I teach these two last because they're harder to see in life and therefore not as critical. However, spending just a little time thinking about them can help you master the illusion of depth in your art!

To make an object look farther away, make it less detailed and less crisp. Some of this is caused by the limitation of our eyes, but even with binoculars we see less detail due to all the atmosphere we're looking through. When you're drawing objects that are very far away, make them a little fuzzy around the edges.

Some people call this effect 'aerial perspective' or 'atmospheric perspective.' How strong of an effect the atmosphere has depends on what's in it. Is it humid, dusty, or foggy? Teaching this concept has 'science' written all over it!

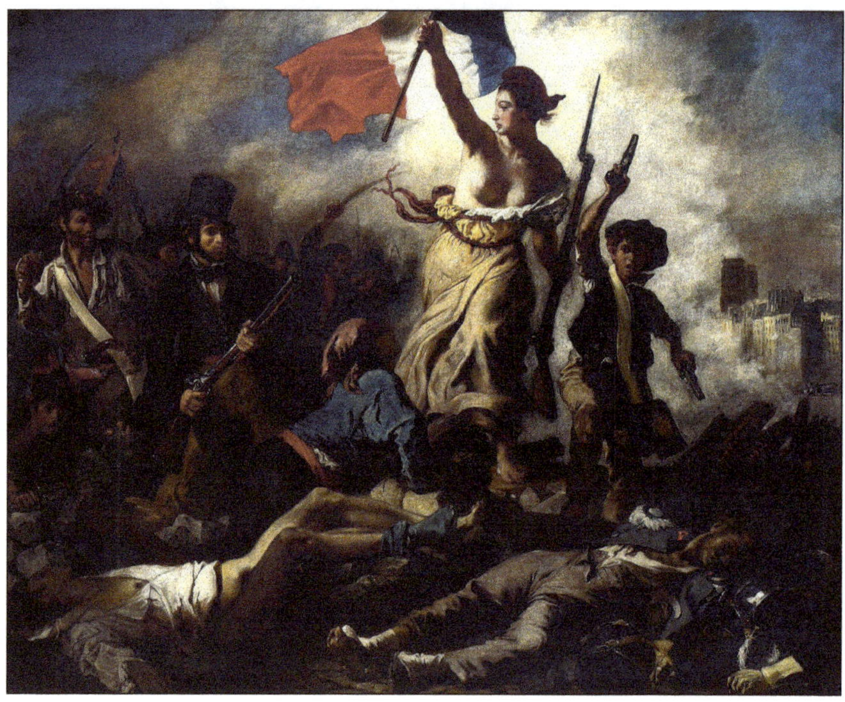

Fig. 23.7 - In *Liberty Leading the People* (1830), Eugene Delacroix paints the far away objects with less detail, giving a feel of depth to his painting.

In Delacroix's painting, *Liberty Leading the People,* (figure 23.7) you can see degree of detail used—only the people in the foreground are detailed.

7. COLOR

The effect of distance on color, like the degree of detail, is sometimes hard to see. Just as the atmosphere affects the degree of detail, it also affects color. However, when it comes to color, it can also be hard to predict. The key is to look for those effects on color and replicate what you see.

When we look at far away objects, we're looking through layers of atmosphere. Since blue light has the shortest wavelength, it scatters more easily. Mountains and other far away objects tend to look bluer and grayer (lower intensity). You can see this principle at work in Gainsborough's painting, *Mr. and Mrs. Andrews* (figure 23.8). Since the fields are golden yellow, the far away hills are greener and grayer in color.

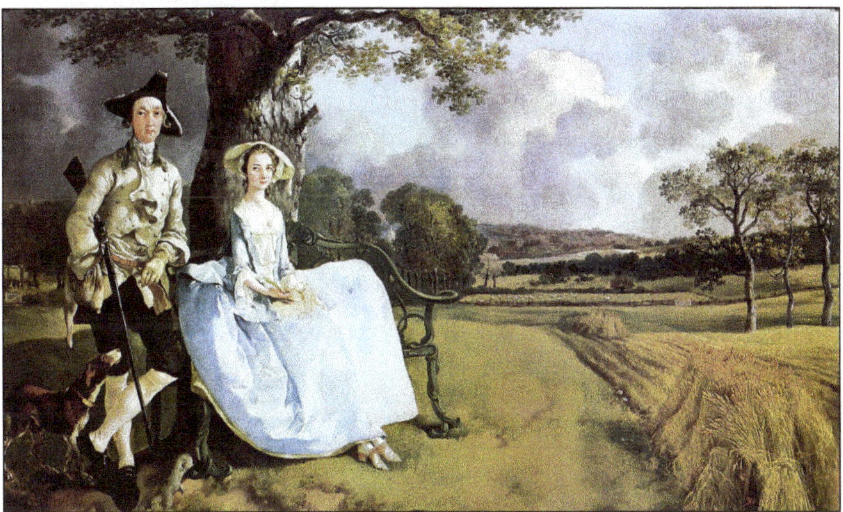

Fig. 23.8 - In *Mr. and Mrs. Andrews* (1749), Thomas Gainsborough uses bright intense color in the foreground and grayer tones in the background, giving the viewer the feeling of depth.

If it's sunset, the light has to pass through the full horizontal length of our atmosphere. This means more light is scattered and mountains turn a breathtaking pink/purple color, beautifully named 'alpenglow,' which is one of my favorite words (figure 23.9)! Always pay attention to the colors of far away objects and how they differs from the colors of nearby objects.

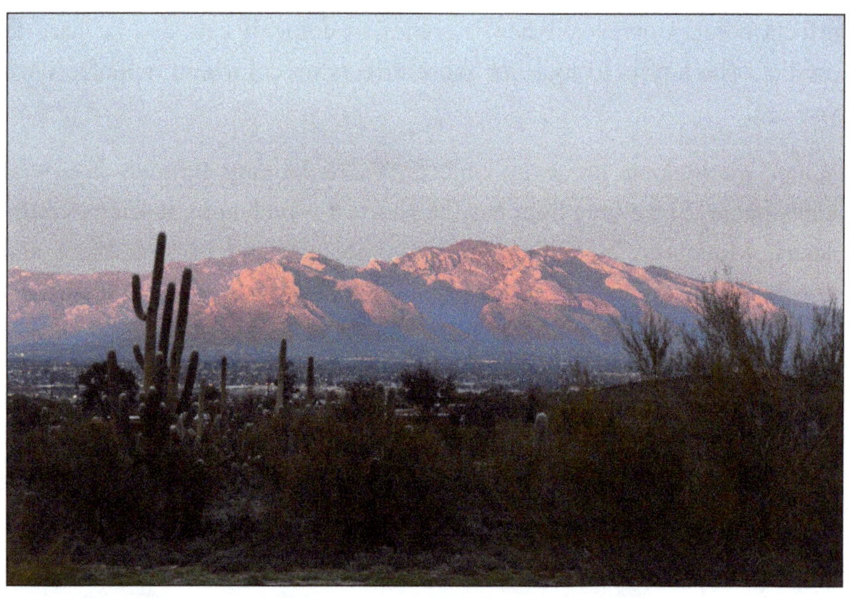

Fig. 23.9 - This photo of Pusch Ridge in Tucson, AZ at sunset shows the effect of sunlight passing through the full horizontal length of our atmosphere. When the mountains turn this beautiful pink/purple color, we call it 'alpenglow.'

8. BONUS: FORESHORTENING

Foreshortening is not really a method of perspective, but instead involves multiple methods of perspective—mainly overlap and size. We tend to use it to draw a subject that is close and is moving either toward or away from the viewer. When we foreshorten a person or object, we draw it counter-intuitively (some say distorted) to show its perspective. Radical foreshortening can look very strange, but if done well, it just looks normal or 'right.'

One of the most famous examples of drastic foreshortening is *The Lamentation of the Dead Christ* by Andrea Mantegna (figure 23.10).

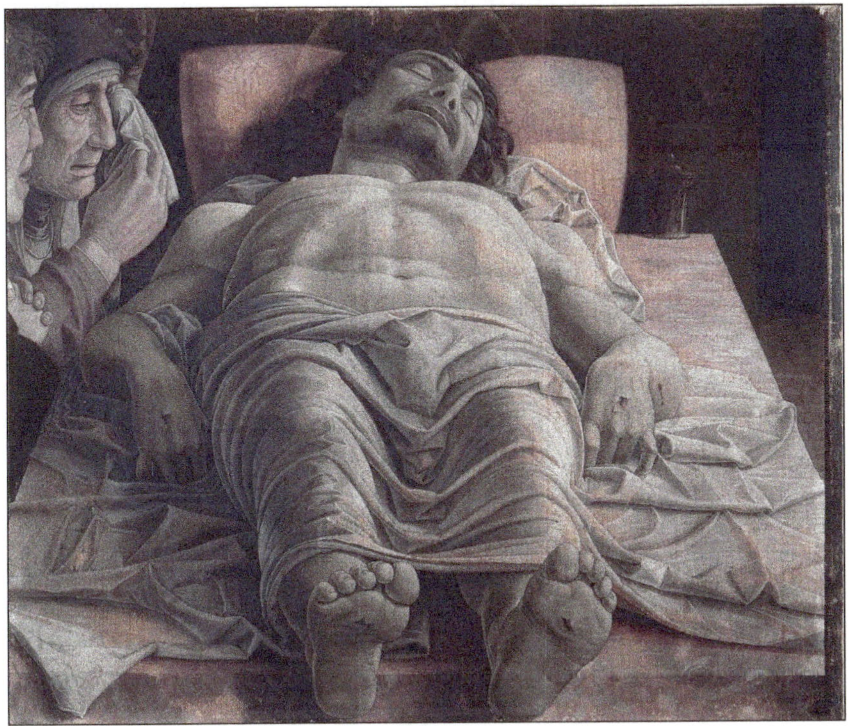

Fig. 23.10 - *The Lamentation of the Dead Christ* by Andrea Mantegna (1474) is a famous example of foreshortening from the Renaissance period.

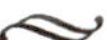

Now you know how to introduce your students to the methods of perspective to add realism and depth to their artwork!

This part of the book about practical art creation could be a library of books all on its own. There are so many great art projects we can do! I've tried to focus on art projects that help with specific art skills, but know that every time you or your students create art, you're working on art skills.

The internet is a treasure trove of art projects. One of my favorite things to do is look through Pinterest with my children and let them pick out an art project! (If you follow RidgeLightRanch on Pinterest, you'll be able to see all our favorite art projects.)

There's something about picking it out themselves that gives kids ownership of a project and makes them much more likely to work hard. When we do this, I start by giving my kids some parameters. For example, I may say, "We're going to do an art project with clay that's small and has something to do with the planets and stars, since we're studying astronomy." It's really fun to see how they will stretch their brains to make a project they're interested in fit the topic at hand. They don't even realize how valuable that simple activity of making connections is!

Now that you have a solid overview of what kind of simple projects you can use to teach your students to create art, let's turn our attention to art appreciation and learn about famous artists, the works they created, and the art periods they've been classified into.

CHAPTER SUMMARY

Use the methods of perspective to add depth to any art project:

- **Overlap**: To make an object look farther away, draw a second object overlapping it.
- **Size**: To make an object look farther away, make it smaller.
- **Horizontal placement:** To make an object look farther away, place it closer to the horizon line.
- **Value**: To give depth, darken the areas away from the light. Create a gradual change on curved surfaces.

- **Color**: To make an object look farther away, make the colors bluer and more faded.
- **Degree of detail**: To make an object look farther away, make it less detailed and less crisp.
- **Linear perspective**: Use linear perspective to precisely portray the angle of lines and the size and spacing of objects.

24

PRACTICAL ART APPRECIATION

What does art appreciation look like practically? How do you create opportunities to look at art together and have interesting discussions?

The best way to start is to simply look at some art with your children. As you look at art together, engage your students with the art appreciation questions listed in Part Two of this book for the grammar, dialectic, or rhetoric layers. The internet, art books, and museums are a great place to start looking for art.

THE INTERNET

There are countless websites with art you can print, but I like to start with Wikipedia. I know some people don't like Wikipedia because it's openly editable and not a peer reviewed journal. However, Wikipedia has more eyes on it than any peer reviewed journal and I've found it to be a very reliable source of information, not to mention a great source for links to do extended research.

Wikiart.org is a great place to view art without as much text. You can view a whole screen full of works of art and even sort them chronologically. They usually have a great collection of art for each famous artist, including art that is still protected by copyright.

I also find the websites of big art museums like The National Gallery of Art in Washington, D.C., and The Metropolitan Museum of Art in New York City to be great resources. They have high resolution images of art that you can download and print (if the art is out of copyright) and they often have additional information about the art and artist to accompany it.

Khan Academy has compiled a wonderful collection of art articles and videos from several sources. I've been really impressed with how their topics move along systematically and keep the content interesting.

ART BOOKS

There are so many great books of art. The first place I'd suggest you look is your local library. Search the online catalog or ask your librarian for help finding some children's art books.

My next favorite place for art books is at the Friends of the Library. These are non-profit groups that accept donations of books (sometimes from the libraries), sell them, and then use the proceeds to help libraries and other similar organizations. A good percentage of the books in our home (and I don't even want to know how many books we own) have come from these sales.

The Metropolitan Museum of Art has a nice series of books designed for young children. Each book has a title that starts with *Can You Find It...* You'll find about a dozen different works of art in each book with little rhymes of pertinent questions to think about as you look at the picture. For example, while looking at *Peaceable Kingdom* (figure 24.1) by Edward Hicks, it starts, "Do you see him stare at you? A golden lion is in view?" At the back of each book is the information about the name of the painting, the artist, and other pertinent details.

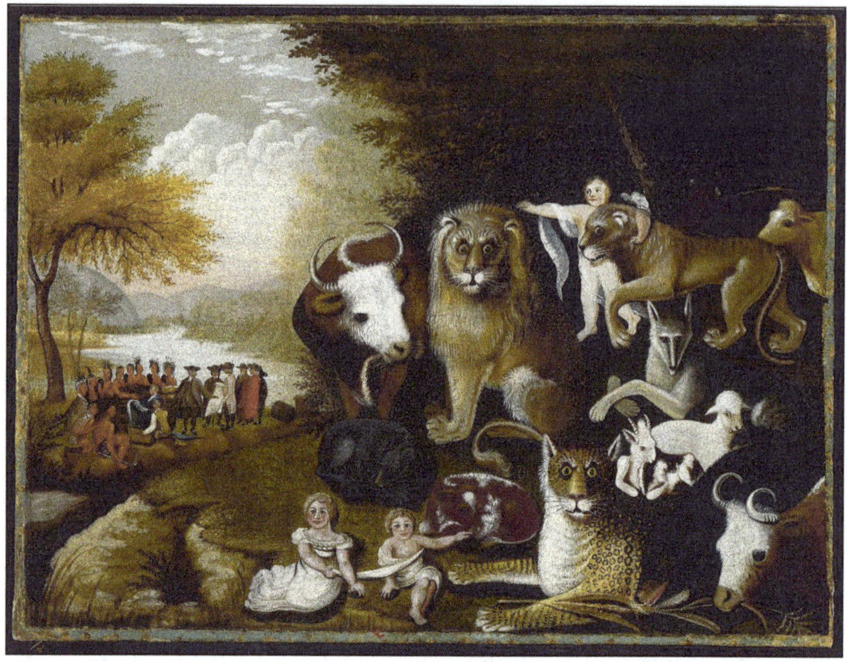

Fig. 24.1 - *Peaceable Kingdom* (1845) by Edward Hicks, is one of the works of art featured in one of the Metropolitan's Museum of Art's children's books.

Some of our favorite books have been in the *Getting to Know the World's Greatest Artists* series by Mike Venezia. Venezia makes art fun and interesting as he tells readers all about famous artists, using lots of comic book style pictures. My late elementary kids like these books best.

The *Come Look with Me* series is great for looking at art within a certain theme, like *Art in Early America*, *American Indian Art*, or *Animals in Art.* Each book has about a dozen paintings in it and coordinating questions for discussion. For example, in the *Art in Early America* book, when looking at *Cotopaxi, Ecuador* (figure 24.2) by Frederic Church, the author asks, "Which are the lightest areas of this painting? Which are the darkest? What effect does the light have on the mood of this painting?" The information about the painting is on the same page as the art print. These books seem to be designed for late elementary or middle school students.

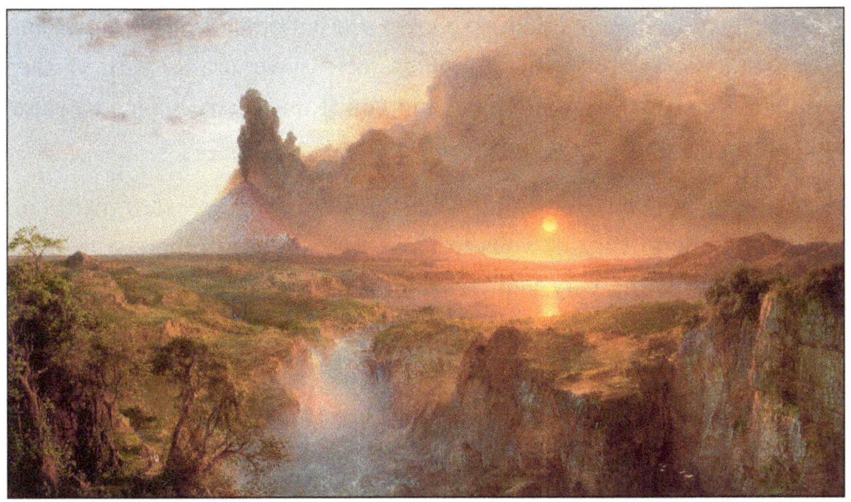

Fig. 24.2 - *Cotopaxi, Ecuador* (1862) by Frederic Church is one of the paintings featured in *Come Look with Me; Art in Early America* by Randy Osofsky.

I also love the Usborne books about great works of art. I've checked them out from the library many times and I own one, but I look forward to owning a few more soon. (I love books!)

For high schoolers and adults, I highly recommend *The Annotated Mona Lisa: A Crash Course in Art History from Prehistoric to Post-Modern* by Carol Strickland. Strickland manages to insert enough personality to make you laugh while still doing a great job of leading you through a "crash course in art history."

MUSEUMS

Another great source of art is your local art museum. Almost every city has a museum of some kind and most also have an art museum. Art museums typically have a rotation of exhibits that change monthly or quarterly, so you can go many times and always see new art! Art museums will often borrow collections of art that travel from city to city as well. Find your local museums online and sign up for their mailing lists so you won't miss something awesome!

Obviously, art museums will have great art, but other kinds of museums, like historical or scientific museums, also have art as part of their exhibits. Be on the lookout for art and you'll find many hidden treasures in unexpected places.

Art galleries also have stunning collections of art. However, it makes me (and the owners) very nervous to have my children in there with me—probably due to the very high price tags on everything. I find museums are more kid-friendly than galleries.

How to Have a Successful Art Museum Visit

1. Study the art ahead of time.

I have found that the visit goes smoother and the students (and teachers) are more interested in the museum if they've done some studying of the subject ahead of time. Ideally, you'd read a bit about the artist, time period, or genre first. Then you'd visit the art museum and follow up with some more studying to answer any questions that you may have had during the visit.

For example, during my latest trip to the National Gallery of Art in Washington, D.C., I was delighted to see works of art by Giotto (figure 11.1) and El Greco (figure 6.2), mostly because I had just spent a few months preparing lesson plans about them. I hardly noticed the *Voyage of Life* (figure 23.3) series by Thomas Cole because I didn't know much about it. Later, when I started reading about the Hudson River School (American Romantic artists of the mid 1800s), I came across Thomas Cole's paintings and thought that I'd seen them in the National Gallery of Art. Sure enough, there's a photo of them on my phone! Now I'd really love to go back and spend more time with those paintings.

2. Look online and determine what the museum allows.

Is food and drink allowed? (Usually, no.) Is there a café inside the museum? Is photography allowed? (Usually, yes.) Will you be allowed to take your backpack? Stroller? Does the museum offer discounts for school groups? If so, call up your homeschool friends and arrange to meet there as a field trip! If you can't find the answer to these questions online, pick up the phone and call.

3. Take advantage of the resources provided by the museum.

Many museums provide art lesson materials online. Check them out ahead of time to learn about the artists featured.

Try to schedule a tour ahead of time with a docent (an in-house guide). The docents are very knowledge about the art and really help it come to life!

If there isn't a docent tour, look for an audio tour. It seems like we should be able to read every plaque, but it gets old and the audio tours often have additional interesting information about each piece of art.

4. Set a timer.

If it's your first visit to an art museum with your students, plan on only staying an hour or so. If you have a guided tour, the students will probably enjoy the museum for a little longer—maybe two hours. I know it's hard to spend the money to get in and then leave after such a short amount of time, but it's better to have a fun experience than to stay too long. You don't want to make students think they hate art museums just because you wanted to get your money's worth. You can always stay longer if *everyone* wants to, but a set time will help those who are not as enthralled to be patient with the experience.

5. Bring a sketch book and camera.

Most museums allow you to bring a sketch book and camera. There's something about the process of taking photos of paintings that really encourages some kids to slow down and look.

Some museums will not allow photography (or not allow flash photography, thereby making it very hard to get a good photo), but they will allow you to stop and sketch a painting. This is another way to help students really spend time looking at the work of art, while simultaneously building their sketching skills. It's also a great way to internalize a variety of excellent compositions, and it provides a goal for students to work towards. Copying great works of art is a time-honored tradition!

6. Look for creative ways to have fun

Head to the museum gift shop and ask if they have postcards of any works of art that are on display that day. Buy one or more (postcards are some of the cheapest souvenirs and make great bookmarks later), and then go on a hunt for those works of art.

TIPS FOR LOOKING THROUGH ART BOOKS AT HOME WITH YOUR CHILDREN

Most of the suggestions I give in this book work just as well in a homeschool classroom, traditional classroom, or at home with your child. However, there are some extra things you can do at home with your own children while looking through art books.

1. Pace Yourself

Pick two works of art and compare them. (Don't try to look through a big book of 100 works of art all in one sitting.)

2. Pick Favorites

There's something about asking someone which is their favorite that makes them take a closer look at the options. Write each family member's name on a sticky note and ask them to place it on the page in your art book with their favorite painting. Tell them they're welcome to move the sticky note at any time. When you're done, leave the book out and available for your kids to leaf through if they want.

3. Create a Family Story for a Work of Art

Pick a piece of art and consider what might have happened right before that moment. Make up a story and tell the first part of it. Let the person to your right make up the next part of the story and so on.

DECIDE AHEAD OF TIME HOW YOU'LL HANDLE NUDITY

It's inevitable—both art books and art museums will have some nudity. Some of the world's most famous art has nudity in it, like most of Michelangelo's Sistine Chapel fresco (figure 24.3). If you decide ahead of time how you'll handle it, it won't be so uncomfortable. Nudity means different things to different cultures, and you should consider how your culture handles nudity as you decide how your family wants to handle nudity in art.

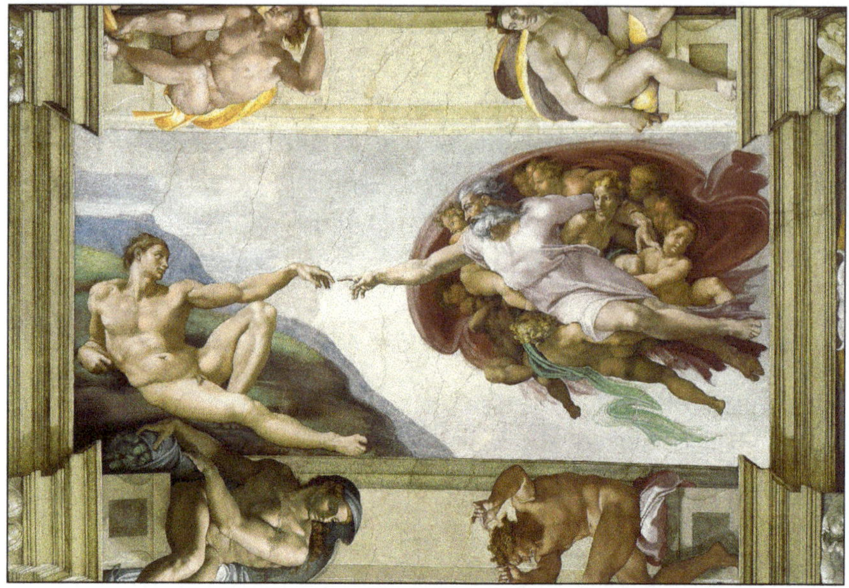

Fig. 24.3 - Michelangelo's fresco on the ceiling of the Sistine Chapel is one of the world's greatest works of art, but the nudity in it sometimes scares parents away from showing it to their kids.

Here's what I said to my own children about nudity. You can use this verbatim, consider it a starting point, or ignore it completely:

> Yes, that's the human body. Most of the time we keep our private parts private because they are special. However, there are other times, like at the doctor's office, when we have to show our private parts so the doctors can help us stay healthy. When they are training, doctors study the human body extensively so they can be skilled and confident in healing human bodies.
>
> Artists also want to be very skilled at what they do. In order to draw people accurately, artists often sketch every component of a person. An artist who wants to draw horses will draw the muscles, ligaments, tendons, and bones of a horse so they can understand how best to draw a horse as it runs through the field.

> In the same way, artists who draw people, often draw nude bodies so they can be extra skilled at drawing how the human body moves.
>
> Everything God made is good, including private body parts. We can recognize the artistic talent of the artists who created works of art, including nudes, while still respecting each individual and keeping our own private parts private.

Drawing Nudes

The next thing to consider is if you'll allow your children to draw nudes. If so, what parameters will you give to guide them? Little boys drawing penises all over everything is not the same thing as Michelangelo's nudes on the ceiling of the Sistine Chapel. Our family has decided that you need to be an adult before you draw adult things, like nudes. My children will one day make the decision for themselves, but as long as they are children, I've asked them not to draw private parts.

This is what I said to my kids:

> I've decided not to draw nude bodies, but I can still appreciate the skill of the artists who do. You're too young to be drawing nudes, but when you're an adult you'll make that decision for yourself

How about older kids? You may never have to deal with this, but it's good to think ahead of time—is it okay for your high schooler to take an art class with live nude models? This is seen differently in different cultures, so I'm not one to judge others for their decisions. I personally do not attend classes with live nude models, because I don't think it's mentally healthy for the model. I've seen some statistics about how, in America, nude modeling is often a gateway to prostitution and exploitation. As someone who consistently supports organizations dedicated to the anti-slavery and anti-sex-trafficking movement, I don't want to risk it.

I've heard people say that a good test for whether or not you should do something is to ask yourself if it would be okay with you if it was published on the front page of the newspaper—or these days, posted on Facebook—for all to see. Perhaps you and your children will never get to this point in your art career, but it's always good to think about something before it happens so you're not caught off-guard.

You might also caution your children to be respectful of the sensitivities of those around them. What one person views as art may be seen as sexual harassment to others. As they become adults and move into the workspace, they'll need to be aware of what their employer considers acceptable as well.

ART HISTORY

With so many sources of art and great questions you can ask your students while looking at works of art, you'll find you and your students curious about the people who created the art and the times they lived in. This is what art history is all about!

If art history sounds daunting or boring, let me assure you that it's really all about the fascinating stories of real people who interacted with their culture through the art they created. Art both reflects and influences culture, so it really acts as a historian throughout the ages. On the 'Anyone Can Teach Art' podcast, many of our episodes focus on a particular artist. We have a lot of fun chatting about their life and the time period they lived in!

Pick out a famous artist and then, with your students, research their life and culture.

- When did they live? What was their life like?
- What else was going on in their part of the world then?

- In what art period/movement do art historians classify this artist?
- What are the artist's most famous works of art?
- What media did they typically use?

Then ask all your grammar, dialectic, or rhetoric questions about the artwork and discuss the way history played a role in the creation of this artwork. As you expose your students to a variety of art periods, remind them of the art periods listed in chapter 12, Art Grammar: Art History and Art Appreciation.

At RidgeLightRanch.com/Art-Periods-and-Movements/ you'll find a list of the major art periods along with the art movements contained in each period, as well as a list of the key artists from that period. This can serve as a great list of core artists to introduce your students to over their school years.

Use these practical art creation exercises and art appreciation activities to help your students internalize art grammar so you can have great discussions.

CHAPTER SUMMARY

- Start your journey into art appreciation by finding art on the internet, in art books, and at museums to look at with your students.
- Make the artist come alive for your students by learning about the artist's life and personality alongside their art.
- Be sure to consider ahead of time how you'll handle nudity in art.
- Key into the personal stories of specific artists to keep art history engaging and intriguing.

EPILOGUE

In our modern, industrial, testing-obsessed culture, it's easy for a homeschooling parent to get nervous that they aren't covering everything their child needs. I want to encourage you to step back and consider how the classical model of education approaches the idea.

Remember that the purpose of education is "the cultivation of wisdom and virtue by nourishing the soul on truth, goodness, and beauty, so that, in Christ, the student is better able to know, glorify, and enjoy God."

Our students need art in their education to nourish their soul on truth, goodness, and beauty, but you don't have to hit every single component of art grammar to nourish the soul. Find ways to enjoy art and sprinkle art vocabulary into your projects. The most important thing is to just start creating and looking at art with your students!

RESOURCES

- WikiArt.org is one of my favorite places to view art online. There are multiple ways to sort the art and the images are high quality!
- CIRCE, the Center for Independent Research on Classical Education, is a great source for general knowledge and resources for classical educators (CirceInstitute.org).
- Leigh Bortin's books, *The Core*, *The Question,* and *The Conversation* provide an in-depth look at classical education apart from art.
- Betty Edwards' website, DrawRight.com, as well as her book, *Drawing on the Right Side of the Brain*, have wonderful exercises aimed at helping adults learn to draw.
- RidgeLightRanch.com is my website:
- You can find a list of some of my favorite art supplies at RidgeLightRanch.com/Art-Supplies/.
- You can find a growing glossary of art terms at RidgeLightRanch.com/Art-Glossary.
- You can find a full list of art periods and movements with short descriptions at RidgeLightRanch.com/Art-Periods-and-Movements/.

Don't forget to download your free Art Teacher Kit with printable posters and famous works of art at RidgeLightRanch.com/Art-Teacher-Kit/.

GLOSSARY

This is a core list of the art vocabulary used in this book to help you as you read.

As you teach art, you may run across additional art terms. Learning the vocabulary of a subject is one of the main goals of the grammar layer of learning. So, in an effort to make teaching art as easy as possible, I keep a more extensive glossary on my website with definitions designed for the grammar stage. Bookmark this page and whenever you encounter an art word you're not sure about, look it up in our free glossary: Ridge-LightRanch.com/Art-Glossary.

Abstract Art: art that does not try to visually represent reality.

Architecture: the art of designing buildings.

Art Movement: a collection of artists and their works of art with a common philosophy or goal, technique, style, or time period. Many movements formed a club with a manifesto, a spokesperson, and an exclusive art show. (You can find a full list of art periods and movements with short descriptions at RidgeLightRanch.com/Art-Periods-and-Movements/).

Art Period: a longer block of time encompassing many different artists and their works of visual art, music, theater, and literature. An art period usually includes several art movements with a shared focus or goal. Artists and their works of art are usually grouped into an art period by art historians after the period has come and gone. (You can find a full list of art periods and movements with short descriptions at RidgeLightRanch.-com/Art-Periods-and-Movements/).

Balance: the equal arrangement of visual weight on each side of a work of art.

Botanical Illustration: scientifically accurate art, depicting the form, color, and details of a single plant species or a group of plant species.

Caricature: a recognizable drawing of a real (not imaginary) person with certain exaggerated features.

Cartoon: a simplified, humorous drawing or animation—cartoons can include simple humor, satire, or caricature.

Color Harmony: the pleasing arrangement of color leading to a visual harmony. At one extreme, bland colors tend to look boring. At the other extreme, too much color complexity will feel chaotic. Harmony is the balance between the two extremes.

Color: the reflections of light, varying in hue, value, and intensity.

Color Wheel: a color circle based on primary colors (red, yellow, and blue), which includes secondary and sometimes tertiary colors.

Commission (n): payment for the creation of a work.

Commission (v): to request that an artist create a specific work of art, often with payment made in advance—commissions can be made by individuals or organizations.

Complementary Colors: a pair of colors that are directly across from each other on the color wheel (e.g. purple and yellow). Complementary colors are made of one primary color paired with a mix of the other two primary colors.

Context of Color: how colors appear relative to each other. (Red appears vibrant next to yellow, but dull next to orange.)

Contrast: the use of opposite elements of art together to create interest.

Education: the purpose of education is "the cultivation of wisdom and virtue by nourishing the soul on truth, goodness, and beauty, so that, in Christ, the student is better able to know, glorify, and enjoy God." (from The Mother of Divine Grace School)

Elements of Art: the tools used to make art (line, shape, form, color, space, texture, value).

Emphasis: the creation of a dominant visual area to which the eye is drawn, the focal point.

Foreshorten: to distort a subject in order to give the illusion of depth.

Form: the three dimensions of an object that take up space.

Genres: (see Hierarchy of Genres)

Gradient: a gradual transition from one color, texture, or value to another.

Hierarchy of Genres: an Italian Renaissance idea that some types of painting were nobler than others. The genres, in order of most noble to least, were historical, portrait, lifestyle, landscape, animal, and still life.

Horizontal Line: a line lying flat (like the horizon).

Hue: the purest form of a color.

Illustration: a picture that tells a story, often found in books and magazines.

Intensity: the brightness or saturation of a color.

Landscape: a single view of a large area of land.

Line of Symmetry: the imaginary line where you could fold the image and have both halves match exactly.

Line: the path created when a dot moves from one point to another.

Linear Perspective: the geometric techniques that dictate the angle of lines used to make two-dimensional drawings look three-dimensional.

Methods of Perspective: the ways to create the illusion of form/depth in a work of art.

Movement: how the eye moves through the composition. (Alternatively, this word is sometimes used to mean a feeling of action within the art.)

Negative Space: the space surrounding the subject.

Neutral Colors: a color made from mixing complementary colors together. Artists have many terms for these colors: mud colors, mouse colors, semi-neutrals, grays, browns, or earthen colors. A true neutral color will not show any of the primary or secondary colors in it, but will look truly gray/brown. True neutrals are hard to create. A semi-neutral will show a hint of one of the primary or secondary colors.

Pastels: similar to chalk crayons, but made from colored powder and gum.

Patron: a person who gives financially to support a cause or activity.

Pattern: repeating, predictable, and identical elements of art.

Perspective: the appearance of form/depth in a two-dimensional picture.

Point of View: the position from which something or someone is observed.

Portrait: a drawing or painting of a person.

Primary Colors: red, yellow, and blue. (The primary colors of light are different from the primary colors in art.)

Principles of Design: how to use the elements of art to make art (balance/symmetry, emphasis, movement, unity, contrast, pattern, rhythm, variety).

Proportion: the size of one part of the subject in comparison to (relative to) the size of the whole subject.

Realist: an artist who creates art accurately reflecting reality.

Relief: a sculpture where the three-dimensional pieces are attached to a solid flat background of the same material.

Repetition: recurring similar elements of art.

Rhythm: the use of pattern or repetition to create a visual tempo.

Secondary Colors: orange, green, and purple—the colors that can be made by mixing two primary colors.

Self-portrait: a drawing or painting made by the artist of him/herself.

Shape: the enclosed space that occurs when a line connects to itself or another line. A shape has both a positive and negative image. There are geometric and organic shapes.

Space: the area around and within the subject.

Still Life: art with a subject matter of inanimate (not-alive) objects (not people, animals, or landscapes).

Symmetry: when one half of a shape becomes exactly like the other half if you flip or turn it. Thc simplest type of symmetry is reflection symmetry, also known as mirror symmetry or line symmetry. (Rotational symmetry and point symmetry are a little different.)

Texture: the actual, or appearance of, three-dimensional raised areas.

Tone: (see Value)

Unity/Harmony: the feeling that everything works together.

Value (Tone): the light to dark gradient of a color, typically created by adding white or black.

Variety: the use of dissimilar elements of art.

Vertical Line: a line standing up straight.

INDEX OF GREAT WORKS OF ART

NOTES

1. WHAT'S THE PURPOSE OF EDUCATION?

1. CIRCE, the Center for Independent Research on Classical Education, can be found at www.circeinstitute.org.

2. WHAT DOES ART TEACH US?

1. Scudder, Samuel Hubbard. *In the Laboratory With Agassiz* (also referred to as *Look at Your Fish)*. 1874 essay.
2. This interview, titled "Ira Glass on Storytelling," was done by Creative TV. Part three includes Glass's words about persistence and can be found at https://youtu.be/X2wLP0izeJE.

3. USING ART TO LEARN OTHER SUBJECTS

1. We mention several of these studies in the Anyone Can Teach Art podcast, episode #22: "Why Include Art in Education." RidgeLightRanch.com/Podcast-22-Why-Art-Education/.

5. WHAT IS THE CLASSICAL MODEL?

1. Caleb Skogen. "A Quadrivium Developed." *Classical Conversations*, 24 Feb. 2015. members.classicalconversations.com.

16. THE RHETORIC LAYER

1. While Jane Goodall never earned an undergraduate degree, she was accepted into Cambridge Univerity's PhD program in 1962 after her work become well-known and she was already a success. Learn more at janegoodall.org.uk/jane-goodall/biography.
2. Learn more at cnbc.com/2016/08/11/nearly-a-third-of-the-worlds-billionaires-didnt-graduate-college.html.

ACKNOWLEDGMENTS

I want to start by thanking God and giving Him all the glory: Every time I'm filled with self-doubt, You are my refuge, my calm in the storm. You give me the courage to step out, be vulnerable, and try, even if I flail a bit as I go.

To my sister, Deanna Munger: Thank you for always being interested in my life. I can't imagine anyone more supportive. Thank you for the countless hours you spend being my co-host on the *Anyone Can Teach Art* podcast and for your encouragement to write this book. It's your turn to write a book now!

To my husband: Thank you for sharing me with my business and thank you for not letting it swallow me whole. I might never step away from my desk if it weren't for your gentle reminders to keep living life.

To my older son: Thank you for your excitement over my endeavors and your constant exuberance. Your energy and joy are contagious.

To my younger son: Thank you for your honesty and insight. You have an impressive mix of silliness and wisdom beyond your years.

To my parents: Thank you for raising me to believe all things are possible with God. You gave me the best foundation a kid could hope for and I seriously love being able to call you friends now. Thank you, Dad, for taking art classes with me. Thank you, Mom, for reading every art lesson plan before anyone else!

To my friends in the Right Table Mastermind: Thank you for your company. Entrepreneurship can be lonely. I look forward to each of our group calls and I love how much we've all grown to know and care about each other's lives and businesses. Thank you for your honest appraisal of my crazy ideas and your push to write this book.

To my cover designer, Jonathan Lewis of Jonlin Creative: Thank you for your vision and execution of a beautiful cover.

To my editors, Emily Magone and Kara Warren: Thank you for your enthusiasm for this book and your efforts to make it perfect!!

Lastly, I want to give a big thank you to all my customers and (dare I say it?) fans. Your kind words, stories, and photos inspire me to keep at it. Thank you for all your feedback and thank you for bravely joining me on this adventure of teaching art!

HELP!

Thank you so much for taking the time to read this book. Would you be so kind as to leave an honest review wherever you buy books, so other people know if this book would benefit them as well?

Thank you so much. Your reviews really do mean the world to me!

HOW CAN I HELP YOU?

Do you have questions about teaching art? You're welcome to contact me. I love talking about art! I'd also love to see photos and hear stories about your art adventures. You can email me or connect with me on Facebook or Instagram as 'Ridge Light Ranch.'

Beyond helping you teach art, I also have a passion for supporting other entrepreneurs! Have you considered writing a book to share what you know with the world? Or perhaps you have a business idea you want to run by someone? If so, I invite you to contact me. I'm happy to share my experience of running an online business, teaching local classes, and writing a book with you and encourage you to go for your dreams too!

Julie Abels, Founder of Ridge Light Ranch

julie@ridgelightranch.com

Google voicemail/text: (234) 405-0029

ABOUT THE AUTHOR

Julie B. Abels is a Christian, a wife, and a homeschooling mom of two boys. She and her family live in Tucson, Arizona, on 3.3 acres she likes to call the Ridge Light Ranch. In her life before children, she earned a degree in environmental science and a master's in business and worked as an environmental consultant in the corporate world. Now she's found her calling homeschooling her boys and teaching art to anyone who will listen.

In between church activities and camping with her family, you'll usually find her sketching, teaching an art class, or working on her website at RidgeLightRanch.com and her podcast, Anyone Can Teach Art. She loves to create and teach art and she's on a mission to help you learn to love teaching art so that you can give your children all the benefits of art and creativity in their education. She makes it simple with fun, easy, no-prep art lesson plans and tons of free help found on her blog and podcast.

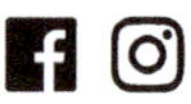

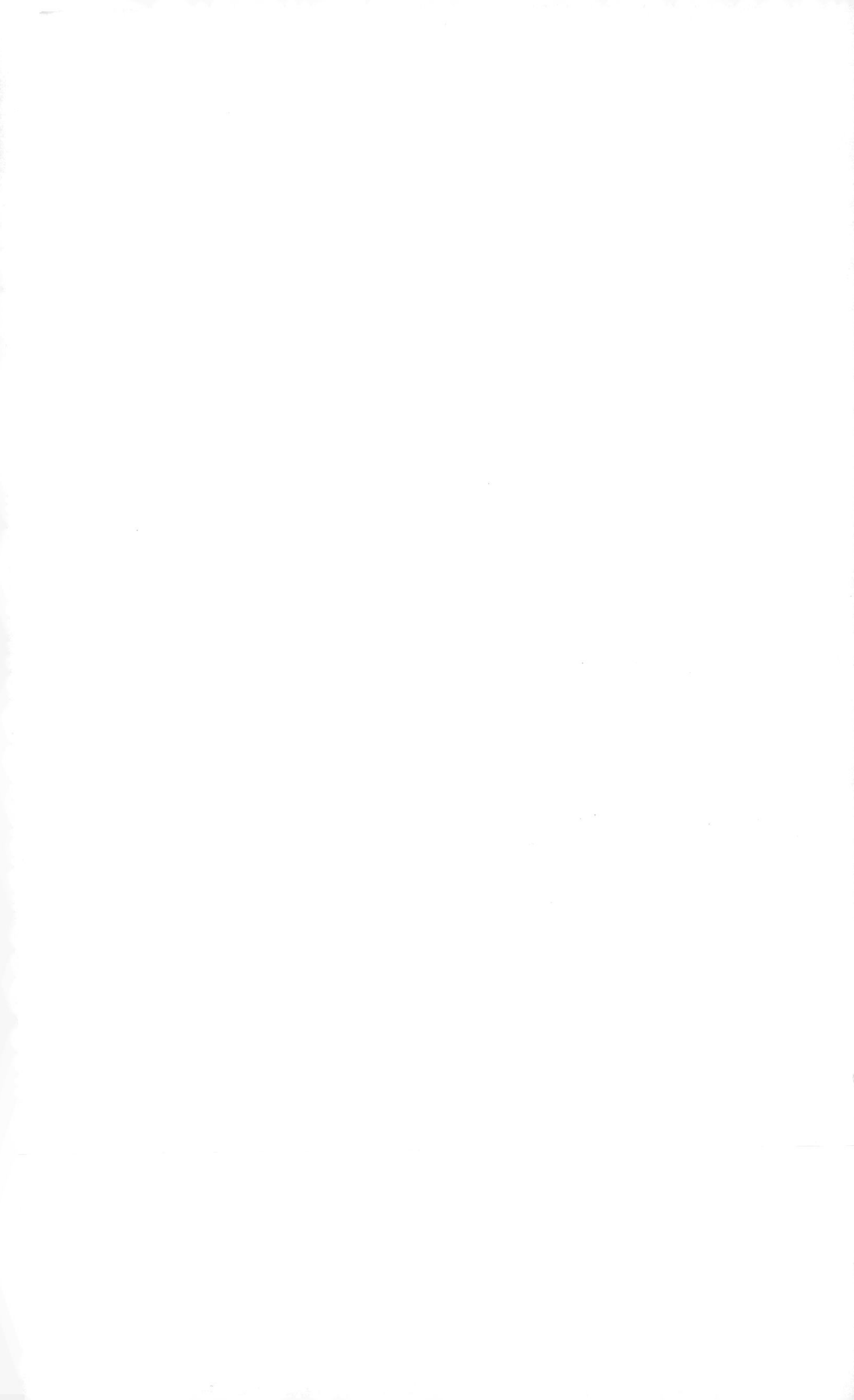

www.ingramcontent.com/pod-product-compliance
Ingram Content Group UK Ltd.
Pitfield, Milton Keynes, MK11 3LW, UK
UKHW021838270726
14058UKWH00002B/216

9 781952 390005